The *Pianist's* **Dictionary**

The Pianist's **Dictionary**

Maurice Hinson

INDIANA UNIVERSITY PRESS

Bloomington & Indianapolis

This book is a publication of
Indiana University Press
601 North Morton Street
Bloomington, IN 47404-3797 USA

http://iupress.indiana.edu

Telephone orders	800-842-6796
Fax orders	812-855-7931
Orders by e-mail	iuporder@indiana.edu

Library of Congress Cataloging-in-Publication Data
Hinson, Maurice.
The pianist's dictionary / Maurice Hinson.
p. cm.
Includes bibliographical references (p.).
ISBN 0-253-34405-0 (cloth : alk.
paper)—ISBN 0-253-21682-6 (pbk. : alk. paper)
1. Piano—Dictionaries. 2. Pianists—Biography.
3. Music—Terminology. I. Title.
ML102.P5H46 2004
786.2'03—dc22
2003025350

ISBN 978-0-253-21682-3 (pbk.)

4 5 6 7 8   14 13 12 11 10 09

To our daughter Susan

Contents

Preface

This music dictionary aims to assist the pianist in all aspects of his or her art. It is a practical guide that covers definitions of terms, performance directions, names of well-known piano pieces, nicknames of pieces, forms, and styles, plus brief biographies of leading pianists, composers of piano music, and piano manufacturers as well as parts of the piano (action, soundboard, etc.) and neglected repertoire the author feels is important. I have also included the names of some college and university faculty members who are outstanding teachers, performers, or both, or who have made some unusual contributions to the piano world by their writing or editing. It is impossible to include some of the most interesting instructions from composers: Satie suggested the pianist should play "like a nightingale with a toothache"; Messiaen urged the performer to sound "like someone sharpening a scythe."

To be sure, there is more to interpretation than just recognizing the terms. The pianist has to know that *allegro* means a style as much as a tempo and that a Brahms *grazioso* is quite different from a Mozart *grazioso*. This dictionary aims to help with the other "part of the meaning" besides speed and tempo.

How many times has a pianist worked so diligently on a passage or piece only to realize there was a term or directions present all along that would have steered him or her in the right direction if only they had been properly understood? These words cannot be ignored, for they help bring a score to life.

I owe special thanks to Dr. Charles Timbrell for his assistance with death dates and students of listed pianists, and to Suzie Collins and Linda Durkin for typing the manuscript.

I have tried to keep the language as simple as possible as relates to the topic. The information contained covers the subject from around 1700 (the beginning of the history of the piano) to the present day. This is information I have worked with while teaching piano for almost 60 years.

Maurice Hinson
Louisville, Kentucky

The Pianist's **Dictionary**

A

a (It.). At, in, to.

à deux (Fr.). For two (as a duet). *à deux mains:* for two hands.

à l'aise (Fr.). With ease; in a relaxed manner.

à la manière de (Fr.). In the style of.

à la mesure (Fr.). A tempo; in strict time.

à peine (Fr.). Slightly, scarcely.

à peu (Fr.). A little.

à peu près sans pédale (Fr.). Almost without pedal, with very little pedal.

a piacere (It.). At pleasure, as desired. The pianist is to use his or her discretion as regards the rhythmic or dynamic nuance; play freely.

à quatre mains (Fr.). For four hands.

a tempo (It.). In the original speed, resume the original tempo after having made some deviation from it.

à temps (Fr.). In time.

à un temps (Fr.). In one beat.

à volonté (Fr.). At will, at pleasure.

à 2 mains (Fr.). With or for two hands (R.L.R.L.).

***Ab Irato* (In a Rage).** Franz Liszt, S. 143, 1852. This piece first appeared in 1842 as *Morceau du salon*. It was expanded and reappeared in 1852 with the new suggestive title. It is an effective octave and chord study in a mainly violent mood.

ABA. Analysis term used to describe sections of a piece: *A* = first section, followed by contrasting section *B*, followed by repeat (sometimes modified) of *A* section.

Abegg Variations. Robert Schumann, op. 1, 1829–30. A set of variations on a theme based on the notes A—B♭—E—G—G and dedicated to his friend Meta Abegg.

aber (Ger.). But.

Abridged Sonata Form/Modified Sonata Form. A form based on sonata form but not containing a development section.

accarezzevole (It.). Caressingly.

accelerando, accel. (It.). Increasing the speed, accelerating, becoming faster.

accélerer (Fr.). To speed up, get faster.

acciaccatura (It.). A type of grace note indicated by a small note with its stem crossed through. It is a "crushed note," to be played a split second before the principal note and released at once.

accompaniment. Musical background for a principal part or parts.

accusé (Fr.). With emphasis.

action. Mechanism of the piano that causes a string to sound when a key is depressed.

ad libitum (Lat.). At will, freely; strict time not required, "make yourself at home"; extemporize a cadenza or a section.

adagietto (It.). Slightly faster than *adagio*, of which term it is the diminutive.

adagio (It.). At ease, leisurely; slowly with great expression. "To play an *adagio* well, enter into a calm and almost melancholy mood" (Quantz, p. 163).

adagio non troppo (It.). Slow, but not too slow.

Adieu. Felix Mendelssohn, op. 85, no. 1, in A Minor, one of the *Songs without Words*.

Adieu Valse, L' (Farewell Waltz). Frédéric Chopin, Waltz in A-flat Major, op. 69, no. 1, 1835. Composed as a "farewell" present to Maria Wodizínska on the breakup of their romantic relationship.

Adieux, l'absence et le retour, Les (The Farewell, Absence, and Return), *Das Lebewohl, Abwesenheit und Wiedersehn.* Ludwig van Beethoven, Sonata in E-flat Major, op. 81a.

Title given by Beethoven's publisher to this *sonate caractérestique*, dedicated to the Archduke Rudolph, who had to leave Vienna when it was under attack by the French. Beethoven wrote *Lebewohl* (farewell) over the opening phrase, and he referred to it as the *Lebewohl* Sonata.

"Aeolian Harp" Etude. Frédéric Chopin, Etude in A-flat Major, op. 25, no. 1, 1836. Perhaps this title came from a remark made by Robert Schumann comparing Chopin's playing to an Aeolian harp, a stringed instrument that when placed outside or in a window makes vague, eerie harmonies when the wind blows through it. Chopin is supposed to have referred to this etude as the "Shepherd Boy" Etude. See "Shepherd Boy" Etude.

aérien (Fr.). Light, airy.

affabile (It.). Affable, pleasing, politely, pleasantly, gentle.

affettuoso (It.). Affectionately, with feeling or tender feeling, warm, emotional.

affretando (It.). Hurrying, increasing the speed, pushing on.

agevole (It.). Easy, relaxed, smooth, comfortable, facile.

Agitation. Felix Mendelssohn, op. 53, no. 3, in G Minor, one of the *Songs without Words.*

agitato (It.). Excited, agitated, hurriedly, at a slightly faster tempo.

agité (Fr.). Agitated, restless.

agrémens, agréments (Fr.). Grace notes, in particular the "small ornaments" found in 17th- and 18th-century French music.

aigre (Fr.). Harsh, shrill.

aigu (Fr.). Sharp, acute.

aimable (Fr.). Kindly, pleasant, nice.

air. A tune, a simple melody, sometimes in the style of a folksong. In suites of the Baroque and Classical eras, the air was an optional piece, in general as opposed to the dance-based pieces in the suite. J. S. Bach used the term for the fourth movement in his French Suite no. 2 in C Minor, BWV 813, and the fifth movement in his French Suite no. 4 in E-flat Major, BWV 815.

air with variations. See theme and variations.

Airplane Sonata. George Antheil, Sonata no. 2, 1922. Sonata in two movements, its rhythms are aggressive and motoristic, but also sometimes reminiscent of ragtime. It is characterized by clusters and strident harmonies and is deliberately noisy; material is repeated either wholly or in fragments.

aisé (Fr.). Easy.

aisément (Fr.). Unhurried, with ease.

al, alla (It.). To the, at the, in the (manner, style, etc.).

al fine (It.). To the end (go).

al niente (It.). Dying away to nothing, gradually fading away.

al segno (It.). To the sign: locate the sign in the score and play from there.

Albéniz, Isaac (1860–1909). Spanish composer and pianist, he studied with Liszt. Albéniz composed over 200 piano pieces with strong rhythmic Spanish features, including *Iberia,* a cycle of 12 pieces, and the popular Tango in D.

Albert, Eugen d' (1864–1932). German composer, he was born in Glasgow, Scotland. A student of Liszt and highly regarded as a piano virtuoso and composer, d'Albert's piano works include two piano concertos, a sonata, a suite, and miscellaneous piano works. He also edited piano music.

Alberti bass. An accompaniment figure, located mainly in the left hand. It gets its name from Domenico Alberti (1710–40), who used it frequently. A good example is found in the first movement of the Mozart Sonata in C Major, K. 545.

alborada (Sp.). Music at dawn, a morning song. Ravel's *Alborada del gracioso* (The Fool's Dawn Song) from his *Miroirs* is a good example.

Albumblatt (Ger.). Album leaf: a title used for short character pieces, mainly for piano, by Romantic composers.

alcun, alcuna (It.). Some, a little.

alegria (Sp.). Mirth, merriment, gaiety, joy.

Alhambra Suite no. 1. Isaac Albéniz, 1897. This suite contains only one movement (*La Vega*) and was left unfinished. It is based on impressions of Grenada and contains colorful native rhythms and melodies.

Alkan, Charles-Valentin (real name Morhange) (1813–88). French composer, pianist, and teacher, he wrote mainly for the piano. His best works display technical challenges and musical imagination. He was killed when a bookcase fell on him.

alla breve (It.). In a concise manner, indicated by a sign ¢ which means instead of four beats to a measure there should be only two; also called "cut time."

alla marcia (It.). In march style.

alla tedesca (It.). In the style of a German dance.

alla turca (It.). In the Turkish style. See the last movement of Mozart's Sonata in A Major, K. 331.

alla zingarese (It.). In a gypsy style.

allant (Fr.). Stirring, going, moving.

allargando (It.). Broadening, getting slower and having a more dignified style, sometimes with a simultaneous *crescendo*.

allégrement (Fr.). Gaily, merrily, fast, briskly.

allegretto (It.). Rather cheerful, somewhat jolly, light, a moderately brisk speed; a little slower than *allegro*.

allegrezza (It.). Joyous, cheerfulness.

allegrissimo (It.). Very fast.

allegro (It.). Cheerful, merry, happy, upbeat, quick, lively, brisk, swift, good humored; a rather fast speed.

Allegro barbaro. Pieces by Alkan and Bartók that contain plenty of vigor and storm and stress.

allegro di molto, allegro molto (It.). Very fast.

allegro non tanto (It.). Fast, but not too fast.

allemande (Fr.). 1. A French word meaning German. 2. A German dance in ¾ meter, somewhat like the Ländler. Often used as the first movement in Baroque suite, for example, in J. S. Bach's French Suites. It makes frequent use of an upbeat at opening, is written in ⁴⁄₄ meter, and is rather cheerful and sprightly.

alquanto (It.). Somewhat, a little, rather.

amabile (It.). Graceful, tender, sweet, gentle.

American Ballads. Roy Harris, 1946. Five settings of American folk tunes, something of American equals to Bartók's folksong arrangements: *Streets of Laredo, Wayfaring Stranger, The Bird, Black Is the Color of My True Love's Hair,* and *Cod Liver Ile.*

amoroso (It.). Tenderly, lovingly.

amoureusement (Fr.). Lovingly, tenderly.

amplitude (Sp.). Greatness; full sound.

anacrusis. Term for unstressed up-beat, note(s) preceding the first strong beat of a measure; pickup.

ancora (It.). Again, once more, still, yet.

andante (It.). Steadily moving (walking), literally "going." The steady quality is more appropriate to the 18th century. Not slow or fast: in between.

Andante favori (Favorite Andante). Ludwig van Beethoven, WoO 57, 1803–4. Composed by Beethoven as a slow middle movement for the "Waldstein" Sonata, op. 53. After a friend suggested the movement was too long for the sonata Beethoven withdrew it and composed a shorter one. Beethoven used the Andante alone, and it was published as *Andante Favori.*

andante spianato (It.). 1. Flowing and smooth. 2. The title of Chopin's op. 22 for piano and orchestra (1834). Linked by Chopin to the Polonaise in E-flat Major; the whole work appeared as *Grand Polonaise brillante précédée d'un Andante spianato.*

andantino (It.). In the 18th century, a little slower than *andante;* in the 19th century, a little faster than *andante.*

anglaise (Fr.). English dance, in the English style. This word has been used for many types of dances: hornpipe, country dance, *écossaise.* They are usually strongly accented. See J. S. Bach's French Suite no. 3, BWV 814.

angoisse (Fr.). Anguish, with anguish.

angosciosamente (It.). Anguish, painfully.

anima (It.). Soul.

animando (It.). Becoming animated, more lively.

animant (Fr.). Becoming lively, animated.

animato (It.). Animated, lively; to be performed in a rather quick tempo.

animé (Fr.). Animated, spirited, in a moderately quick tempo.

animez (Fr.). More lively (slightly).

Années de pèlerinage (Years of Pilgrimage/Travel) Franz Liszt. Three collections of piano music. The first (1835–52), an extensive revision of his *Album d'un voyageur,* is entitled *Suisse* (Swiss), S. 160; the second (1838–49) *Italie* (Italy, with a three-piece supplement entitled *Venezia e Napoli*—Venice and Naples), S. 161 and 162; and the third (1867–77) is untitled, S. 163. Descriptive titles reflecting Liszt's travels are used with many of the pieces.

Añoranza (Longing for Home). Enrique Granados, 1888–90. From *Seis piezas sobre cantos populares españoles* (Six Pieces on Spanish Folk Themes). This piece, like many of his earlier works, is a picture post card in sound.

apaiser (Fr.). To sooth, calm, appease.

Aperçus désagréables (Unpleasant Observations). Erik Satie, 1912. For piano duet. 1. *Pastorale,* 2. *Choral,* 3. *Fugue.*

appassionato (It.). Impassioned, in a passionate intense style. *Sonata appassionata* is the title given to Beethoven's Sonata in F Minor, op. 57, 1805, by the publisher Cranz in the four-handed arrangement published in 1838. The sonata (in its original solo form) is usually called the *Appassionata.*

appena (It.). Scarcely, very little, hardly.

appoggiatura (It.). A "leaning" note appears as a small note slurred to the main note. In music of the Baroque and Classical periods it is played as an accented dissonance on the beat. In Romantic and 20th-century music, it normally is played slightly before the beat.

appuie sur la clé (Fr.). Stay (or press) on the key.

âpre (Fr.). Harsh, violent.

Arabeske (Ger.), **arabesque** (Fr.). 1. An ornate figuration, a curved, flowing line derived from Moorish art and architecture. 2. In music, a piece that uses a decorative design of florid material. Schumann, MacDowell, and Debussy, among others, used this word as titles for piano pieces.

Argerich, Martha (b. 1941). Argentinean pianist, she studied with Friedrich Gulda (1930–2000), Nikita Magaloff, and Michelangeli. She won the Chopin Competition in Warsaw in 1965 and has enjoyed a distinguished international career.

aria (It.). Air, song, tune, songlike piece. Used as titles for piano pieces by Alfredo Casella, Dohnányi, Handel, Peter Mennin, Selim Palmgren, and Scarlatti, among others.

Aria with Variations in the Italian Manner. J. S. Bach, BWV 989, 1709. Aria with 10 contrasting variations. This early set and the *Goldberg Variations* are Bach's only two separate sets of keyboard variations.

arietta (It.). Little aria or song. Used as title of small pieces by Clementi, Grieg, Johann Pachelbel, and Poulenc, among others.

arioso (It.). A melodious short piece in singing style. This title is used for pieces by Arthur Honegger, Meyer Kupferman, and George Rochberg, among others. Beethoven used it in his Sonata in A-flat Major, op. 110, in the slow movement, indicated *Arioso dolente* (in the style of a sad song) to distinguish it from the preceding *recitativo* (recitative).

armonioso (It.). Harmonious. When Chopin and Liszt use this term it means to use full (all the way down) pedal in the section so marked.

arpège (Fr.). Arpeggio.

"Arpeggio" Study. Frédéric Chopin, Etude in E-flat Major, op. 10, no. 11, 1829. This etude is often referred to by this title because of the continual use of arpeggiated (rolled) chords.

arrangement. The adaptation of a work from one medium to another. J. S. Bach was very active in arranging his own works and those of other composers. Liszt arranged his *Concerto Pathétique,* S. 258, from his solo piano piece *Grosses Konzertsolo,* S. 176. Arrangements have come from some of our greatest composers.

Arrau, Claudio (1903–91). Chilean pianist, he studied in Berlin with the Liszt student Martin Krause and won several international prizes. Arrau was known for broad, poetic readings of the major repertoire. He settled in the United States in 1941.

arrêt (Fr.). Stop; pause.

articuler (Fr.). To play clearly, distinctly.

Ashkenazy, Vladimir (b. 1936). Russian pianist, he studied with Lev Oborin at the Moscow Conservatory. He won first prize at the Brussels Competition in 1956, and in 1962 he was first-prize winner with Ogdon of the Tchaikovsky Competition in Moscow. Ashkenazy has played worldwide as an outstanding all-around interpreter.

aspramente (It.). Harshly.

assai (It.). Very, enough, extremely, much.

assez (Fr.). Rather, fairly, sufficiently, enough.

assez lent (Fr.). Rather slowly.

atonality. Organizing harmonic system for a piece not based on a tonal (or key) center.

attacca (It.). Attack, start, go on, begin the next. Continue for one movement (section) to the next without pause.

attaquez de suite (Fr.). Go on immediately.

attendez (Fr.). Wait, pause.

au loin (Fr.). Far away, in the distance.

au même tempo (Fr.). At the same tempo.

au moins (Fr.). At least.

au mouvement (Fr.). *A tempo.*

au signe (Fr.). To the sign.

au temps (Fr.). *A tempo.*

aubade (Fr.). Morning music, dawn; the same as *alborado*. Used for titles of piano pieces by Peter Fricker, Richard Franco Goldman, Rubinstein, and Satie, among others.

augmenter (Fr.). To increase, crescendo.

ausdrucksvoll (Ger.). With expression.

aussi (Fr.). Also, as.

Australian Forest Pictures. Roy Agnew (1891–1944). Six colorful character pieces.

Auszug (Ger.). Extract, abridgement; arrangement.

avant (Fr.). Before.

avant-bras (touches noirés) (Fr.). Forearm (black keys).

Avant-dernières pensées (Next-to-Last Thoughts). Erik Satie, 1915. 1. *Idylle,* 2. *Aubade,* 3. *Méditation.*

avant-garde (Fr.). New, "cutting-edge" ideas or techniques not yet commonly known and/or accepted by most pianists.

avec (Fr.). With.

avec colère (Fr.). Angrily.

avec humour (Fr.). With humor.

avvivando (It.). Becoming enlivened.

Azulejos (Mosaics or Tiles). Isaac Albéniz, 1909. The only piece in this intended set of short pieces is a *Prelude,* completed by Granados.

B

Babbitt, Milton (b. 1916). American composer, he is an important teacher who has expanded serial technique by using mathematical applications to rhythm, form, etc. For piano: *Partitions, Playing for Time, Post-Partitions, Reflections* (for piano and tape), *Semisimple Variations, Tableaux,* and *Three Compositions for Piano.*

Bacchanale. John Cage, 1938. Cage's earliest work for prepared piano. Composed for a dance by Syvilla Fort.

B-A-C-H. The letters of the name Bach correspond to the notes B♭-A-C-B in German. (The note B is called H in German.) They have been used as a musical motive (theme) in J. S. Bach's *Art of Fugue* and in works by Busoni, Liszt, Reger, Schumann, and Webern, among others.

Bach, Anna Magdalena (1701–60). The second wife of J. S. Bach, who compiled the "Anna Magdalena Books" of 1722 and 1725 for her musical education.

Bach, Carl Philipp Emanuel (1714–88). German composer, he was the third son of his famous father J. S. Bach. He was court musician to Frederick the Great of Prussia for 27 years, then became church organist in Hamburg. He composed over 200 sonatas and concertos plus an outstanding treatise on keyboard playing: *Ver-*

such über die wahre Art das Clavier zu spielen (Essay on the True Art of Playing Keyboard Instruments, 1753).

Bach, Johann Christian (1735–82). The youngest son of J. S. Bach, he spent time in Italy and London and is known as the "London Bach." He composed mainly opera but also close to 40 concertos and a number of piano sonatas. Bach exercised a major influence on Mozart. He wrote a piano method for the Naples Conservatory with Francesco Pasquale Ricci entitled *Méthode ou recueil de connaissances élémentaires pour le forte-piano ou clavecin* (Method or Collection of Elementary Studies for the Forte-piano or Harpsichord, 1786). Ricci wrote the text, and Bach provided the 100 pieces.

Bach, Johann Christoph Friedrich (1732–95). Known as the "Bückeburg Bach" (since he was active at the Bückeburg court), this ninth son of J. S. Bach wrote 15 solo sonatas and smaller works for the keyboard. His style combines German and Italian elements with a compositional technique characteristic of both Baroque and Classical styles.

Bach, Johann Sebastian (1685–1750). One of the greatest composers, he was organist in a number of small towns, then at the courts of Weimar and Cöthen before he was appointed Kantor (organist and choir master) at the Thomaskirche (St. Thomas Church) in Leipzig. Bach composed a large amount of music for the keyboard including concertos with and without accompaniment, numerous suites, separate pieces, plus the two volumes of the *Well-Tempered Clavier* or "The 48," among others. He was well known as an organ virtuoso.

***Bachianas brasileiras* (Brazilian Bach Pieces).** Heitor Villa-Lobos. Nine suites combining Brazilian folk music with Bachian techniques. No. 3 (1938) is for piano and orchestra, and no. 4 (1930–36) is for solo piano.

Backhaus, Wilhelm (1884–1969). German pianist, he studied with d'Albert in Frankfurt. He won the 1905 Rubinstein Prize and soon established an international reputation. He was one of the greatest interpreters of Beethoven, Brahms, and Chopin. Backhaus recorded most of the Classical and Romantic piano repertoire.

Bacon, Katherine (1896–1982). English pianist, she made many tours of the United States and Canada. In 1927 she gave recitals in New York of all 32 Beethoven sonatas. In 1928 she gave a Schubert series with 10 sonatas and other works. She appeared with many orchestras and was a member of the faculty of The Juilliard School from 1940 until her death.

badinage (Fr.). Childlike playfulness, lightness; pleasantry. *Badinerie* is an 18th-century term indicating a playful or coy movement.

Badura-Skoda, Paul (b. 1927). Austrian pianist, teacher, and author, he studied at the Vienna Conservatory and with Fischer. He has toured extensively and is well known through his many recordings. Although he is identified with Mozart, he has also performed many contemporary works. He has written *Interpreting Mozart on the Keyboard* and *Interpreting Bach at the Keyboard,* plus many articles.

bagatelle (Fr.). Trifle, a short unpretentious piece; sketch. Beethoven composed three sets of *Bagatelles:* opp. 33, 119, and 126.

Bagatelle ohne Tonart (Bagatelle without Tonality). Franz Liszt, S. 216a, 1885. Liszt selected this title since the piece constantly modulates toward a key that never materializes.

Baker, Joanne (b. 1923). American pianist and teacher, she studied at the University of Michigan with Brinkman. She taught for many years at the University of Missouri–Kansas City and turned out class after class of exceedingly fine pianists. She was also chair of the judges at the Gina Bachauer International Piano Competition for a number of years.

Balakirev, Mily (1837–1910). Russian composer, pianist, and teacher, he was the leader of the group of Russian nationalist composers known as "The Five." His piano works include the virtuosic "Oriental fantasy" *Islamey,* plus mazurkas, nocturnes, scherzos, waltzes, and two piano concertos.

Baldwin Piano Company. Leading American piano manufacturer founded in 1862 by Dwight Hamilton Baldwin (1821–99) in Cincinnati, Ohio.

ballade (Fr.). A composition which suggests a story. Chopin, Brahms, Liszt, Grieg, and others have written ballades for piano. Chopin's ballades are thought to have been inspired by the Polish poet Mickiewicz.

Bamboula. Louis Moreau Gottschalk, op. 2, probably 1844–45. A picturesque dance featuring the stamping of African American slaves mixed with the delicate arabesques of Chopin. It is a brilliant rondo on *Sweet Potatoes,* a Creole folk song.

Banjo, The. Louis Moreau Gottschalk, op. 15, 1855. The composer's most famous piano piece. The banjo is imitated in this piece, which shows the influence of Stephen Foster (1826–64).

Banowetz, Joseph (b. 1935). American pianist, author, and teacher, he was trained at The Juilliard School and the Vienna Academy of Music (First Prize). He has toured worldwide for many years and has made more than 25 recordings. Banowetz is one of the last exponents of the great Romantic keyboard tradition. He is also author of the widely known book *The Pianist's Guide to Pedaling*, published in four languages. He has taught at the University of North Texas for a number of years.

Banshee, The. Henry Cowell, 1925. The piece is played entirely on the strings inside the grand piano.

Barber, Samuel (1910–81). American composer, his accessible idiom is based on a lyrical, neoclassical music style. He used a broad spectrum of color in writing for both solo instruments and orchestra. Piano works: *Ballade* (composed for the 1977 Van Cliburn Competition as the commissioned piece), *Excursions, Love Song, Nocturne, Souvenirs* (originally for piano duet, solo version by the composer), and an outstanding piano sonata. He also composed a highly effective concerto for piano and orchestra.

barcarolle (Fr.). From *barca* (It.) meaning boat. A composition usually in swaying ⅜ time, imitating the boat songs of the Venetian gondoliers. Bartók, Chopin, Fauré (who wrote 13), Mendelssohn, and Rachmaninoff, among others, have composed barcarolles.

Barenboim, Daniel (b. 1942). Argentinean pianist and conductor, he studied with Boulanger and Fischer. He was a child prodigy who went on to enjoy an international career. He was married to the cellist Jacqueline du Pré.

Baroque. The term Baroque is used to designate a historical period and style in music, art, and architecture that covered roughly the years 1590–1750. Many musical forms involving the keyboard came into being during this time: fugue, concerto, suite, variations, toccata, passacaglia, chaconne, rondo, da capo form (ABA), and solo sonata. Keyboard composers active during this time included J. S. Bach, Couperin, Handel, Rameau, and Scarlatti.

Barr, Jean (b. 1942). American pianist and teacher, she studied with Gwendolyn Koldofsky at the University of Southern California. She was the first person in the United States to earn a doctoral degree in accompanying. She has been much in demand as a collaborative pianist and master teacher of chamber music. She has performed worldwide and has appeared in concert with many distinguished artists. Prior to assuming her present position at the Eastman School of Music, Barr taught at the University of Texas—Austin, Arizona State University, and the Music Academy of the West. Barr plays the full range of chamber music with astonishing attention to detail and beauty in all she does.

Bartók, Béla (1881–1945). Hungarian composer, he is one of the half-dozen major composers of the 20th century. He was also an outstanding pianist and teacher. Bartók was greatly influenced by the folk music of Central Europe. He wrote three piano concertos, *Bagatelles, Burlesques,* many pieces based on folk songs, six volumes of progressive piano pieces entitled *Mikrokosmos,* and a sonata in addition to suites.

basses légèrement expressive, les (Fr.). The bass notes should be lightly expressive.

basso continuo (It.). Continuous bass. This is a shorthand guide to the harmonic background of a keyboard piece. Bass notes were written with numbers above or beneath indicating the correct chords to be added. It was widely used during the Baroque period.

Battista, Joseph (1918–68). American pianist, he studied at the Philadelphia Conservatory of Music and with Samaroff at the Juilliard School. He won six major musical awards, and his career was launched when he appeared with the Philadelphia Orchestra. He was in the armed services during World War II but quickly resumed his career as a soloist and with numerous major orchestras with tours in the United States, Canada, Mexico, and South America. He taught at Indiana University until his death.

Bauer, Harold (1873–1951). English pianist, he started out to be a violinist, but Paderewski advised him to switch to piano. He had an international career and settled in the United States during World War I, where he exerted a strong influence on the musical life of that country. He was head of the piano department at the Manhattan School of Music. Ravel dedicated his *Ondine* to Bauer, and he later gave the premiere of Ravel's Concerto in G. He also edited music for Schirmer.

Bax, Arnold (1883–1953). English composer, he wrote prolifically for the piano. His style always shows great facility and a Romantic temperament. A love of the great Irish poets and Celtic folklore plus an early visit to Russia proved to be major influences. Piano works: *Lullaby, Nereid, Toccata, Two Russian Tone Poems, Whirligig, Winter Waters,* and four piano sonatas. For piano and orchestra: *Concertante* (for piano left-hand and orchestra), *Morning Song, Symphonic Variations.* For two pianos: *The Devil That Tempted St. Anthony, Hardanger, Moy Mell, The Poisoned Fountain, Red Autumn,* and a sonata.

Beach, Amy Marcy (1867–1944). The most famous American woman composer, she was an outstanding pianist and made her debut with the Boston Symphony Orchestra in 1885. Piano works: *Ballad, Five Improvisations, Four Sketches, Hermit Thrush at Eve, Morceaux Caractérestiques, Scottish Legend, Variations on a Balkan Theme,* and numerous other pieces, plus a piano concerto and much chamber music involving the piano.

bearbeitet (Ger.). Worked over, arranged. *Bearbeitung:* arrangement.

Bebung (Ger.). 1. A stroking. 2. A vibration used on the clavichord that gives a wavering of the true pitch where the finger repeatedly depresses the key without releasing it. Beethoven used this technique in the Adagio introduction to the last movement of his Sonata in A-flat Major, op. 110.

Bechstein, Friedrich Wilhelm Carl (1826–1900). German piano manufacturer, he founded his firm in Berlin in 1856. Bechstein pianos are considered to be outstanding.

Bee's Wedding, The. Felix Mendelssohn, op. 67, no. 4, in C Major, one of the *Songs without Words.* This name was given (though not by the composer) in early editions; it is better known as the *Spinning Song.*

Beethoven, Ludwig van (1770–1827). One of the most important composers for the piano, his piano works occupy a unique place in piano literature and demand the attention of both the teacher and the serious student. He worked in Vienna as a pianist and a composer. His 32 sonatas for the piano have been called the "New Testament" of piano literature. He composed five piano concertos, many single pieces, and sets of variations, especially the large set entitled the "Diabelli" Variations.

Bells of Moscow, The. Sergei Rachmaninoff, Prelude in C-sharp Minor, op. 3, no. 2. An editor actually introduced this title; the composer had nothing to do with it. The piece does seem to create the impression of bells with their overtones.

Belt, Philip (b. 1927). American fortepiano maker, he has made successful reproductions of Dulcken, Stein, and Walter fortepianos. During the 1970s his replicas of various fortepianos added to the interest and knowledge of Classical keyboard performance practice in the United States.

bem ligado (Port.). Very connected.

ben, bene (It.). Well, thoroughly. *ben marcato:* well marked, play in an accented manner.

berceuse (Fr.). Lullaby, cradle song. Brahms, Busoni, Chopin, Debussy, Fauré, Gottschalk, Grieg, Liszt, and Schumann, among others, have used this title for piano pieces.

Berceuse héroïque **(Heroic Lullaby).** Claude Debussy, 1914. This solo piano piece was written as a tribute to King Albert of Belgium and his soldiers during World War I. The Belgian national melody *La brabançonne* is quoted briefly. Distant bugle calls add atmosphere.

bergamasque (Fr.). A lively peasant dance from Bergamo, Italy. The word was used by Debussy in the title of his *Suite bergamasque* (1890–1905).

Bernstein, Leonard (1918–90). American composer, conductor, and pianist, his style was a mix of Broadway popular music and Mahler's chromaticism. The Sixth Van Cliburn International Competition (1981) commissioned Bernstein's largest work for piano: *Touches—Chorale, Eight Variations and Coda.* He wrote numerous pieces for the piano called *Anniversaries,* each dedicated to one of his (famous) friends.

Bernstein, Seymour (b. 1927). American pianist, composer, teacher, he studied with Alexander Brailowsky and Curzon. He has received numerous awards and has concertized in Asia, Europe, and North and South America, receiving accolades for his technical brilliance and interpretive skills. He is well known for his lectures and master classes. Many of his compositions appear continually on the bestseller lists. He has written a very popular book, *With Your Own Two Hands,* and has made videos. He is a private teacher in New York.

bestimmt (Ger.). With energy, decisively; prominent.

bewegt (Ger.). Moved (with motion), emotionally; fast moving.

"Biblical" Sonatas. Johann Kuhnau (1660–1722), 1700. These six sonatas (all based on scripture from the Old Testament) are among the most famous examples of Baroque keyboard program music.

bien articulé (Fr.). Clearly defined.

bien lent (Fr.). Moderately slow.

bien lié de pédale (Fr.). Very legato pedaling.

bien lier le thème (Fr.). Very legato melody.

bien modéré (Fr.). Rather moderate.

bien rhythmé (Fr.). With rhythmic emphasis.

Bilson, Malcolm (b. 1935). American pianist and fortepianist, he studied at Bard College and the University of Illinois. He has taught at Cornell University since 1968. Bilson was one of the first to make a persuasive case for using the fortepiano in the performance of Viennese Classical keyboard music. He has performed throughout the United States and Europe and has received high praise for recording many keyboard works of Haydn, Mozart, and Beethoven.

binary form. Two-part form, AB, meaning the musical material is completely different in each part; often each part is repeated. It may also just mean music in two parts.

bis (Lat.). 1. Twice, used to indicate a passage to be repeated. 2. Shouted by an audience to request an encore.

bisbigliando (It.). Whispering, murmuring. Used when a delicate effect is required.

bitonality. Organizing harmonic system of a piece based around two tonal (or key) centers.

"Black Key" Etude. Frédéric Chopin, Etude in G-flat Major, op. 10, no. 5, 1830. The right hand plays mainly black keys. Chopin authorized the name in a letter to Julian Fontana dated 23 April 1839.

"Black Mass," The. Alexander Scriabin, Sonata no. 9, op.68, 1913. One of Scriabin's friends, Podgaetsky, gave the sonata this nickname. A diabolical element present with the theme develops more "evilly": as the performance notation reads, "a sweetness gradually becoming more and more caressing and poisonous." Perhaps this is the reason for the subtitling it the "Black Mass," the perversions of the sacred mass associated with worship of the Devil (Berkowitz, p. 14).

Blind octaves. A piano technique where the hands alternate playing octaves in a unique way whereby the thumbs combine to create a scale, arpeggio, trill, etc., alternating notes which are doubled at the octave above or below.

Bloch, Joseph (b. 1917). American pianist, he studied with Mollie Margolies and Ganz in Chicago and Samaroff in New York. He received degrees from the Chicago Musical College and Harvard University. His Town Hall debut took place in 1950, and he has concertized in the United States, Europe, and Asia. He has made recordings and taught piano literature at the Juilliard School for many years. He has featured the music of Alkan on many of his programs and has a sensitive musical mind, always playing with authoritative grace and suppleness.

blues. A slow, melancholy jazz song, usually lamenting an unhappy love affair. The music is usually in a major key and uses the flattened third and seventh (the blue notes). Barber, Copland, Gershwin, Ravel, and Tansman, among others, used characteristics of the blues in some of their piano compositions.

Blumenstück (Ger.). 1. Flower piece. 2. Solo piano piece by Robert Schumann, op. 19, 1839.

Blüthner. German firm of piano manufacturer founded by Julius Blüthner (1824–1910) in Leipzig in 1853.

bolero (Sp.). Spanish dance in triple meter. Alfredo Casella, Chopin, Mikhail Glinka, and Carlos Surinach, among others, have composed boleros for the piano. Ravel's *Boléro* for orchestra is perhaps the most famous example.

Bolet, Jorge (1914–90). Cuban born, this American pianist studied with Saperton at the Curtis Institute. He toured worldwide and was an outstanding interpreter of Liszt and the 19th-century repertoire. He was the pianist in the film *Song without End*, based on the life of Liszt.

boogie-woogie. A type of fast jazz piano playing characterized by split (broken) octaves in the repeated bass line.

Bösendorfer. Viennese firm of piano manufacturer founded by Ignaz Bösendorfer (1796–1859) in 1828.

Boulanger, Nadia (1887–1979). French teacher, conductor, and pianist, she attracted leading musicians from throughout the world who came to study with her. She also lectured and conducted worldwide. Her outstanding American students included Copland, Roy Harris (1898–1979), and Walter Piston (1894–1976).

Boulez, Pierre (b. 1925). French composer, conductor, and teacher, he studied composition with Messaien at the Paris Conservatoire. Boulez's importance and originality has been as an *avant-garde* composer. He has composed three piano sonatas and *Douze Notations* for solo piano plus *Structures* for two pianos.

bourrée (Fr.). A lively French dance in duple time beginning with a quarter note upbeat. In the Baroque period it was one of the optional dances used in keyboard suites. Alkan, Chabrier, Chopin, Poulenc, and Albert Roussel, among others, composed *bourrées* for piano.

Brahms, Johannes (1833–97). German composer and pianist, this last of the great German composers composed during the later Romantic period. His music reflects the seriousness of his North German home (Hamburg) as well as the sensuous charm of Vienna, his home from 1863 until his death. The piano was his choice of instrument for his earliest works—the three sonatas and the scherzo—and his penultimate works, the groups of short character pieces of opp. 116–19, which include ballades, capriccios, intermezzos, and rhapsodies. He also composed eight sets of variations plus numerous pieces of chamber music that include the piano.

"Brahms Piano Method." See *Übungen* (Fifty-one Exercises).

bravura (It.). Skill, bravery, courage. Bravura playing requires great skill displaying virtuosic technique in difficult, showy passages.

breit (Ger.). Broadly; sometimes the equivalent of *Largo.*

Breitkopf & Härtel. German music publishers probably established on 24 January 1719 by the printer Bernhard Christoph Breitkopf (1695–1777). Gottfried Christoph Härtel (1763–1827) joined the Breitkopf firm in 1795. In 1796 he bought the firm and took over the running of the publishing house, now known as Breitkopf & Härtel. The firm is well known for its complete and excellent editions.

Brendel, Alfred (b. 1931). Austrian pianist, born in what was then called Czechoslovakia, he studied at the Vienna Academy of Music and with Fischer. He is regarded as one of the great pianists of our time. Brendel is famous for interpretation of the Viennese classics, especially Beethoven. He has recorded most of Beethoven's piano music twice.

bridge. A connecting (transitional) passage, frequently involving a change in key, that links together two important sections of a large-scale work.

brillant (Fr.), *brillante* (It.). Brilliant, bright, sparkling.

Brinkman, Joseph (1901–60). American pianist and teacher, he studied at the American Conservatory of Music and was a faculty member of this institution. He taught at the University of Michigan School of Music from 1930 to 1960, where he was instrumental in bringing Schnabel to teach from 1940 to 1945, with whom he studied and assisted in teaching. He gave the European premier of Leo Sowerby's Piano Concerto no. 2 in 1937. His students include Baker, Hinson, Race, and Marilyn, Nelita, and Wesley True.

brio (It.). Vigor, spirit, fire.

Broadwood. Founded in London in 1728 by John Broadwood to make harpsichords, the company began making pianos in 1773. Beethoven enjoyed the Broadwood piano sent to him by the piano maker.

Brook, The. Felix Mendelssohn, op. 30, no. 5, in D Major, one of the *Songs without Words.*

Brouillards **(Fog).** Claude Debussy, *Préludes,* book 2, no. 1, 1913. Atmospheric figuration accompanies a vague melodic line.

Brown Index. Maurice J. E. Brown's 1960 index of the works of Frédéric Chopin in chronological order. Commonly referred to as the "BI" number.

Browning, John (1933–2003). American pianist, he studied privately with Rosina Lhévinne as a youngster and later with her at The Juilliard School and with Lee Pattison in Los Angeles. He received numerous national and international awards and established an international career. He gave the world premiere of Barber's Piano Concerto in 1962 and played it hundreds of times. Browning played a broad range of repertoire from Bach to the 20th century. He had a superb technique, was an outstanding craftsman, and took nothing for granted in his performances.

brusco (It.). Rough, harsh, brusque, rude.

bruyant (Fr.). Noisy.

Bruyères **(Heather).** Claude Debussy, *Préludes,* book 2, no. 5, 1913.

This idyllic landscape may be regarded as a companion piece to the "Girl with the Flaxen Hair," book 1, no. 8.

"Bückeburg Bach." See Bach, Johann Christoph Friedrich.

Bull, John (1562–1628). English composer and outstanding keyboard performer, some of his works require immense finger dexterity. Bull was organist of the Chapel Royal and the first professor of music at Gresham College, London (1596–1607). Some of his keyboard pieces are contained in the collection *Parthenia* (1611). Others have been reprinted in the *Fitzwilliam Virginal Book* (2 vols., 1894–1899).

Bülow, Hans von (1830–1894). German pianist and conductor, he studied piano with Wieck and Liszt and conducting with Richard Wagner. He was well known for his interpretations of Beethoven and specialized in playing enormous programs, such as the last five piano sonatas of Beethoven. He edited extensively for Universal Edition. His edition of the Beethoven sonatas is thought to represent the way Liszt taught these works.

Burge, David (b. 1930). American pianist and teacher, he studied at Northwestern University, the Eastman School of Music, and with Pietro Scarpini in Florence while he was there on a Fulbright scholarship. He has performed 20th-century piano music extensively, including first performances of many American works. He has taught at the University of Colorado and the Eastman School of Music. He has written a book entitled *Twentieth-Century Piano Music.*

burla, burlesca (It.), **burlesque** (Fr.). Burlesque, jocular, in joking style. A *Burlesca* is found in J. S. Bach's Partita no. 3 in A Minor, BWV 827. The style is also used in extended compositions in a playful mood, such as Richard Strauss's *Burleske* for piano and orchestra, op. 16. Other composers of burlesques include Bartók, Dohnányi, MacDowell, Messiaen, Ned Rorem, and Tansman.

Burgmüller, Johann Friedrick (1806–1874). German composer, he wrote mainly light salon music as well as some useful studies for the pianist.

Busoni, Ferruccio (1866–1924). Born in Italy and educated in Germany, he was always pulled between these two traditions. He was one of the greatest and most creative pianists of all times. Busoni composed many works for the piano including a five-movement concerto that uses a male choir, *Fantasia contrappuntistica* (Contrapuntal Fantasia, inspired by Bach), *Indianisches Tagebuch* (Indian Diary), *7 Elegies,* six sonatinas, and many transcriptions of works by other composers.

"Butterfly" Etude. Frédéric Chopin, Etude in G-flat Major, op. 25, no. 9, 1832–34. This imaginative title, which came from a publisher, seems appropriate since the piece is fluttery and light, perhaps suggesting the whirr of a butterfly.

"butterfly" pedaling. See *vibrato.*

BWV. *Bach-Werke-Verzeichnis* (Index to Bach's Works). Numbering system for the works of J. S. Bach taken from Wolfgang Schmieder's *Thematisch-systematisches Verzeichnis der musikalischen Werke von Johann Sebastian Bach* (1950).

Byrd, William (1543–1623). Great English composer, this "Father of Musicke" had more influence than any other composer on the development of English music. Over 120 pieces of his keyboard music for the virginal survive in collections such as *My Ladye Nevells Booke* and *Parthenia.* Others have been reprinted in the *Fitzwilliam Virginal Book.*

C

cadenza (It.). A brilliant passage introduced near the end of a composition, either improvised by the performer or written by the composer or editor. Allusion to previously used themes is the norm. Sometimes cadenzas can be very short and may be used at any point in solo works, usually extemporized (impromptu) by the pianist. This practice took place from the Baroque through the Classical and Romantic periods.

Cage, John (1912–92). American composer, he was occupied for some time with the prepared piano, which he invented in 1938, where various objects are placed between the strings to obtain unusual sound effects. He assimilated elements of the 12-tone school and was influenced by Oriental philosophy. Toward the end of his life his interest in the aleatoric or "random" element was supreme. Piano works: *Musical Changes* (which uses the Chinese book of numbers *I Ching*), *Music for Amplified Toy Pianos, Music for Piano 4–84, Sonatas and Interludes, Winter Music, 32 études australes,* and *4′ 33″*, where the pianist does not make any "music"; the only music is the sounds in the performing space.

cakewalk. A dance that began among American plantation slaves in the 1840s that involved parodying their white owners' manners and fancy dancing. The cakewalk was associated with ragtime and appealed to Europeans. Debussy's *Golliwogg's Cake-walk* is a well-known example of this American influence.

calando (It.). Becoming quieter (softer) was the meaning in the 18th century. In the 19th century the term generally involved becoming quieter *and* a gradual decrease (getting slower) in tempo; dying away.

calando nel tempo. Decreasing in respect to the tempo. In Mozart's works *calando* normally meant only becoming quieter (softer).

calcando (It.). Hurrying the time, accelerando.

calma (It.). Tranquil, calm.

calmant, en se (Fr.). Subsiding, becoming calm.

calmato (It.). Calmed, quieted.

calore (It.). Warmth, passion.

caloroso (It.). Warm, passionately, animated; heat.

camminando (It.). Strolling, at a moderate pace.

Campanella, La (The Little Bells). Franz Liszt, no. 3 of the "Paganini" Etudes, 1838. Well-known piece by Liszt in which the sound of little bells is imitated. It is based on the finale (*Rondo alla campanella*) of Paganini's Violin Concerto in B Minor.

canarie (Fr.). A 17th-century French dance that originated in the Canary Islands, written in $\frac{3}{8}$ or $\frac{6}{8}$ time and employing dotted rhythms. It is somewhat related to the gigue and characterized by jumping and foot stamping.

Canin, Martin (b. 1930). American pianist, he studied at the Juilliard School with Rosina Lhévinne and Samaroff. He has toured in the United States and Europe and is an expert chamber musician as well as soloist. His performances display a polished technique, great attention to structure, and a beautiful sound.

canon. The most strict form of counterpoint where two or more voices present the same melody in overlapping succession.

Canope (Canopic Urn). Claude Debussy, *Préludes*, book 2, no. 10, 1913. The title refers to an Egyptian burial urn. The piece is mysterious and atmospheric, with a subtle evocation of Eastern music using slow chords and a haunting melody.

cantabile (It.). In a singing style; play in a melodious and graceful manner; smoothly.

cantilena (It.). 1. Play in a smooth, flowing style. 2. A songlike melody.

canzona (It.). An instrumental form among the precursors of both the *sonata* and *fugue,* in contrasting sections. J. S. Bach, Girolamo Frescobaldi, Froberger, and Handel, among others, wrote *canzonas.* The term is used by later composers such as Liszt, Nicolai Medtner, and Peter Mennin to refer to pieces of a songlike character.

capriccio (It.), **caprice** (Fr., Eng.). Whim, caprice; humorous, fanciful. In piano music a piece in free form of a light or humorous character. Bach, Brahms, Dohnányi, Dvořák, Fauré, Mendelssohn, Poulenc, and Prokofiev, among others, composed pieces with this title. Stravinsky wrote a piano concerto entitled *Capriccio* (1929).

Capriccio on the Departure of a Beloved Brother. J. S. Bach, BWV 992, 1704. Bach's only (known) example of programmatic keyboard music, in six sections with programmatic titles. It was written to mark the departure of his brother Johann Jakob as oboist in the Swedish service.

Capriccio on Five Notes. Lee Hoiby (b. 1926). The commissioned piece for the 1962 Van Cliburn Piano Competition.

capriccioso (It.). Capricious, whimsical, fancifully; at the player's whim, in a playful style.

caressant (Fr.). Tender, caressing.

Caresse dansée (Danced Caress). Alexander Scriabin, op. 57, no. 2, 1907. A delicate, lilting waltz, in a suggestive mood, this piece needs a sensuous and sensitive performance. One of the very best of Scriabin's smaller works.

Carnaval (Carnival). Robert Schumann, op. 9, 1834–35. A variegated suite of 21 character pieces, subtitled "Little Scenes on Four Notes." Most of the pieces are variations on the four notes A—E♭—C—B (ASCH in German) or alternatively A♭—C—B, musical letters in Schumann's name. ASCH was the name of a Bohemian town where Schumann's girlfriend Ernestine von Fricken lived.

Carnaval de Pesth (Carnival in Pest). Franz Liszt, Hungarian Rhapsody no. 9, S. 244-9, 1848. This piece has been so nicknamed because of the festive character of the music.

Carnaval des animaux (Carnival of the Animals). Camille Saint-Saëns, 1886. This "grand zoological fantasy," originally intended as a musical joke for family and friends and not published until after his death, is composed for two pianos and chamber orchestra. Each descriptive movement is named for an animal: swan, fish, even pianists!

Carreño, Teresa (1853–1917). Venezuelan pianist, she was taught by her father and studied with Gottschalk and Anton Rubinstein. She was called the "Valkyrie of the Piano" because of her virtuoso technique. One of her four husbands was the pianist d'Albert.

Casadesus, Robert (1899–1972). French pianist, he studied at the Paris Conservatoíre and lived in the United States from 1940 to 1946. He was especially respected for his interpretations of Chopin, Debussy, Mozart, Ravel, and Scarlatti. His wife Gaby (1901–99) and son Jean (1927–72) were also pianists.

Cass, Richard (b. 1931). American pianist, he studied with Wendell Keeney at Furman University and with Boulanger and Cortot in Paris. He has won important contests and has concertized extensively in the United States and Europe. He taught at the University of North Texas and presently at the University of Missouri—Kansas City (Conservatory of Music).

Catalogue d'oiseaux **(Catalog of Birds).** Olivier Messiaen, 1956–58. Seven books of large-scale pieces based on bird calls. A unique set of pieces, perhaps unprecedented in the history of music.

Cathédrale engloutie, La **(The Sunken Cathedral).** Claude Debussy, *Préludes,* book 1, no. 10, 1910. A vision in sound of the legendary submerged Cathedral of Ys off the coast of Brittany.

Cat's Fugue. Domenico Scarlatti, Sonata in G Minor, K. 30 1738. Nickname for a fugue in this sonata, whose subject suggests a cat walking over the keyboard.

cedendo (Sp.). Yield; get slower, *ritard.*

cédez (Fr.). Yield, give way; get slower, diminish the speed.

celeramente (It.). Rapidly.

celere (It.). Quick, rapid, swift.

Celestial Railroad, The. Charles Ives, 1924. This fantasy for piano was arranged by Ives from the second movement of his Symphony no. 4.

cembalo (It.). Term for harpsichord, abbreviation of *clavicembalo.*

Ce qu'a vu le vent d'ouest **(What the West Wind Saw).** Claude Debussy, *Préludes,* book 1, no. 7, 1910. A brilliant Listzian showpiece, it takes its title from a Hans Christian Andersen story.

Chabrier, Emmanuel (1841–94). French composer, he wrote music that has a certain uninhibited quality and is easily accessible. All of his compositions are vigorous, unpretentious, expressive, and pianistic. His music is a bridge between Saint-Saëns and Impressionism. Some of his better-known works include *Bourrée fantasque* (Fantastic Bourrée), *España* (Spain), *Habanera,* and *Pièces pittoresque* (Picturesque Pieces).

chaconne (Fr.), **ciacona** (It.). A graceful Baroque form of composition in triple meter with a continuous set of variations over a ground bass (*basso ostinato*) of eight measures. Beethoven's C Minor Variations for piano (WoO 80) are in the form of a chaconne. Louis Couperin, Girolamo Frescobaldi, Handel, Carl Nielsen, Henry Purcell, Halsey Stevens, and Stefan Wolpe, among others, have composed *chaconnes* for keyboard.

chiaro, chiara (It.). Clear, unconfused. *chiaramente:* clearly, distinctly. *chiarezza:* clarity, distinctness.

chamber music. "Room music." Music written for a small group to be played in a room or small hall, for three to eight performers, one instrument on each part. Groups larger than eight require a conductor, and a conductor is not a part of true chamber music. The piano in chamber music involves an enormous repertoire: trio, quartet, quintet, etc. Haydn and Mozart were the first two composers to establish a true chamber music style involving the piano.

chantant (Fr.). Melodious, *cantabile.*

Chapitres tournés en tous sens (Chapters Turned Every Which Way). Erik Satie, 1913. *Celle qui parle trop* (The Woman Who Talks Too Much), *Le porteur parle trop* (The Bearer of Large Stones), *Regrets des enfermés (Jonas et Latude)* (Regrets of the Immured Men [Jonah and Latude (a historical prisoner in the Bastille)]). Written in barless notation.

character piece. A term used for a large repertoire of small 19th-century pieces. They often are programmatic or express a definite mood and are usually short. Examples include bagatelles, impromptus, intermezzi, musical moments, preludes, rhapsodies, and songs without words. Schumann constructed cycles of small character pieces as seen in his *Carnaval, Davidsbündlertanze, Kreisleriana,* and *Papillons.*

chaud (Fr.). Warm, passionate.

Cherkassky, Shura (1911–95). Russian pianist, he studied with Hofmann and was renowned for his interpretation of 19th- and mainstream 20th-century works, but he also included music of Berg, Bernstein, Messiaen, and Stockhausen on his programs in his later years.

Chester: Variations for Piano. William Schuman (1910–92). The commissioned piece for the 1989 Van Cliburn Piano Competition.

Chickering. American firm of piano makers founded by Jonas Chickering (1798–1853) in Boston in 1823. They made some of the finest pianos during the 19th century.

Children's Corner. Claude Debussy, 1908. Six-movement suite written for his three-year-old daughter, Chouchou (Little Cabbage): *Doctor Gradus ad Parnassum, Jimbo's Lullaby, Serenade for the Doll, The Snow Is Dancing, The Little Shepherd, Golliwogg's Cake-walk.*

Chopin, Frédéric (1810–49). Polish composer and pianist, he settled in Paris. Chopin's highly original writing made a unique contribution to piano literature. He composed more than 200 works, mostly for the piano including two concertos, four ballades, 27 etudes, four impromptus, 57 mazurkas, 21 nocturnes, 26 preludes, 10 polonaises, three rondos, four scherzos, three sonatas, among various other pieces. Most great pianists play Chopin.

Chopsticks. An anonymous, quick waltz tune for piano to be performed with two forefingers or with the hands held flat perpendicularly, the keys being struck by the sides of the hands. The name refers to the chopping-like action. A collection for four hands (based on this tune) entitled *Paraphrases* was published in 1893 including pieces by Alexandre Borodin, César Cui, Anatoli Liadov, and Liszt.

chorale. A hymn tune or sacred tune; it may also refer to a piece in simple four-part harmony. Many composers of piano music have used this term in their keyboard music: J. S. Bach, Bartók, Busoni (who transcribed a number of chorales for piano), Johann Krebs, Mel Powell, Hermann Reutter, Vittorio Rieti, Kaikhosru Sorabji, Villa-Lobos, and Richard Yardumian, among others.

Christmas Tree Suite. Franz Liszt, S. 186, 1874–76. This is a mixed collection of 12 religious and genre pieces: *An Old Noel, O Holy Night, Shepherds at the Manger, March of the Magi, Sherzoso: Lighting the Candles on the Christmas Tree, Carillon, Berceuse, Old Noël* (carol), *Evening Bells, In the Olden Days, Hungarian, Polish* (polonaise with mazurka characteristics). Liszt also prepared a piano duet version.

Chromatic Fantasia and Fugue. J. S. Bach, BWV 903, 1720–23. A piece written in an expansive harmonic language, highly sectionalized and free in construction. The three-voice fugue is a magnificent example of dramatic cumulative effect.

Ciaccona dei tempi di guerra. Erich Itor Kahn (1905–56), 1943. Chaconne "in time of war" is a large-scale work (40 variations) in nonstrict serial technique that is powerful in its combination of anger, strength, and poignancy. The straight row is presented between the fantasy-like introduction and the beginning of the *ciaccona* proper. Very pianistic but a challenge for the finest performers.

Ciccolini, Aldo (b. 1925). Italian pianist, he studied at the Naples Conservatory and became professor there in 1947. His Paris debut was in 1949, and he has toured Europe, United States, and the Far East. He taught at the Paris Conservatoire from 1971 to 1988 and plays a wide repertoire from Bach to modern French composers. His style of playing is brilliant, robust, and colorful.

clair (Fr.). Light, brightness.

***Clair de lune* (Moonlight).** Claude Debussy, the third piece in his *Suite bergamasque* (1890–1905).

clarté (Fr.). Clarity.

classical music. 1. A term used to denote works which are considered perfect in content and form and have enduring value. 2. Music composed during the Classical era (ca. 1750–1820). Haydn, Mozart, Beethoven, and Schubert represent the highest standards during this time. 3. "Art music" as opposed to popular and folk music.

clavecin (Fr.). Harpsichord; spinet.

clavicembalo (It.). Harpsichord, abbreviated *cembalo*.

clavichord. A predecessor of the piano with a mechanism that uses metal wedges rather than hammers, very popular in J. S. Bach's time.

clavier (Fr.). Any stringed keyboard instrument, such as the piano, harpsichord, clavichord. Bach used the term in his famous work the *Well-Tempered Clavier*.

Clementi, Muzio (1752–1832). Italian composer, teacher, pianist, music publisher, and piano manufacturer, his well-known collection of 100 studies *Gradus ad Parnassum* (Steps to Perfection) has influenced generations of pianists. Clementi's compositions also profoundly influenced Beethoven. Clementi composed over 100 sonatas and sonatinas.

Cliburn, Van (Harvey Lavan, Jr.) (b. 1934). American pianist and student of Rosina Lhévinne, he became an international celebrity when he became the first American to win the Tchaikovsky Competition in Moscow in 1958. In 1962 he founded the Van Cliburn Piano Competition in Fort Worth, Texas. Cliburn specializes in 19th-century repertoire, has a big technique, and knows how to use it effectively.

cloches (Fr.). Bells or chimes. Composers have been fascinated by bell or chime sonorities: Debussy, *Cloches à travers les feuilles* (Bells [Heard] through the Leaves) from the second book of *Images;* Dohnányi, *Cloches* from *Six Piano Pieces;* Liszt, *Cloches de Genève* (Bells of Geneva) from book 1 (Swiss) of *Années de pèlerinage, La cloche sonne* (The Bell Tolls), *Cloches du soir* (Evening Bells), and *La campanella* (The Little Bells); Saint-Saëns, *Les cloches du soir* (The Evening Bells).

Clouds. Felix Mendelssohn, op. 53, no. 2, in E-flat Major, one of the *Songs without Words.*

clusters. See tone cluster.

coda (It.). Literally tail: a short section that concludes a work after the main body of the piece.

codetta (It.). A short coda.

col, colla (It.). With the.

colla destra (It.). With the right hand.

colla sinistra (It.). With the left hand.

colla voce (It.). With the voice, direction to the pianist to follow the singer.

Collines d'Anacapri, Les (The Hills of Anacapri). 1910. Claude Debussy, *Préludes,* book 1, no. 5, 1910. The piece has brilliant writing that uses a tarantella rhythm.

come (It.). As, like, the same as.

come da lontano (It.). As if from a distance.

come prima (It.). As at first, play the same way as previously.

come sopra (It.). Play a note or passage as before.

comme (Fr.). As, like.

commosso (It.). Moved, excited, affected, stirred, touched.

comodo (It.). Convenient; at a convenient, comfortable or leisurely manner (without haste), an easy rate of speed, moderate tempo.

compass. The range of a voice or instrument, from its lowest note to its highest.

compiacevole (It.). Agreeable, pleasing.

Composition for Piano with Pianist. Robert Moran (b. 1937), 1965. The score reads: "A pianist comes onto the stage and goes directly to the concert grand piano. He climbs into the piano and sits on the strings. The piano plays him." An *avant-garde* piece.

con (It.). With.

con alcuna licenza (It.). With some degree of freedom.

con anima (It.). With soul.

con animato (It.). With animation.

con brio (It.). With spirit, vigor, fire.

con grazia (It.). With grace.

con lancio (It.). With gusto, bounding, springing.

con lentezza (It.). With slowness and delay.

con rabbia (It.). With rage, fury.

con solemnita (It.). With solemnity.

con sordino (It.). With the mute or damper. Used by Beethoven to indicate not to use the damper pedal—so the dampers (mutes) are on the strings.

concertino (It.). A small concerto.

concerto (It.). A piece of several movements, for one or more solo instruments with orchestra.

Concerto pathétique ("Pathetic" Concerto). Franz Liszt, Concerto for Two Pianos in E minor, S. 258, 1856. A bold one-movement form similar to a symphonic poem in three contrasting sections and virtuosic throughout. Two solo piano and orchestra versions survive, one in the original (1850) one-movement form and the other in Liszt's revised multisectional form.

Concord Sonata. Charles Ives, 1909–15. Ives's second piano sonata, it contains four pragmatic movements: *Emerson, Hawthorne, The Alcotts, Thoreau.* The work is Ives's impression of the spirit of transcendentalism that is associated with Massachusetts in the 19th century. It is an early example of the use of clusters.

Concertstück (Ger.). See *Konzertstück.*

Confidence. Felix Mendelssohn, op. 19, no. 4, in A Major, one of the *Songs without Words.*

Connoisseurs and Amateurs. C. P. E. Bach, W. 55, 56, 57, 58, 59, and 61, 1779–87. Sonatas, fantasies, and rondos for keyboard.

These 37 large-scale works (in spite of the title) are eminently suitable for recitals. The fantasies contain some of Bach's most original writing. See especially the Sonatas in C Major, W. 55:1, and A Major, W. 55:3.

Consolation. Felix Mendelssohn, op. 30, no. 3, in E Major, one of the *Songs without Words.*

Consolations. Franz Liszt, S. 172, 1850. Six *pensées poétiques* (poetic thoughts) or nocturnes, the best known being number three. Number 4, the so-called *Stern-Consolation,* is on a theme by the grand duchess Maria Pavlovna. They were inspired by poems of Charles Sainte-Beuve entitled *Les consolations* (1830) that deal with consoling—hence the title.

Contemplation. Felix Mendelssohn, op. 30, no. 1, in E-flat Major, one of the *Songs without Words.*

Contemporary period. This period of music history extends from around 1910 to the present time. A good deal of the music of this period is anti-German (and particularly the music of Richard Wagner) or anti-19th century. This period is often called the Modern period. A distinction should be made between modern music and music that was written recently. Any music which still clings to the Romantic style is not genuinely modern even if written yesterday. Many styles of music have been written during this period.

continuo (It.). An abbreviated form of the term *basso continuo.*

contredanse (Fr.). See country dance.

copla (Sp.). A contrasting short lyrical section following a faster section. It consists of phrases that begin with two upbeats. *Rubato* is appropriate.

Copland, Aaron (1900–1990). American composer and pianist, he was one of the most influential musicians of the 20th century. He studied with Rubin Goldmark (1872–1936) and Boulanger and composed for most media. His best-known works for piano include his Piano Concerto, *Four Piano Blues, Night Thoughts,* composed for the 1973 Van Cliburn International Piano Competition, *Piano Fantasy, Piano Variations,* and a sonata.

coranto (It.). See *courante.*

corda (It.). String. In piano music, *una corda* (one string, literally one less string) means to use the left pedal (soft pedal), while *tre corde* or *tutte de corde* (all the strings) means to stop using the *una corda.*

Corelli, Variations on a Theme of. Sergei Rachmaninoff, op. 42,

1932. Work for solo piano involving 20 variations: in reality it is two sets of variations, generally of parallel construction, separated by an *Intermezzo* and concluded by a *coda.*

"Coronation" Concerto. W. A. Mozart, K. 537, 1790. This concerto was called the "Coronation" because Mozart performed it in Frankfurt in October 1790 at the coronation festivities of Holy Roman Emperor Leopold II.

corrente (It.). See *courante.*

Cortot, Alfred (1877–1962). Swiss pianist, he lived most of his life in Paris. He studied at the Paris Conservatoire and became famous both as conductor and pianist. In 1905 Cortot associated with violinist Jacque Thibaud and cellist Pablo Casals to form a celebrated piano trio. Cortot edited the piano works of Chopin, Liszt, and Schumann and wrote several books including *French Piano Music.* He was a great interpreter of Chopin and Schumann, but he also played works of Beethoven, Debussy, Liszt, and French composers extensively.

Couleurs de cité celeste **(Colors of the Celestial City).** Olivier Messiaen, 1963. Work for piano and chamber orchestra. These "inner colors" spring from five quotations from the Apocalypse (Book of Revelations, given in the score). The form of each piece depends entirely on colors, and they include bird songs of different countries.

coulant (Fr.). Flowing.

country dance (Eng.), *contredanse* (Fr.), *Kontretanz* (Ger.). An English dance of popular origin. A form of the English country dance also became popular on the European continent as the *contredanse.* Beethoven, Chopin, Mozart, Prokofiev, and Weber, among others, composed *contredanses.*

Couperin, François (1668–1733). French composer and harpsichordist, he was a most original and versatile composer. He influenced J. S. Bach and Handel as well as many of his younger contemporaries. Couperin composed over 220 pieces that are contained in his four books of *Pièces de clavecin* (Harpsichord Pieces). His treatise *L'Art de toucher de Clavecin* (The Art of Playing the Harpsichord) was written to help performers know how to perform his works.

courante (Fr.), *corrente, coranto* (It.). A lively 16th-century dance which became one of the standard movements of the classical suite.

The Italian version (*corrente*) is in quick time with running passages; the French type (*courante*) is slower and has shifting rhythms. Most of the great Baroque composers composed works in these forms.

court (Fr.). Short, brief.

Cowell, Henry (1897–1965). American composer, he was a founding father of 20th-century American music and multiculturalism. He composed over 1,000 works, including many short piano pieces. His music covers an enormous range, in both technique and expression. Cowell's clusters and use of the prepared piano are well known, and his technique of manipulating the strings directly has become standard fare with many contemporary composers.

Cramer, Johann Baptist (1771–1858). German composer, pianist, and teacher, he studied with Clementi and had a successful career as a touring virtuoso. Cramer started a publishing firm in London in 1824 that later began manufacturing pianos. His *84 Studies for Piano*, the fifth and last part of his *Grosse praktische pianoforte Schule* (Large Practical Piano School), are still used today, and he composed seven concertos and over 100 sonatas. His musical compositions are characterized by solid musical taste. Beethoven, who greatly admired Cramer's pianistic abilities, made annotations in 21 Cramer etudes; perhaps they were to be used in Beethoven's projected *Klavierschule*.

crescendo (It.). A direction to increase volume, gradually get louder (stronger); abbreviated *cresc.* Often written as a sign: ⟍

Cristofori, Bartolomeo (1655–1731). Italian keyboard instrument maker and designer. He constructed the first piano around 1700 in which strings were struck by hammers, and the performer could control dynamics by the use of more or less weight on the keys.

croiser (les moins) (Fr.). Crossing hands. Scarlatti was one of the earliest composers to use this technique frequently.

Croquis et agaceries d'un gros bonhomme en bois (Sketches and Provocations of a Big Wooden Boob). Erik Satie, 1913. *Tyrolienne turque* (Turkish Yodel Song), *Danse maigre* (*à la maniére de ces messieurs*) (Thin [or Lenten] Dance [in the style of their Lordships]), *Españaña* (a kind of waltz). Parodies of Mozart, Chabrier, Scott, and Debussy. Written in barless notation.

crotchet. In British terminology, a quarter note.

Crumb, George (b. 1929). American composer, he constantly seeks new sonorities from both the keyboard and the inside of the piano. He is one of the most original voices in new music. His most important piano music includes *Makrokosmos I and II* (which involve singing, whistling, speaking, and groaning as well as playing both inside the piano and on the keyboard), *Gnomic Variations, A Little Suite for Christmas,* and *Processional.*

csárdás, czárdás (Hung.). A Hungarian dance in duple meter and two sections: a melancholy section (*lassús* or *lassan*) and a cheerful section (*friss,* or *friska*). Liszt's *Hungarian Rhapsodies* provide fine examples.

cupo (It.). Obscure, dark, pensive, hollow, gloomy, somber.

Curzon, Clifford (1907–82). English pianist, he studied at the Royal Academy of Music in London and with Schnabel and Landowska. An international concert star for three decades, he played Beethoven, Mozart, Schubert, and Schumann with great success and premiered a number of works by English composers.

cycle. A name used with a group of compositions that are sometimes (and sometimes not) related in some way and are usually meant to be performed together. Parts may be linked thematically or based on a common subject. Schumann composed cycles of pieces strung together under a name, such as *Papillons* (Butterflies), *Davidsbündlertanze* (Dances of the League of David), *Carnaval* (Carnival), and *Kinderszenen* (Scenes of Childhood).

cyclic form. The formal structure of a composition wherein a later movement reintroduces material (sometimes in varied forms or guises) of an earlier movement. A few piano examples are Beethoven's Sonata in A Major, op. 101, Schubert's *Wanderer Fantasy,* Liszt's Sonata in B Minor, and Franck's *Prélude, chorale et fugue.*

Czárdás macabre (Dance of Death). Franz Liszt, S. 224, 1884. An excellent piece for budding virtuosi!

Czerny, Carl (1791–1857). Austrian pianist, teacher, and composer, he studied with Beethoven, Clementi, and Hummel and taught Liszt and Leschetizky. His piano studies will always benefit young pianists. He wrote approximately 1,000 printed compositions, including 11 piano sonatas. His piano method, *Vollständige theoretisch-practische Pianoforte-Schule* (Complete Theoretical and Practical Piano Forte School, 1839), is still the finest piano method ever written.

D

d. dessus (Fr.). Right hand above (over).

da capo, D.C. (It.). From the head, repeat from the beginning. *da capo al fine:* repeat from the beginning and end at the word *fine*. *da capo al segno:* return to beginning and play to the sign ℅. *da capo sin' al segno:* return to beginning and play to the sign, then go to the coda.

Da Motta, José Vianna (1868–1948). Portuguese pianist, he studied with von Bülow, Xaver Scharwenka, and Liszt. He was a superb pianist who had much influence on Portuguese pianistic tradition and wrote many articles in French, German, and Portuguese. He was director of the Lisbon Conservatory from 1919 to 1938 and taught many outstanding students, including Laires. He also composed many piano pieces.

dal segno, D.S. (It.). From the sign. *dal segno al fine:* repeat from ℅ to the word *fine*.

damper. A device used on pianos to dampen, or terminate, string vibrations. Usually operated as a pedal device.

damper pedal. The name applied to the right-hand-side pedal on a piano.

Dance Suite. Béla Bartók, 1923. Originally written for orchestra, transcribed for piano by Bartók. Six movements: *Moderato, Allegro molto, Allegro vivace, Molto tranquillo, Comodo, Finale—Allegro*. Written to celebrate the 50th anniversary of the merging of the cities of Buda and Pest, it contains some of Bartók's most arresting and invigorating writing.

dans la tête (Fr.). In the head.

dans l'expression (Fr.). In the expression, with feeling.

dansant (Fr.). Like a dance.

Danse de Puck, La (The Dance of Puck). Claude Debussy, *Préludes*, book 1, no. 11, 1910. This is the airy and elfish Puck of *A Midsummer Night's Dream*.

Danseuses de Delphes (Dancers of Delphi). Claude Debussy, *Préludes*, book 1, no. 1, 1910. A statue in the Louvre inspired this slow, hypnotic dance characterized by steady, flowing metric shifts.

Dante Sonata. Franz Liszt, S. 161, 1837–49. Three contrasting themes are developed in free rhapsodic style in this one-movement sonata from book 2 of his *Années de pèlerinage*. It is characterized by many powerful octaves; shimmering treble tremolos depict Paradise.

Danzas fantásticas (Imaginary Dances). Joaquin Turina, op. 22, 1920. Three dances (*Ecstasy, Daydreams,* and *Revel*) with pictorial excerpts from the Spanish poet José Más are used to preface each dance.

de très loin (Fr.). From afar.

Debussy, Claude (1862–1918). French composer, he extended the heritage of Liszt in his daring exploitation of the keyboard. His highly individual style is often compared with the Impressionistic style of certain painters. His major piano works include *Children's Corner, Estampes, 12 Etudes,* two books of *Images, Pour le piano,* two books of *Préludes, Suite Bergamasque.* For piano duet: *Epigraphes antiques, Petite suite.* For two pianos: *En blanc et noir.* For pieces in the two books of preludes, see listings for the individual titles.

début (Fr.), **debut** (Eng.). First public appearance for a soloist.

décidé (Fr.), **deciso** (It.). Decisively, energetic, boldly, *marcato.*

declamando, declamato (It.). In bold declamatory style.

decrescendo (It.). Gradually getting quieter; abbreviated *descresc.* Often written as a sign: ⎯⎯⎯⎯⎯⎯

dehors (Fr.). Outside; *en dehors* indicates the part or melody that should be emphasized or brought out.

Delaborde, Élie Miriam (1839–1913). This French pianist studied with Alkan (his father) and Moscheles. He toured Europe concertizing, and during the Franco-Prussian War he settled in London. He returned to Paris and became professor of piano at the Paris Conservatoire. Saint-Saëns dedicated his third piano concerto to him, and by all accounts he was a most admirable pianist. Samaroff studied with him.

delicato (It.). Delicate, smooth. *delicatissimo:* very delicately.

Delirium. Felix Mendelssohn, op. 85, no. 3, in E-flat Major, one of the *Songs without Words.*

Dello Joio, Norman (b. 1913). American composer, his style emphasizes strong melodies, vigorous rhythmic practice, and great communication. None of his piano works are overly demanding, yet some of the movements call for a much-above-average technique and fine musical equipment. Piano works: *Capriccio "On the Interval of a Second"* (written for the 1969 Van Cliburn International Piano Competition), *Concert Variants, Diversions, Lyric Pieces for the Young, Nocturne, Prelude: To a Young Dancer, Prelude: To a Young Musician, Salute to Scarlatti, Short Intervallic Etudes for Well-Tempered Pianists, Suite for the Young,* three sonatas. For piano and orchestra: *Ballad of the Seven Lively Arts, Fantasy and Variations, Ricercari.*

dengosa (Sp.). Fastidious, overly nice.

Departure, The. Felix Mendelssohn, op. 62, no. 2, in B-flat Major, one of the *Songs without Words.*

Des pas sur la neige (Footprints in the Snow). Claude Debussy, *Préludes,* book 1, no. 6, 1910. Persistent, stumbling rhythms evoke a gray horizon over a pale expanse of ice.

desafiando (Port.). Defiantly.

Descriptions automatiques (Automatic Descriptions). Erik Satie, 1913. *Sur un vaisseau* (On a Boat), *Sur une lanterne* (On a Lantern), *Sur un casque* (On a Helmet). Written in barless notation.

Désir (Desire). Alexander Scriabin, op. 57, no. 1, 1907. Evocative in mood, many augmented sonorities, with a sense of nostalgic longing; one of Scriabin's finest small works.

despacio (Sp.). Slowly, leisurely, gently.

Desperate Measures. Robert Muczynski, op. 48, 1994. Subtitled "Paganini Variations," this piece contains 12 variations on the famous Paganini etude, which is given as the theme, though it is not always easily heard. The piece holds many contrasts and a blues influence. No. 8 is a tango, no. 9 a waltz.

destra (It.). Right.

determinato (It.). Determined, resolute.

Deutscher Tanz (Ger.). See German dance.

deux (Fr.). Two.

deux pédales, les (Fr.). The two pedals: use both *una corda* and damper pedals.

development. The middle section in sonata-allegro form, preceding the return of the exposition (the recapitulation). In the development section, some or all of the themes are expanded or elaborated. New material may also be introduced. Development of a theme may take place anywhere and in any form.

devozione (It.). Devotion, piety.

Dexter, Benning (1915–96). American pianist and teacher, he received degrees from San Jose State University and the Juilliard School and studied with Siloti and Gorodnitzki. Dexter's solo and chamber music performances include television and many radio broadcasts, the latter including a series of several dozen on Radio Tokyo, and network broadcasts in the United States on NBC and NPR. He gave premieres of the music by Leslie Bassett, Paul Cooper, Ross Lee Finney, Charles Jones, Milhaud, and George Wilson. Dexter, an outstanding teacher, was a member of the University of Michigan music faculty from 1949 until his retirement. His students included Doppmann, Hinson, and Timbrell.

di (It.). Of, with, from, by.

di molto (It.). Very much, extremely. An expression to intensify further directions.

di nuovo (It.). Once more or again.

Diabelli, Anton (1781–1858). Austrian composer and publisher whose style includes all of the techniques of the Classical period. He wrote a waltz that Beethoven used as the basis of his "Diabelli" Variations. Diabelli published works by Beethoven and Schubert.

"Diabelli" Variations. Ludwig van Beethoven, *33 Variations on a Theme of Diabelli for Piano*, op. 120, 1823. The Viennese composer and publisher Diabelli wrote a very simple waltz and invited Beethoven and Schubert (among some 50 others) to write variations on it. Beethoven took up the challenge to splendid effect. Brendel considers this the greatest work in all piano literature. It invites comparison with Bach's "Goldberg" Variations.

Dichter, Misha (b. 1945). This brilliant American pianist was born in China and is of Polish descent. He studied at The Juilliard School with Rosina Lhévinne and won second place in the Third International Piano Competition in Moscow in 1966. He has toured the world extensively playing a large range of repertoire, especially that from the 19th and early 20th centuries. He appears frequently in two-piano recitals with his pianist wife, Cipa Dichter (b. 1944).

Dick, James (b. 1940). American pianist, he studied at the University of Texas with Frantz and at the Royal Academy of Music in London with Curzon. He won top prizes in the Busoni, Leventritt, and Tchaikowsky international piano competitions. He has concertized in the world's premier concert halls and performed with major orchestras. In 1971 he founded the International Festival-Institute at Round Top, Texas, which has grown to be one of the most respected music festivals in the world.

***Didone abbandonata* (Dido Abandoned).** Muzio Clementi, Sonata in G Minor, op. 50, no. 3. This name was used in the first edition of Clementi's sonatas published in London in 1821. This is the only example of a programmatic piece by Clementi; it is based loosely on an operatic text by Matastasio which relates the tragedy of Dido deserted by Aeneas at Carthage.

diluendo (It.). Fade away into silence, dying away; dissolving.

diminuendo (It.). Getting quieter (softer), *descrescendo;* abbreviated *dim.* or *dimin.*

disinvolto (It.). Careless; direction to play in a free and easy manner.

divertimento (It.). Diversion or pastime. A work for the piano in light style, performed in a cheerful and light-hearted manner. Cramer, Jacques Ibert, Prokofiev, Satie, and Soulima Stravinsky, among others, have composed pieces in this genre.

do (It.). The first degree of the scale, or the note or tonality (key) C.

doch (Ger.). But, yet, still.

dodecaphonic. Twelve sounds. See twelve-tone music.

"Dog" Waltz. See "Minute" Waltz.

Dohnányi, Ernö (or Ernst) (1877–1960). Hungarian composer and pianist, most of his well-constructed music is in the Brahmsian tradition, pianistic and effective. His piano works include *Passa-caglia,* rhapsodies, *Suite in the Olden Style,* variations, a concerto, and *Variations on a Nursery Song* ("Twinkle, Twinkle, Little Star") for piano and orchestra.

dolce (It.). sweet, delicate, gentle; suggests the use of *poco rubato.* Brendel suggests "tenderly committed." *dolcissimo:* very gently.

dolcezzo (It.). Sweetness, gentleness.

dolente (It.). Sadly, mournful, grieving, doleful.

Dolly. Gabriel Fauré, op. 56, 1894–97. Suite for piano four-hands with six movements: *Berceuse* (Lullaby), *Kitty-Valse* (Kitty Waltz), *Le jardin de Dolly* (Dolly's Garden), *Le pas espagnol* (The Spanish Step), *Mi-a-ou* (Meow), *Tendresse* (Tenderness). Characterized by charming, elegant, and refined writing. Inspired by his friend Dolly Bardac.

doloroso (It.). Sorrowful, mournful; expressing grief or pain.

doppio (It.). Double.

doppio movimento (It.). Double movement, twice as fast.

Doppmann, William (b. 1934). American pianist and composer, he appeared with the Cincinnati Symphony Orchestra when he was 10 and again as a high school senior. He studied with Goldsand and, after entering the University of Michigan, with Dexter. In 1954 he won both the Naumberg Foundation and the Michaels Awards and concertized extensively. He has taught at the Universities of Iowa and Texas. More recently his interest has turned to composition, but he continues to perform.

Dorfman, Ania (1899–1983). Russian-born American pianist and teacher, she studied at the Paris Conservatoire with Philipp. She had a brilliant career in Europe before coming to the United States, where she appeared with major orchestras as well as soloist in many American cities. She made recordings, and in her later years she taught at The Juilliard School.

Doscher, John-David (b. 1935). American pianist and publisher, he studied with Saperton, George Kochevitsky, and Vladimir Padwa. He was an outstanding publisher who began Musical Scope Publishers and brought out some first-rate books and several superb series: *Virtuoso Piano Works, Salon Series, Romantic Piano Concerto,* and *The Art of the Cantilene.* In 1989–90 he published two volumes of previously unpublished manuscripts of Field.

double (Fr.). Variation.

double movement, le (Fr.). Twice as fast.

douce, doux (Fr.). Sweet, soft. *doucement:* sweetly, softly.

doucement marqué (Fr.). Gently accented.

doucement timbre (Fr.). Gently but slightly stressed.

Drake, Kenneth (b. 1930). American pianist and teacher, he studied at the Eastman School of Music with José Echaniz and at the University of Illinois with Stanley Fletcher. He also studied at the Vienna Academy of Music on a Fulbright scholarship. He has specialized in piano music of the Classical era and owns an early Broadwood piano. He taught at Drake University and the University of Illinois and has written *The Beethoven Sonatas and the Creative Experience.* He is a highly sensitive performer with a superb command of voicing.

Dubal, David (b. 1940). American pianist and teacher, he attended The Juilliard School and studied privately with Loesser. He has concertized throughout the United States and has made recordings. Since 1967 Dubal has been director of classical music station WNCN in New York. In 1983 he joined the faculty of The Juilliard School, where he teaches piano literature. He has written *Reflections from the Keyboard* and *The Art of the Piano.*

due corde (It.). Two strings, with the soft (left) pedal. When the soft pedal is depressed on a grand piano, the hammer mechanism is shifted to "one less string" from the regular three strings, hence two strings are struck by the hammer. *Tre corde* (three strings) cancels the *due corde* direction.

duet. A work for two performers. A piano duet is played by two pianists at the same piano. Georges Bizet, Brahms, Clementi, Czerny, Fauré, Ravel, and Schubert are a few composers who have composed for this medium.

Duetto (Duet). Felix Mendelssohn, op. 38, no. 6, in A-flat Major, one of the *Songs without Words.* So named by the composer: perhaps Mendelssohn thought of this piece being a duet between himself and Cécile Jeanrenaud, his future wife.

Dumm, Robert W. (b. 1928). American pianist, teacher, and writer, he received degrees from the University of Michigan and studied with Maurice Dumesnil, John Kollen, and Loesser. He was Dean of the Boston Conservatory for 10 years. Dumm has written a number of books and has been a contributing editor of *Clavier* magazine and has written for numerous periodicals. He has also conducted 500 taped interviews with pianists for the International Piano Archives.

dummy keyboard. Silent keyboard. See Virgil Clavier.

***D'un cahier d'esquisses* (From a Sketchbook).** Claude Debussy, 1903. This lovely solo piano piece is a sketch for his tone poem *La Mer,* charming and ethereal. It contains a mixture of styles.

d'une manière très particulière (Fr.). In a very unusual manner.

d'un rythme—trés enveloppé de pédales (Fr.). With a simple rhythm—very enveloped with pedal.

duo. A duet; two performers.

duolo (It.). Grief, sorrow, pain.

duple time. Two beats in the measure: $\frac{2}{2}$, $\frac{4}{4}$, $\frac{6}{8}$, etc.

dur (Ger.). Major (key), e.g., C dur: C major.

duramente (It.). Harshly.

durchkomponiert (Ger.). See through-composed.

Dussek, Jan Ladislav (1760–1812). Bohemian pianist and composer, he was the first performer to sit with his right side to the audience. He exploited the piano and anticipated later Romantic traits. He composed over 25 piano sonatas and 15 piano concertos, variations, and numerous smaller pieces.

Dvořák, Antonin (1841–1904). Great Bohemian composer, he came to New York City in 1892 to serve as the director of the National Conservatory of Music, where he served for three years. He returned to Prague in 1895 to become director of the Prague Conservatory. His piano works include a concerto, *Album Leaves, Humoresques, Poetic Tone Pictures, Silhouettes,* a suite, and a set of variations. For piano duet: *Slavonic Dances.*

Dvorsky, Michael. Pseudonym used by Josef Hofmann for a few piano compositions written in a fluent and florid post-Romantic style.

dynamic marks. Signs used in music to indicate the degree of variation of intensity (loud or soft) of the sound from fortissimo (*ff*) to pianissimo (*pp*).

E

écart (Fr.). A wide stretch on the piano.

éclatant (Fr.). With brilliance; dazzling, sparkling, sunny.

écossaise (Fr.). 1. Scottish. 2. An English or Scottish country dance in $\frac{2}{4}$ time that was popular in England and France in the early nineteenth century; there is no obvious connection to Scotland. Beethoven, Chopin, Schubert, and Weber wrote *écossaises*.

"Edward" Ballade. Johannes Brahms, op. 10, no. 1, in D Minor. This piece is the first of a set of four ballades with the subtitle coming from the Scottish ballad *Edward*. It is a grisly story of a son who kills his father; a ghostly march rhythm ends the piece with a whisper.

effet (Fr.). Interpretation or realization.

effleuré (Fr.). Lightly touched.

effrayé (Fr.). Frightened.

egal (Ger.). Same, even. *egal zu spielen:* play evenly, equal.

également (Fr.). Equally, even-flowing.

égalité (Fr.). Evenness, smoothness.

"Egyptian" Concerto. Camille Saint-Saëns, Concerto for Piano no. 5, op. 103, 1896. The *Andante* (second movement of this work) was influenced by the composer's impressions of a visit to Luxor on the Nile River. This is the reason this concerto has been nicknamed "Egyptian."

einfach (Ger.). Simply, plain.

élan (Fr.). Verve, temperament, dash, enthusiasm, burst.

élargir (Fr.). To broaden or slow the tempo.

electronic piano. An electronically amplified keyboard instrument capable of imitating acoustic piano sounds.

élégie (Fr.). A lament, mournful composition. Bartók, Busoni, Grieg, Liszt, Rachmaninoff, and Reger, among others, have composed elegies for the piano.

Élégie harmonique sur la mort du Prince Louis Ferdinand. J. L. Dussek, Sonata in F-sharp Minor, op. 61, 1806–7. Dussek was a close friend of Prince Louis Ferdinand of Prussia. When the prince was killed prematurely on the battlefield in 1806, Dussek wrote this work in his memory.

Elegy. Felix Mendelssohn. Piano piece, op. 85, no. 4 in E Major. See *Songs without Words.*

éloignant (Fr.). Becoming more distant.

embellishment. Improvement; ornamentation or the act thereof, ornament.

Embryons desséchés (Dried Embryos). Erik Satie, 1913. *D'holothurie* (Of a Holothurian), *D'edriophthalma* (Of an Edriophthalma), *De podophthalma* (Of a Podophthalma). Written in barless notation.

empâter (Fr.). Produce a very smooth legato.

"Emperor" Concerto. Ludwig van Beethoven, Piano Concerto no. 5 in E-flat Major, op. 79, 1809. Origin of the nickname is unknown, although it appears early in the work's history. Beethoven would not have approved of this "Emperor" reference to Napoleon, especially after Napoleon's seizure of Vienna in 1809. The work was published in 1811, with a dedication to Beethoven's patron the Archduke Rudolph.

Empfindung (Ger.). Feeling, play with expressive feeling.

emporté (Fr.). Passionate, carried away with passion.

empressé (Fr.). Hurried, eager.

ému (Fr.). With feeling, touched, sensitive.

en accusant (Fr.). Emphasizing.

en affaiblissant (Fr.). Weakening, a steady softening.

en allant (Fr.). Flowing.

en augmentant (Fr.). Crescendo.

en badinant (Fr.). Playfully, *scherzando*.

en blanc et immobile (Fr.). White and motionless.

En blanc et noir **(In White and Black).** Claude Debussy, Suite for Two Pianos, 1915. Three movements: *Avec emportement; Lent. Sombre; Scherzando.* Written during World War I, this suite reflects Debussy's great depression and anxiety over the turmoil and his eventually fatal cancer. The title perhaps suggests a state of half-mourning. This entire suite is prophetic of later developments in two-piano writing by Bartók and Stravinsky.

en blousant (Fr.). With a burst (of passion).

en commençant (Fr.). At first, in the beginning.

en conservant le rythme (Fr.). Keep the tempo.

en croisant (Fr.). Crossing (of hands, of parts).

en dédoublant (Fr.). Twice as slow; divided into two.

en dehors (Fr.). Bring out.

en élargissant (Fr.). Broadening, becoming *largo*.

en général, sans nuances (Fr.). In general, without nuances. This suggests a rather straightforward interpretation of a passage.

en glissant le doigt (Fr.). Sliding the finger.

En habit de cheval **(In Riding Habit).** Erik Satie, 1911. For piano duet: *Choral* (Chorale), *Fugue litanique* (Litany-fugue), *Autre chose* (Another chorale), *Fugue de papier* (Paper Fugue).

en laissant (Fr.). In a free and easy way.

en maintenant toujours la pédale appuyée (Fr.). Holding the sustaining pedal throughout.

en pesant un peu (Fr.). A little stressed.

en retenant (Fr.). Holding back, slowing down.

en s'apaisant (Fr.). Suggests quieting down, getting softer.

en s'effaçant (Fr.). Fade away.

en se perdant (Fr.). Disappearing, fading.

en serrant (Fr.). Becoming quicker, *stringendo*.

en sourdain (Fr.). Muted; with muted strings or pedaling.

en un mouvement assez lent de valse, et très tendrement (Fr.). In a rather slow waltz tempo, and very tenderly.

en valeur et sostenu (Fr.). In the foreground and sustained.

enchaîner (Fr.). To join with the following, *segue. enchaînez:* continue without pause.

encore (Fr.). 1. Again. 2. A number given after the regular program is completed, at the request of the audience.

encore plus animé (Fr.). Yet more lively.

encore plus lent (Fr.) Still slower.

encore plus vif (Fr.). Still faster.

energico (It.). Energetically, vigorously.

enforcée (Fr.). (The pedal) deeply depressed.

enforcer sans jouer (Fr.). Push down (the key/s) without playing.

English Suites. J. S. Bach, BWV 806–11, ca. 1722–26. Six keyboard suites in A Major, A Minor, G Minor, F Major, E Minor, and D Minor. Each suite begins with a prelude. The designation "English Suite" is not original with Bach.

enivré (Fr.). Elated, ecstatic.

enlevez brusquement (Fr.). Lift (the pedal) abruptly.

ensemble (Fr.). 1. Together. 2. A group of players or an indication for all to play together (teamwork). Agreement between performers.

Entremont, Philippe (b. 1934). French pianist and conductor, he studied at the Paris Conservatoire. He has toured throughout the world and has appeared with many American orchestras and was conductor of the New Orleans Philharmonic from 1979 to 1986 and the Denver Symphony Orchestra. He has recorded a wide variety of repertoire including Ravel's complete piano works.

entschlossen (Ger.). Play resolutely and with much determination.

épais (Fr.). Somber, heavy, thick.

epigram. A word used by numerous composers for the title of a piano composition. Jean Françaix, Pál Kadosa, Georges Migot, Robert Palmer, Günther Ramey, Roger Reynolds, Knudæge Rüsager, Pedro Saenz, Roger Smalley, and Egon Wellesz among others have composed works with this title.

épinette (Fr.). 1. Name for a small 17th- and 18th-century harpsichord. 2. A modern upright piano.

episode. 1. A middle or intermediate section. 2. A digression from the main theme in a fugue. 3. The contrasting sections that occur between the recurring material in a rondo. Some composers have used this term as titles of self-standing pieces, such as Arthur Berger, Copland, Cowell, Nicholas Flagello, Carlisle Floyd, Peter Fricker, Norman Lloyd, Josef Tal, Tcherepnin, Lester Trimble, and Ben Weber.

equal temperament. The system of tuning used today, established by the International Agreement of Temperament in 1677. It is based on dividing the octave into 12 equal semitones (half steps).

equalmente (It.). Smoothly, evenly, steadily.

Erard, Sebastian (1752–1831). French firm of piano and harp makers and music publishers. Of all the French piano manufacturers, Liszt preferred Erard.

erhaben (Ger.). Lofty, elevated.

ernst (Ger.). Earnest, serious.

"Eroica" Sonata. Edward MacDowell, Sonata in G Minor, op. 50, 1895. This work contains the motto "Flos regum Arthuris": MacDowell had the King Arthur legend in mind when he composed this sonata. He used the name "Eroica" as a subtitle. MacDowell said the first movement suggests the coming of Arthur, the second was suggested by a Gustave Doré picture showing a knight surrounded by elves in the woods, and the third came from MacDowell's thoughts of Guinevere.

"Eroica" Variations. Ludwig van Beethoven, Piano Variations in E-flat Major, op. 35, 1802. This title refers to a theme used in both the op. 35 and the finale of the "Eroica" Symphony first used in his ballet *Die Geschöpfe des Prometheus* (The Creatures of Prometheus). Op. 35 was composed before the symphony, but this piece has always been called the "Eroica" Variations.

esercizio (It.). Exercise, a study.

esitando (It.). Hesitating, wavering, uncertain.

España **(Spain).** Emmanuel Chabrier, 1883. A rhapsody for piano on original Spanish airs. Originally a piano solo but later orchestrated.

espressivo (It.). See *expressif*.

Essay on the True Manner of Playing Keyboard Instruments. *Versuch über die wahre Art, das Clavier zu spielen*, C. P. E. Bach, 1753, 1762. A major treatise on performance practice in the 18th century.

Estampes (Prints). Claude Debussy, 1903. Three pieces for piano: *Pagodes* (Pagodas), *La soirée dans Grenade* (Evening in Granada), *Jardins sous la pluie* (Gardens in the Rain). The title refers to images printed from engraved copper or wood plates.

estinguendo (It.). Dying away.

estinto (It.). Hardly audible.

estomper (Fr.). To tone down, soften, blur.

États d'âme **(Soul States).** Alexander Scriabin, Sonata no. 3 in F-sharp Minor, op. 23, 1898. The composer used this subtitle with this work because he felt this music represented his own emotional biography. He was going through a very difficult time when this work was composed.

éteindre (Fr.). To die out, fade away.

étendre (Fr.). To stretch out, extend, expand.

étincelant (Fr.). Sparkling.

étude (Fr.), **etude** (Eng.). Study or exercise with some special technical problem stressed. Brahms, Clementi, and Czerny composed etudes that focused on specific technical problems. Piano etudes of Chopin, Debussy, Liszt, and Scriabin are mainly performed as concert pieces.

Études d'execution transcendente **(Transcendental Etudes).** Franz Liszt, S. 139, 1851. Twelve virtuosic pieces for piano: 1. *Preludio* (Prelude), 2. Untitled, 3. *Paysage* (Landscape), 4. *Mazeppa,* 5. *Feux follets* (Will o' the Wisps), 6. *Vision,* 7. *Eroica,* 8. *Wilde Jagd* (Wild Ride), 9. *Ricordanza* (Remembrance), 10. Untitled, 11. *Harmonies du soir* (Evening Harmonies), 12. *Chasse-neige* (Sleigh Ride). These pieces could have been named ballades or poems, since most of them are programmatic.

Études d'execution transcendante d'après Paganini **(Transcendental Etudes after Paganini).** See "Paganini" Etudes.

Études symphonique **(Symphonic Etudes).** Robert Schumann, "Etudes in the Form of Variations" in C-sharp Minor, op. 13, 1837. Schumann used as the theme a melody sent to him by Hauptman von Fricken, elaborated and improved upon it, and composed this superb set of variations.

etwas (Ger.). Somewhat.

éveillé (Fr.). Brisk, lively.

Evening Star, The. Felix Mendelssohn, op. 38, no. 1, in E-flat Major, one of the *Songs without Words.*

exalté (Fr.). With enthusiasm.

Excursions. Samuel Barber, 1944. These are four "excursions" into regional American idioms using small classical forms: *Un poco allegro* (Boogie-woogie style), In Slow Blues Tempo, *Allegretto* (Western song with variations), *Allegro molto* (Square dance).

execution (Fr.). Performance.

exposition. 1. The first section in sonata-allegro form, which contains the main thematic material. 2. In fugue, the presentation of the subject by all voices.

expressif, expressive (Fr.), *espressivo* (It.). 1. With emotion and feeling. Turned inward, more personal involvement of the performer. 2. "Tell it to the world" (Artur Schnabel).

expressif en récit (Fr.). Expressive as a recitative.

expression. Represents the elements of music regarding musical shading in performance. It is mainly up to the performer, using musical sense and taste, to execute the composer's intentions to the best of his or her abilities.

expression marks. Directions to a performer indicating tempo, dynamics, phrasing, mood, etc. It is impossible for a composer to notate all "expression" terms; this is where the interpreter must become involved.

Expressionism. A term borrowed from 20th-century paintings that depicts real objects in distorted forms that express the composer's inner feelings as opposed to Impressionism, which expressed the composer's outer feelings of the world. Expressionistic music is generally more harsh and dissonant than impressionistic music. Examples may be found in the early works of Schoenberg, Berg, and Webern.

exquis (Fr.). Refined, delicate; delightful.

extemporize. To improvise.

F

_f._ Abbreviation of _forte:_ loud, strong. _ff, fff,_ etc., indicate increasing degrees of loudness or strength.

_fa_ (It.). The fourth degree of the scale, or the note or tonality (key) F.

Fables. Composers use this word for descriptive pieces. Some composers who have written pieces for piano using this title are Pierre-Octave Ferroud, Jacobo Ficher, Martinů, Georges Migot, Robert Muczynski, and Øistein Sommerfeldt.

facile (Fr.). Easily, fluently.

faible (Fr.). Weak.

faire ressortir le chant (Fr.). Bring out the melody.

faites vibrer (Fr.). See _vibrer._

Faith. Felix Mendelssohn, op. 102, no. 6, in C Major, one of the _Songs without Words._

"Fall of Warsaw" Etude. See "Revolutionary" Etude.

Falla, Manuel de (1876–1946). Spanish composer and pianist, he used the piano for profound compositional statements, yet his music is atmospheric and evocative of his homeland. His best-known works for piano are _4 Pièces espagnoles_ (4 Spanish Pieces), _Fantasia Bética_ (Andalusian Fantasy), and _Noches en los jardines de España_ (Nights in the Gardens of Spain) for piano and orchestra. He also composed a concerto for piano (or harpsichord) and flute, oboe, clarinet, violin, and cello for Landowska.

false octaves. A device used in which the effect of octaves is faked. Octaves are used alternately with single notes.

Famous Pianists and Their Technique. Reginald R. Gerig, 1974. The finest book in English on the subject.

fandango (Sp.). A Spanish dance in fast triple time. Antonio Soler (1729–83) and Granados wrote highly effective fandangos.

fanfare. A flourish or call of trumpets. Some composers, such as Ingolf Dahl, Charles Jones, Gioacchino Rossini, and Carlos Surinach, have written pieces for piano using this title. The pieces have much rhythmic interest.

Fantasia contrappuntistica. Ferruccio Busoni, 1910. One of Busoni's major works, using the Contrapunctus XVIII from Bach's *Kunst der Fuge* (Art of Fugue), his attempt to complete the unfinished fugue. There are four versions: the first three are for solo piano, the fourth version is arranged for two pianos. This work represents a summing up of Busoni's interest in Bach.

Fantasiestücke **(Fantasy Pieces).** Robert Schumann, op. 12, 1837. Eight piano pieces, each with a descriptive title. Schumann composed three more *Fantasiestücke* (op. 111, 1851), but without descriptive titles. Griffes also composed three *Fantasy Pieces* (1912–15) with titles: *Barcarolle, Nocturne, Scherzo.*

fantasy. An imaginative composition in free form written according to the composer's fancy. Composers who have written fantasies include Bach (Chromatic Fantasy and Fugue), Beethoven (Choral Fantasy), Brahms (*Fantasies,* op. 116), Crumb (*Fantasy Pieces after the Zodiac for Amplified Piano*), Mozart (three fantasies), Schubert (Fantasy in C Minor).

Fantasy on an Ostinato. John Corigliano, 1985. Commissioned by the Seventh Van Cliburn Competition, this piece has intense emotional expression, energetic sections, strong minimalist structure, colorful, atmospheric keyboard textures, and superb craftsmanship. Based on the repeated-note theme from Beethoven's Seventh Symphony.

Fantasy Pieces after the Zodiac for Amplified Piano. See *Makrokosmos.*

Farewell, A. Felix Mendelssohn, op. 85, no. 2, in A Minor, one of the *Songs without Words.*

"Farewell" Sonata. J. L. Dussek, Sonata in E-flat Major, op. 44, 1800.

"Farewell" Waltz. Frédéric Chopin, Waltz in A-flat Major, op. 69, no. 1, 1835. Chopin composed this waltz for Maria Woedziňska, with whom he had fallen in love. On the autograph Chopin wrote "pour Mlle Marie" and added the date and place. Maria entitled her copy "l'Adieu" (the farewell).

***Faschingsschwank aus Wien* (Viennese Carnival Pranks).** Robert Schumann, op. 26, 1839. This suite of five character pieces (Schumann subtitled them *Fantasiebilder:* Fantasy Pictures) is a direct result of the composer's visit to Vienna in the interest of his music periodical *Die Neue Zeitschrift für Musik.* The movement titles are *Allegro, Romanze, Scherzino, Intermezzo, Finale.*

fastoso (It.). Pompous.

Fauré, Gabriel (1845–1924). French composer whose individual and instinctive pianism make him one of the great 19th-century composers for the piano. His piano works demand musicianship and pianistic maturity. His piano works include a *Ballade,* 13 barcarolles, six impromptus, 13 nocturnes, nine preludes, theme and variations, four valse-caprices, and a late set of short pieces. For piano duet: *Dolly Suite.*

Fay, Amy (1844–1928). American pianist, she studied with Tausig and Theodor Kullak (1818–82) in Berlin, then worked with Liszt in Weimar. She wrote a book, *Music-Study in Germany,* which includes many vivid impressions of Liszt's teaching.

Federal Overture. Benjamin Carr (1768–1831), 1794. This piece contains eight tunes of Revolutionary times, including the earliest printing of *Yankee Doodle.* Written in the style of the period and an excellent contribution to early musical Americana.

***Fées sont d'exquises danseuses, Les* (The Fairies are Exquisite Dancers).** Claude Debussy, *Préludes,* book 2, no. 4, 1913. The title comes from Arthur Rackham's delightful illustrations for the children's book *Peter Pan in Kensington Garden,* a favorite of Debussy's daughter Chouchou. The piece requires delicate touch and great clarity.

feintes (Fr.). The black keys on a keyboard.

fermata (It.). Pause, wait; indicated by ⌒. When used over a note it means to hold that note at least one-half the value of the note plus its regular length. The ultimate decision of how long is left to the pianist. When the sign appears over a bar line, a short silence is appropriate.

feroce (It.). Wild, fierce, ferocious.

Feuilles mortes (Dead Leaves). Claude Debussy, *Préludes,* book 2, no. 2, 1913. New use is made of the theme from *Les sons et les parfums* (*Préludes,* book 1, no. 4). It should not be played too fast.

feurig (Ger.). Fiery, excited.

Feux d'artifice (Fireworks). Claude Debussy, *Préludes,* book 2, no. 12, 1913. The piece depicts an exciting illumination over Paris. A reference to the French national anthem *La Marseillaise* brings this festive and dazzling virtuoso finale to a close. This crowning piece of the *Préludes* displays Debussy's indebtedness to Lisztian pyrotechnics.

fiacco (It.). Weak, languishing.

fiducia (It.). Confidence, reliance, assurance.

Field, John (1782–1837). Irish composer and pianist, he opened a completely original path in his piano writing and took piano music into the 19th century. He studied with Clementi. Field's nocturnes, with ornate melodies accompanied by widely spaced left-hand chords, established his reputation as a composer. He lived most of his life in Russia. His piano works include fantasies, 20 nocturnes, rondos, four sonatas, variations, and seven concertos.

fieramente (It.). Wildly, boldly.

Fifty-one Exercises. Set of studies by Johannes Brahms. See *Übungen.*

figuration. A decorative, rhythmic, or melodic figure used to accompany a melody.

Fille aux cheveux de lin, La (The Girl with the Flaxen Hair). Claude Debussy, *Préludes,* book 1, no. 8, 1910. The title comes from the *Scottish Song* of Leconte de Lisle. The piece uses an archaic-sounding (pentatonic) melody, an exquisite portrait.

fin (Fr.), **fine** (It.). End, close. Indicates the end of a piece or of a repeated section.

fin al segno (It.). Return to the beginning and end at the sign.

finale (It.). The final movement of a multimovement work, such as a sonata, or Franck's *Prélude, aria et finale* (Prelude, Aria and Finale).

finger pedaling. The prolonging of chord tones in certain purely accompanimental patterns was a part of Classical period practice (Rosenblum, p. 156). This is especially helpful with Alberti basses:

sustain the first note of the pattern until it has to be released to replay the note. Brahms used this technique. This "prolonged style" of playing comes originally from the Baroque period: how did one pedal when playing the harpsichord? The "prolonged style" of playing was the answer: you pedaled with the fingers by holding notes longer than they were written. See *tenuto* touch.

Fingerfertigkeit (Ger.). Fluent finger technique.

fingering. 1. The art of using the fingers systematically. 2. The identification of fingers by numbers.

Finney, Ross Lee (1906–1997). American composer whose sonatas and smaller sets of pieces are a notable contribution to American piano literature. His piano works include *Games,* 24 inventions, *Medley (Campfire on the Ice), Narrative in Argument, Narrative in Retrospect, Nostalgic Waltzes,* five sonatas, *Variations on a Theme of Alban Berg, Youth's Companion.*

fioritura (It.). Flowering, flourishes, decorations; ornamental decoration of a melody. Chopin used *fioriture* many times in his works; a good example is found in his Nocturne in C-sharp Minor (Posthumous), measures 58–59, where a series of additional notes in small print are played against a series of accompanying eighth notes.

Firkusny, Rudolf (1912–94). Czech pianist and teacher, he studied at the Prague Conservatory and privately with Schnabel. He toured Europe and gave his U.S. debut in 1938; he subsequently settled in the United States. He introduced Gian Carlo Menotti's Piano Concerto in 1945 with the Boston Symphony Orchestra and gave first performances of works by Barber, Carlisle Floyd, Howard Hanson, and Ginastera. He has also championed the works of Dvořák and Martinů. He taught at The Juilliard School until his death.

first movement form. See sonata-allegro form.

Fischer, Edwin (1886–1960). Swiss pianist, he studied with Martin Krause (1853–1918) in Berlin. Fischer was one of the great piano teachers of his day and specialized in the German masters, especially Bach and Beethoven. He taught at the Berlin Conservatory for many years and prepared editions of Bach and Beethoven.

Fisher, Charles R. (b. 1929). American pianist and teacher, he studied with Victor Labunski at the Kansas City Conservatory and with Brinkman at the University of Michigan, where he received his doctorate. He taught at the University of Michigan for 37 years and was chairman of the piano department for the last 18 years. He formed a two-piano team with Eugene Bossart, and they concertized with great success throughout the United States for 22 years. Fisher is also an outstanding painter and silversmith.

Five, The. A group of Russian composers who were active especially during the 1870s. Members were Mily Balakirev (1837–1910), Alexander Borodin (1834–1887), César Cui (1835–1918), Modest Mussorgsky (1839–1881), and Nicolai Rimsky-Korsakov (1844–1908). They all composed for the piano, but the finest work for piano was written by Mussorgsky, *Pictures at an Exhibition.* This group has also been called "The Mighty Five."

Five Studies Arranged from the Works of Other Composers. Johannes Brahms. 1. Chopin, Etude op. 25, no. 2 (1869), arranged with thirds and sixths in the right hand. 2. Weber, Rondo from Sonata no. 1, op. 24 (1869), consists of an inversion of the parts for right and left hands. 3. J. S. Bach, Sonata for Solo Violin, *moto perpetuo* (first arrangement, 1879), consisting of single notes for each hand, contrary motion, and crossing of hands. 4. J. S. Bach, Sonata for Solo Violin (second arrangement, 1879), an inversion of no. 3. 5. Chaconne after J. S. Bach (1879), arranged for the left hand. These arrangements were more for developing advanced technique than for concert performance.

flatteusement (Fr.). Flatteringly.

flebile (It.). Plaintive, mournful.

Fleecy Cloud, The. Felix Mendelssohn, op. 53, no. 2, in E-flat Major, one of the *Songs without Words.*

Fleischer, Leon (b. 1928). American pianist, he was a child prodigy and then studied with Schnabel in Berlin. His New York debut was in 1944, and he subsequently toured with great success. In 1963 he gave the world premiere of Leon Kirchner's Second Piano Concerto in Seattle. He turned to conducting in 1964 because of a physical problem that developed in his right hand. He has recently returned to playing with both hands. Students include Gregory Allen, Meade Crane, Max Lyall, Alan Marks, Nelita True, and Watts.

Flight, The. Felix Mendelssohn, op. 53, no. 6, in A Major, one of the *Songs without Words.*

flottant (Fr.). Floating, flowing.

flou (Fr.). Hazy and blurred; use a great deal of pedal.

Flügel (Ger.). Wing; used to describe a wing-shaped piano.

fluide (Fr.). Fluid.

focoso (It.). Fiery.

fogoso (Sp.). Fiery, fervent, spirited, impetuous.

folksong. Folksong has influenced many composers of piano music. Both J.C.F. Bach and Mozart wrote *Variations on Ah, vous dirai-je, Maman* (what we know as "Twinkle, Twinkle, Little Star"); Bartók wrote *Variations on a Slovakian Folk Tune,* plus he used many folk tunes in his *Mikrokosmos;* Beethoven composed *Easy Variations on a Swiss Folksong;* Clementi wrote a fantasy on *Au clair de la lune* (A French folksong); Ross Lee Finney composed *Medley,* based on American folksongs. The list could go on and on!

Folk Song. Felix Mendelssohn, op. 53, no. 5, in A Minor, one of the *Songs without Words.* This title came from the composer.

follement (Fr.). Extravagantly, dotingly.

Fontana, Julian (1810–65). Polish composer, writer, and pianist, he studied law at Warsaw University and music under Josef Elsner at the Warsaw Conservatory, where he became a friend of Chopin. He lived in France, England, New York, and Havana and composed piano pieces using African American melodies. He copied out about 80 of Chopin's works for publishers. He made a posthumous edition of Chopin's works, which was published in 1855 and 1859. Chopin dedicated to Fontana the two polonaises op. 40.

forlane (Fr.). A lively Venetian dance in $\frac{6}{4}$ or $\frac{6}{8}$ time. A 20th-century example is found in Ravel's *Le tombeau de Couperin.*

form. The shape of a musical structure such as ABA form, sonata form, rondo form, etc.

forte (It.). Loud, strong; abbreviated *f.*

forte pedal. Another term for the damper pedal.

fortepiano (It.). 1. The early piano used by Haydn, Mozart, and Beethoven. Both the Viennese action (light) and the English action (heavier) were popular during the 18th century. 2. The dynamic mark *fp,* which is an accent. 3. The dynamic mark *fp,* which signifies an immediate reduction in sound after a tone or chord has been played.

"Forty-eight, The." See *Well-Tempered Clavier.*

forza (It.). With force, play vigorously, emphatically.

forzando (It.). Forcing, accented. *forzato:* strongly accenting; abbreviated.

Four Duets. J. S. Bach, BWV 802–5, 1739. These pieces are not for two players but one part for the right hand and one part for the left hand. These pieces are mature Bach; their construction is much more elaborate than the *Two-Part Inventions.*

four hands. A work written for two pianists, both at the same piano, is said to be composed for "piano, four hands." See duet; *primo; secondo.*

foxtrot. An American social dance in $\frac{4}{4}$, introduced in 1914. The "fast foxtrot," as opposed to the "slow foxtrot," became known as the *quickstep.* This dance has inspired a few serious composers to call pieces a foxtrot, including Martinů, Mátyás Seiber, and Tansman, among others.

fp. 1. Loud, then immediately soft (quiet); an accent. 2. Abbreviation of *fortepiano.*

Frager, Malcolm (1935–91). American pianist, he was a child prodigy when he made his debut with the St. Louis Symphony Orchestra at the age of 10. He studied at The Juilliard School with Friedberg and won first prize at the Queen Elizabeth Competition in Brussels in 1960. He toured the United States and Europe with great success.

Franck, César (1822–90). Born in Belgium, he spent most of his life in Paris. This composer began his career as a concert pianist but soon turned to the organ and to composing for other instruments. The few piano works he is remembered for came late in his life. They include *Prélude, Chorale et fugue* (Prelude, Chorale and Fugue), *Prélude, aria et final* (Prelude, Aria and Finale), and the *Variations symphoniques* (Symphonic Variations) for piano and orchestra.

Frantz, Dalies (1908–65). American pianist, he studied with Maier at the University of Michigan and with Schnabel and Horowitz. He won the Schubert Memorial Competition and concertized extensively and played with almost every major orchestra. He appeared in minor roles in several movies and taught at the University of Texas from 1943 until his death.

French Suites. J. S. Bach, BWV 812–17, 1722–24. These six suites—

in D Minor, C Minor, B Minor, E-flat Major, G Major, and E
Major—are smaller in size and scope than his English suites and
partitas. The name "French" was not used by Bach.

fret. A small rib or band upon which a string may be pressed for the
raising of its pitch.

frettevole (It.). Hurried.

freudig (Ger.). Joyfully.

Freundlich, Irwin (1908–77). American pianist and teacher, he studied at the Juilliard Graduate School with Siloti and Friskin. He
taught at Juilliard for many years, including courses in piano literature. Freundlich wrote (with Friskin) the book *Music for the
Piano* and edited the first edition of Hinson's *Guide to the Pianist's
Repertoire*. He also published a number of editions. He and his
wife Lillian (also a fine pianist) gave many duet and two-piano
recitals.

Friedberg, Carl (1872–1955). German pianist, he studied with Clara
Schumann and integrated a successful teaching and concert career.
He was a member of the original piano faculty at The Juilliard
School and turned out a number of very successful pianists in-
cluding Frager, Grainger, Bruce Hungerford, Leginska, Masselos,
and Elly Ney.

Friedman, Ignace (1882–1948). Polish pianist and composer, he
studied with Leschetizky in Vienna and became famous throughout Europe and America for his brilliant technique. He composed
many works for piano and made a number of piano transcriptions.
He edited the works of Chopin, Liszt, and Schumann.

friska (Hung.). The fast section of a *csárdás*.

Friskin, James (1886–1967). Scottish pianist and teacher, he studied
at the Royal College in London. He came to the United States in
1914 to teach and to concertize. He was a member of the original
faculty of The Juilliard School, where he taught for many years.
He was a noted Bach specialist and wrote *The Principles of Pianoforte Practice* and, with Freundlich, *Music for the Piano*.

Froberger, Johann (1616–67). This German composer helped establish the standard form for the Baroque suite. He composed canzonas, capriccios, fantasias, ricercari, suites, and toccatas.

Fuga giocosa (Joyous Fugue). John Knowles Paine (1839–1906),
op. 41, no. 3. Based on the baseball refrain "Over the fence is out,

boys," a sprightly fugue shows Paine's love for Bach and identifies him as an American composer.

fugato (It.). A passage treated in fugal style but not in strict fugal form.

fugue (Lat.). 1. Flight. 2. The most mature form of imitative counterpoint.

functional piano. This term is used to cover several important areas with which the college piano major must be familiar: improvisation, keyboard harmony, sight-reading, and other keyboard skills.

fundamental. The tone produced by the full unaltered vibration of a string.

funèbre (Fr.). Mournful, sad, gloomy.

Funérailles **(Funeral Ceremonies).** Franz Liszt, S. 173, 1849. Written in memory of Liszt's friends Prince Felix Lichnowsky, Count Ladislaus Teleki, and Lajos Batthanyi; Batthanyi was killed in the Hungarian Revolution of October 1849. This is a dramatic work with a midsection that uses trumpet calls and galloping octaves. Harmonic clashes and the savage abruptness of the closing are quintessential Liszt. It requires a mature octave technique.

Funeral March. Felix Mendelssohn, op. 62, no. 3, in E Minor, one of the *Songs without Words*.

"Funeral March" Sonata. 1. Ludwig van Beethoven, Sonata in A-flat Major, op. 26, 1801. The second movement of this piano sonata is entitled "Marcia funebre sulla morte d'un Eroe" (funeral march on the death of a hero), which gives the sonata its nickname. It was inspired by the funeral march in a popular opera by Ferdinando Paër (1771–1839) that Beethoven and Paër saw together. 2. Frédéric Chopin, Sonata in B-flat Minor, op. 35, 1837. This sonata is so nicknamed because the third movement is the well-known funeral march.

"Funeral" Waltz. See *Trauerwalzer*.

fuoco (It.). Fire, spirit.

Für Elise (For Elise). Ludwig van Beethoven, WoO 59, 25 April 1810. One of Beethoven's most famous piano pieces.

furiant (Czech.). A lively Czech dance in triple meter, with shifting accent patterns. Dvořák composed for piano a *Furiant with Dumka* and *Two Furiants*.

furieux (Fr.). Furious, raging.

furioso (It.). Furiously, vehement, savagely.

furniture music. *Musique d'ameublement* or background music. A phrase coined by Erik Satie to characterize his aesthetic conception. His three *Gymnopédies* (1888) are good examples.

fuyant (Fr.). Flying, fleeing.

G

g. dessus (Fr.). The left (hand) over.

Gabrilowitsch, Osspi (1878–1936). Russian pianist, conductor and composer, he studied with Anton Rubinstein and Leschetizky. He built reputations in Europe and the United States. He featured a series of six recitals showing the development of piano music from the English virginalists to modern-day composers. He was conductor of the Detroit Symphony Orchestra from 1918 to 1935 and composed works for the piano.

gai (Fr.). Merry, gay.

gallant. A musical style of the period 1710–75 with characteristics such as light textures, ornate melody, and elegant sentimentality. Haydn and Mozart's style of composing in their early works.

gallop. A lively dance in duple meter with a hopping step. Alfredo Casella, Liszt, Schubert, and Carlos Surinach, among others, have written gallops for piano.

Gallop Marquis. Frédéric Chopin, piece for solo piano in A-flat Major, KK p 1240a. Inspired by his lover George Sand's two pet dogs, Marquis and Dib.

Ganz, Rudolph (1877–1972). Swiss pianist and teacher, he studied at the Zurich Conservatory and privately with Busoni. He toured

Europe, the United States, Canada, and Cuba. He was conductor of the Saint Louis Symphony Orchestra from 1921 to 1927 and served as president of the Chicago Musical College from 1933 to 1954. In 1954 he became a faculty member of the Chicago Musical College of Roosevelt University. Ganz also made recordings and composed.

Garden of Eden, The. William Bolcom (b. 1938), 1968. Four rags based on Genesis, a blend of rag characteristics with contemporary compositional technique.

gardez la Ped. jusqu'à * (Fr.). Hold the pedal until *.

gardez la pédale (Fr.). Keep the pedal (depressed).

gardez la sourdine, la pédal forte sur chaque temps (Fr.). Keep the *una corda* and the damper pedals in use for each measure.

Gargoyles. Lowell Liebeman (b. 1961), 1989. Four contrasting movements requiring virtuosic technique.

Gaspard de la nuit (Gaspard of the Night). Maurice Ravel, 1908. Ravel's three-piece showpiece of virtuosic writing: *Ondine* (a water nymph), *Le gibet* (The Gallows), *Scarbo* (a goblin appearing in a hallucination).

gavotte (Fr.). A French dance usually in common time, somewhat fast, strongly accented, beginning on the third beat. It was an optional dance in the Baroque suite. Examples are found for the piano by J. S. Bach, Arthur Benjamin, John Blow, Dohnányi, Pierre Max Dubois, Johann Fischer, Anis Fuleihan, Handel, Prokofiev, Rameau, Saint-Saëns, Schoenberg, Giovanni Sgambati, and Sibelius, among others.

Gebrauchsmusik (Ger.). "Music for use" or "utility music." Easy-to-play serious music, for amateurs, home, or schools, rather than for virtuosos. The term is usually associated with Hindemith, who composed many pieces in this genre. The six pieces for solo piano from his cantata *Let's Build a City* (1931) are an excellent example.

gebunden (Ger.). Smoothly connected, tied, legato.

Gefühl (Ger.). Feeling, sentiment, expression.

Gefühlsduselei (Ger.). No English equivalent, it roughly describes extremes of sentiment, "breast-beating," sentimental indulgence.

gehalten (Ger.). Sustained.

gehend (Ger.). *Andante*, going.

geistvoll (Ger.). Witty, clever.

gemendo (It.). Moaning, lamenting.

genau im Takt (Ger.). Exactly in time.

Général Lavine—Eccentric. Claude Debussy, *Préludes*, book 2, no. 6, 1913. An American comedian, Edward LaVine, who gave himself the name *General Lavine, the Eccentric,* was the inspiration for this piece. Debussy uses mimicry and dance rhythms to capture a facet of American humor.

Genhart, Cecile (1898–1983). Swiss-born pianist and outstanding teacher, she studied with Philipp Jarnach, Emil Frey, and Fischer. Her debut took place in Zurich in 1920 and her Berlin debut in 1922. She joined the faculty of the Eastman School of Music in 1926 and taught there for many years.

genre (Fr.). Style, type of composition; way.

Gerig, Reginald (b. 1919). American pianist, teacher and writer, he studied at The Juilliard School with Friedberg, Gorodnitzki, Raieff, and Freundlich; he received two degrees from that school. His definitive book, *Famous Pianists and Their Technique,* has become a widely used and acclaimed history of piano technical practice. He has traveled throughout the United States and England lecturing on the subject. He taught at the Eastman School of Music and at Wheaton College for 35 years until his retirement.

German Dance. A dance for couples in a fast triple meter, popular in South Germany and Austria during the late eighteenth and early nineteenth centuries. It eventually became the waltz. Beethoven, Haydn, Mozart, and Schubert wrote numerous examples.

German Suites. J. S. Bach, BWV 825–30, 1726–30. This set of six suites was given this nickname since the other sets had been nicknamed "French" and "English," and because Bach's own designation *Partien* suggested that he regarded them as conforming in style to the German tradition.

Gershwin, George (1898–1937). American composer and pianist, he studied composition with Rubin Goldmark. He most famous works include the opera *Porgy and Bess,* a piano concerto, and the *Rhapsody in Blue* for piano and orchestra along with many popular songs. Recently discovered preludes bring the total to seven, four additions to the familiar three we have had since 1934.

geschwind (Ger.). Quickly, rapid.

gestossen (Ger.). Short, staccato, detached.

getragen (Ger.). Slow and sustained; *sostenuto.*

gewidmet (Ger.). Dedicated (to).

Ghost Waltzes. Morton Gould (1913–96). The commissioned piece for the 1993 Van Cliburn Piano Competition.

Gieseking, Walter (1895–1956). German pianist, he studied at the Hanover Conservatory. He became established as a foremost interpreter of German classics and of French Impressionism, especially Debussy and Ravel. He also composed piano pieces and chamber music and wrote articles on piano subjects.

gigue (Fr.), ***giga*** (It.), ***jig*** (Eng.). A fast dance usually in $\frac{6}{8}$ meter which evolved from the English jig. The French type, imitative and in $\frac{6}{8}$ or $\frac{6}{4}$ meter, used dotted rhythms. The Italian type is faster, not as imitative, and contains frequent running passages. The gigue became one of the standard dances of the Baroque suite, usually as the final movement. J. S. Bach, Handel, Brahms, Dvořák, Mozart, Poulenc, Reger, and Schumann are some composers who have written gigues for the piano.

Gilels, Emil (1916–85). Russian pianist, he studied with Neuhaus at the Moscow Conservatory, where he himself was professor of piano from 1951 until his death. He played a wide range of repertoire from Bach through 20th-century composers and established an international reputation.

Ginastera, Alberto (1916–83). Argentinean composer, he was trained in his native country and developed a personal style, a Pan-American (rather than a Latin) language, that combines certain nationalistic traits with advanced contemporary techniques. His contribution to piano literature, while not large, is significant. Piano works include *Danzas argentinas* (Argentine Dances), *Malambo, Róndo sobre temas infantiles argentinos* (Rondo on Argentine Children's Folk Tunes), three sonatas, *Suite de danzas criollas* (Suite of Creole Dances), *Tres Piezas* (Three Pieces), *Twelve American Preludes*. For piano and orchestra: *Concierto Argentino* and two concertos.

gingando (Port.). Swinging.

giocoso (It.). Merry, humorous, playful.

gioioso (It.). Blithe, joyful, gay.

giustamente (It.). Precise, in time.

giusto (It.). Exact, proper, reasonable, correct; in an appropriate tempo, strict tempo (no *rubato*).

Glass, Philip (b. 1937). This American composer studied at the University of Chicago, The Juilliard School, and with Boulanger in

Paris, where he also worked with Ravi Shankar. Indian music inspired his working with ostinato patterns in forms of slow change (minimalist music). Piano works: *Opening, Modern Love Waltz, The Olympian—Lighting of the Torch, Solo Piano,* and *Wichita Vortex Sutra.*

Glazunov, Alexander (1865–1936). Russian composer, student of Nicolai Rimsky-Korsakov and greatly influenced by Liszt, Wagner, and Brahms. He was more successful with smaller forms than with the sonata. He composed three Concert Studies, Nocturne, Prelude and Fugue, two sonatas, and Theme and 15 Variations.

gliss. m.d. sur les touches blanches (Fr.). Glissando R. H. (right hand) on the white keys.

glissando, gliss. (It.). From Fr. *glisser,* to slide. On the piano, a scale produced by quickly sliding the thumb or thumb and one finger up or down over the keys.

glisser avec le pouce (Fr.). Glissando with the thumb.

glissicato (It.). Softly gliding.

Gnomenreigen (Dance of the Gnomes). See *Waldesrauschen.*

Gnossiennes. Erik Satie, 1889–97. Two sets of three pieces each. The title is likely a vague allusion to Knossos, an ancient city on the Island of Crete—the capital of the mythical King Minos. They feature a repeated melody and continual bass rhythm.

Godowsky, Leopold (1870–1938). Lithuanian pianist, he was a child prodigy and made his debut at age nine; he gained masterly control of the piano. He became a U.S. citizen and was internationally famous. His teaching in New York drew pianists from all over the world. His compositions are very difficult, especially the 53 studies based on Chopin's own sets and his transcriptions of Strauss waltzes. He arranged pieces by Bach, Brahms, and Weber and *Lieder* by Schubert. A master musician.

"Goldberg" Variations. J. S. Bach, BWV 988, 1742. Popular name for Bach's towering set of 32 variations, based on a majestic *sarabande* written for harpsichord but frequently performed on the piano today. Written at the request of a count who suffered from insomnia and needed music to get to sleep. The count asked Bach to compose a piece that his harpsichordist Johann Goldberg (one of Bach's best students) could play for him.

Goldsand, Robert (1911–1991). Austrian pianist, he studied with Rosenthal and Joseph Marx (1882–1964). As a young person he toured Europe and South America; he made his United States debut in 1927 at Carnegie Hall in New York. He settled in the United States in 1939 and taught at the Cincinnati Conservatory and the Manhattan School of Music. He was a pianist with great technical brilliance, a refined style (especially with Chopin), and poetic conviction. Students include Richard Fields and Schumacher.

Golliwogg's Cake-walk. Claude Debussy. The sixth and final movement in his *Children's Corner.* The movement is jazzy (ragtime) and spiced with syncopated harmony. A short, witty reference to Wagner's prelude to *Tristan und Isolde* adds to the fun.

Gordon, Stewart (b. 1930). American pianist, teacher, and writer, he studied at the Eastman School of Music and with Samaroff. While chair of music at the University of Maryland, he established and directed the event now known as the William Kapell International Piano Competition. He also established the Savannah Onstage Festival and its American Traditions Competition. He is chair of keyboard studies at the University of Southern California. Books Gordon has written include *Etudes for Piano Teachers* and *A History of Keyboard Literature,* and he is coauthor of *The Well-Tempered Keyboard Teacher.*

Gorodnitzki, Sascha (1904–86). Ukranian-born pianist and teacher, he studied at the Institute of Musical Art from 1919 to 1923 and later at The Juilliard School from 1926 to 1932 with Josef Lhévinne. He made his New York debut with the New York Philharmonic in 1930 and was quickly recognized as an outstanding virtuoso, especially playing the Romantic piano repertoire. He taught at The Juilliard School from 1948 to his death. His students include Nelita True.

Gottschalk, Louis Moreau (1829–69). American pianist and composer, he went to Paris in 1842 to study. He soon became well known playing in Parisian salons, and he studied composition with Hector Berlioz. Known as the "American Liszt," he ranked with the greatest European virtuosi of his time and toured and played at most of the European courts. He spent time in Cuba and the West Indies and died in Brazil. He composed over 100 piano compositions which require a solid technique and display vitality, beauty, and charm. He was the first American "Ambassador of Art" to Europe.

Gould, Glenn (1932–82). Canadian pianist, he studied with Alberto

Guerreo at the Royal Conservatory in Toronto. His repertoire ranged from Byrd to Schoenberg, and his reputation as a pianist mainly rested on his many recordings. Gould tired of the life of a traveling virtuoso and retired to the recording studio in 1964. He made radio broadcasts and documentary programs that were very popular. His style was characterized by true elegance, no matter what he played.

goût (Fr.). Taste, style, manner.

Goyescas. Enrique Granados, 1911. A set of piano pieces inspired by Goya paintings, this is Granados's most famous and grandiose work for piano. He later used the music as the basis for an opera with the same name.

grace note. A note of very short duration, it takes some of the value of the preceding note.

gracieux (Fr.). Graceful.

gradevole (It.). Pleasant, agreeable.

Gradus ad Parnassum (Steps to Perfection). Muzio Clementi, 1817. A collection of 100 studies for the piano, each piece diverse in style and intended for advanced students, it covers almost every aspect of piano technique. Debussy parodied this collection in the opening movement of his *Children's Corner, Dr. Gradus ad Parnassum.*

Graf, Conrad (1782–1851). Austrian piano maker of German birth, he built fine instruments. He made pianos for Beethoven and for the wedding of Robert and Clara Schumann, and he supplied an instrument for Chopin's 1829 concert in Vienna. Liszt also admired the Graf piano.

Graffman, Gary (b. 1928). American pianist and teacher, he studied at the Curtis Institute with Vengerova, and with Rudolf Serkin and Horowitz privately. He won the Rachmaninoff Prize and appeared with the Philadelphia Orchestra in 1947. He quickly established an international reputation as a soloist and with chamber music groups. His right hand became disabled in 1979, but he continued performing works for left hand alone and teaching at the Curtis Institute. He has been president of that institution for a number of years. His memoir, *I Really Should Be Practicing,* was published in 1981.

Grainger, Percy (1882–1961). Australian pianist and composer, he studied with James Kwast (1852–1927) in Frankfurt and briefly with Busoni. He met Grieg in 1906 and became famous for playing the latter's Piano Concerto. He settled in the United States in 1915 and continued concertizing and teaching in various schools. His friendship with Grieg had aroused an interest in British folk music, which he began researching and arranging. Grainger composed a great deal for the piano and made numerous transcriptions for it.

Granados, Enrique (1867–1916). Spanish composer and pianist, he composed a large body of piano music. Most of his piano compositions show him to be a facile improvisator rather than a master craftsman. His piano works include *Allegro de concierto, Bocetos* (Sketches), *Goyescas, Escenas románticas* (Romantic Scenes), *Rapsodia Aragonesa* (Aragon Rhapsody), 10 Spanish dances, and *Valses poeticos* (Poetic Waltzes). Granados was killed when the ship he was on was torpedoed by a German submarine during World War I.

grand. Term used for a horizontal piano.

grand piano. A large, winged-shaped piano in which the strings are placed horizontally over the soundboard.

Grand Sonata in Rag. William Albright (1944–98), 1974. Three movements: *Scott Joplin's Victory, Ragtime Turtle Dove, Behemoth Two-Step.* The piece blends sonata form with rag characteristics. Technically and demanding, each movement can be played alone.

Grandes études de Paganini (Grand Paganini Etudes). Franz Liszt, S. 141, 1851. A set of six brilliant Paganini studies published in 1840 that Liszt transcribed for the piano.

grandioso (It.). Grandly, noble, in a stately manner, imposing, play in a regal manner.

grandisonante (It.). Sonorous, loud, strong.

grave (It.). The slowest musical tempo; solemn, stately, serious.

gravement (Fr.). Seriously; *plus gravement expressif:* more seriously expressive.

Grazer-Fantasie (Graz Fantasy). Franz Schubert, 1818. Thought to have been written when Schubert was almost 21 years old, this work in C major was discovered in 1962 and displays some brilliant writing.

grazia (It.). Grace, elegance.

Gretchaninoff, Alexander (1864–1956). Russian composer, he worked as a piano teacher and folksong arranger. His eclectic style covers a broad gamut of the standard forms, including some charming pieces for young people. His piano works include *Brimborions, Glass Beads, Historiettes, Russian Folk Dances, Suite Miniature,* and two sonatas.

Grieg, Edvard (1843–1907). Norwegian composer and pianist. Nationalistic elements play a large part in his piano works, especially the smaller characteristic pieces, his finest contribution to the piano repertoire. He was a major composer of small pieces, most notably the 10 books of *Lyric Pieces.* Piano works: *Ballad, Holberg Suite, Humoresques, Moods, Norwegian Dances and Songs, Norwegian Dances, Poetic Tone-Pictures, Slätter* (based on Norwegian folk music), one sonata, *Norwegian Dances* and *Valses-Caprices* for piano duet, and the famous Piano Concerto in A Minor.

Griffes, Charles Tomlinson (1884–1920). This American composer's love of oriental subjects and a preoccupation with Impressionist techniques were the major influences on his music. His stature continues to grow. His piano sonata was one of the most important works in that genre to appear in the United States during the first quarter of the 20th century. His piano works include *Fantasy Pieces, Four Roman Sketches, The Pleasure Dome of Kubla Khan, Rhapsody,* and *Three Tone Poems.*

gris (Fr.). Gray. Play without much color (gray tinted).

gruppetto (It.). Little group; a group of grace notes, such as a turn, trill, etc.; a grace.

Guerry, Jack (b. 1931). This American pianist and teacher received his doctorate from Michigan State University and has studied with Robert, Silvio Scionti, Frantz, Marcel Ciampi at the Paris Conservatoire, and Kabos in London. He has appeared as soloist, with orchestras, in chamber music, and as an accompanist in the United States and Europe. He was instrumental in spearheading the development of the Doctorate of Musical Arts degree in piano at the Louisiana State University, where he taught for many years. He is the author of *Silvio Scionti: Remembering a Master Pianist and Teacher* and *Essays on Artistic Piano Playing.*

Guggenheim Jeune. Virgil Thomson, Sonata no. 4, 1940. This sonata is a portrait of Miss Peggy Guggenheim. At the time it was composed she was planning to open an art gallery in New York and call it Guggenheim Jeune. This title is a nickname for her.

gusto (It.). With relish, taste, style, manner, liking.

Gymnopédies. Erik Satie, 1888. Three pieces. The title refers to ceremonial dances to be performed at ancient Greek festivals. Each piece is sad and languorous.

H

H. 1. Abbreviation for hand. *R.H.*: right hand. *L.H.*: left hand. 2. In German the note B is called H, and B♭ is called B. 3. Abbreviation for Helm, used to identify works by C. P. E. Bach in Eugene Helm's *Thematic Catalogue of the Works of Carl Philipp Emanuel Bach* (1990).

habanera (Sp.). A Cuban dance probably of African origin, in duple time with a syncopated rhythm. It was very popular in Spain during the 19th century. Madeleine Panzera and Ravel have composed habaneras for piano, and Mátyás Seiber has written one for two pianos. The most famous example is the aria from Bizet's opera *Carmen.*

Habermann, Michael (b. 1950). American pianist born in Paris, he has lived in Canada and Mexico. He has almost single-handedly (two-handedly!) brought to audiences the music of Kaikhosru Sorabji (1892–1988), who composed fascinating and enormously difficult scores. Sorabji placed a ban on the performance of his music until his later years, when he did give permission to Habermann (and one or two others) to perform his music. Habermann has performed and recorded most of Sorabji's music and is also an outstanding pianist of the standard repertoire.

hairpins. A name sometimes used with the signs `━━◁` and `▷━━` that indicate *crescendo* and *diminuendo*.

hammer. The padded device which sets the strings on a piano in vibration.

hammer head. The padded mallet which strikes the strings.

Hammerklavier (Ger.). Old German name for the piano; hammer keyboard.

Hammerklavier **Sonata.** Ludwig van Beethoven's Sonata in B-flat Major, op. 106, 1817–18. Beethoven did not give it this name. It is an apocalyptic masterpiece.

Handel, George Frideric (1685–1759). This German composer was equally famous as a composer and a keyboard player of unsurpassed ability. His keyboard compositions include two sets of eight suites, variations, and many separate pieces.

Handstück (Ger.). A teaching piece (small form) frequently using certain types of figuration to express the character or affect. Daniel Gottlob Türk composed many such pieces.

Happiness. Felix Mendelssohn, op. 102, no. 5, in A Major, one of the *Songs without Words*.

hardiesse (Fr.). Boldness, daring. *hardiment:* boldly, impudently.

harmonic. An upper partial brought out by touching a node upon the string while the hammer strikes it in the normal manner.

Harmonies poétiques et religieuses **(Poetic and Religious Harmonies).** Franz Liszt, S. 173, 1845–52. Ten pieces inspired by a set of poems by Alphonse de Lamartine. *Invocation; Ave Maria; Benediction de Dieu dans la solitude* (Benediction of God in the Solitude); *Pensée des morts* (Thought of Deaths); *Pater Noster* (Our Father); *Hymne de l'enfant à son reveil* (Hymn of the Child at His Wakening); *Funérailles, October 1849; Miserere, d'apres Palestrina* (Miserere after Palestrina); *Andante lagrimoso; Cantique d'amour* (Song of Love).

harmonieux (Fr.). Harmonious, sweet, melodious.

"Harmonious Blacksmith." This nickname was given to Handel's air and variations contained in his harpsichord Suite in E Major (1720). Handel liked this air since he used a fragment of it in his opera *Almira* and in his Concerto for Organ or Harpsichord in B-flat Major, op. 4, no. 6.

harpégement (Fr.). Arpeggio.

harpsichord. A keyboard instrument in which the strings are plucked by quills of hard leather, a predecessor of the piano.

Harrison, Lou (1917–2003). American composer whose music ranges from the almost primitive through the ecclesiastically archaic, the saucily pleasant, and the more serious 12 tone to the delicacies of scales in pure nontempered intonation and microtonal divisions of utmost sensitivity. Harrison has been called "the father of American Minimalism." Ives was his model. Piano works include *Reel, Homage to Henry Cowell; Homage to Milhaud; Prelude and Sarabande; Six Sonatas; Suite for Piano.* Two-piano and chamber music: *Concerto in Slendro, Concerto with Selected Orchestra, Suite for Piano, Violin, and Chamber Orchestra.*

Harrison, Robin (b. 1932). English-Canadian pianist, he studied at the Royal Academy in London with Harold Craxton and with Carlo Zecchi in Italy. He also studied at the Mozarteum in Salzburg and with Kabos in London. He has appeared with major orchestras, performed in Europe, the United States, and Canada, and taught at the Royal Manchester College of Music and the University of Saskatchewan. He is most identified with the Romantic repertoire, especially Chopin, and he is a great communicator of this composer's art.

Haskil, Clara (1895–1960). Romanian pianist, she studied with Cortot. She played highly successful recitals in Switzerland, Belgium, and the United States. She was recognized especially for performances of Beethoven, Mozart, and Schubert.

hasta (Sp.). Till, until, up to, as far as.

hâte (Fr.). Hurry, haste, eagerness. *hâtant:* hurried.

Hautzig, Walter (b. 1921). American pianist and teacher (born Austria), he studied with Schnabel and Mieczyslaw Munz at the Curtis Institute. He has toured the world a number of times, receiving high praise for his performances. He has made many recordings and has taught at the Peabody Conservatory for a number of years.

Haydn, Joseph (1732–1809). Austrian composer, he was the greatest of the Classical composers responsible for the development of the symphony and string quartet. He was taught on the fortepiano (a predecessor of the piano), and of the 52 keyboard sonatas he composed, it is not certain for which instrument (harpsichord or fortepiano) they were composed. Haydn's other keyboard works include *Adagios, Ariettas,* a *Capriccio,* a *Fantasia,* sets of variations, and 32 pieces for musical clocks (that can be performed on the piano), plus over 15 keyboard concertos.

heftig (Ger.). Insistent, boisterous, vehement, violent, passionate.

heimlich (Ger.). Secret, mysterious.

Heinrich, Anton Philip (1781–1861). This American composer (born in Bohemia) has been called the "Beethoven of America." He was completely untrained musically but wrote some of the most original music of his day. In many ways Heinrich's accomplishments can be equated with those of Ives. Piano works include *The Dawning of Music in Kentucky, or the Pleasures of Harmony in the Solitude of Nature; The Sylviad, or Minstrelsy of North America; Toccatina Capriciosa;* and *The Western Minstrel.*

heiter (Ger.). Cheerful, merry, serene.

Heller, Stephen (1813–88). Hungarian composer, he lived mostly in France. Heller's works include much fine pedagogical material. Like Grieg, Heller was a masterful composer of small forms. His works include over 100 short piano compositions, many of them character pieces.

Henle. German firm of music publishers founded in Munich in 1948 by Günter Henle (1899–1979), who was an industrialist, politician, amateur musician, and collector. This company is well known for its outstanding *Urtext* editions of the Baroque, Classical, and Romantic piano and chamber repertory.

Hensel, Fanny Mendelssohn (1805–47). German composer, she was the older sister of Felix Mendelssohn and composed over 400 works. She and her brother had similar training, and they wrote in similar styles. Her piano works include two sonatas, *Das Jahr* (The Year), *Songs without Words,* and other pieces.

héroïque (Fr.). Heroic, bold, daring.

hervortretend (Ger.). Emphasized, marked.

herzlich (Ger.). Tenderly, heartfelt.

Hess, Dame Myra (1890–1965). English pianist, she studied with Tobias Matthay. She made her London debut in 1907 and slowly built her career. During World War II she performed lunchtime concerts at the National Gallery in London. She premiered many contemporary works by English composers such as Bax, Arthur Bliss, Frank Bridge, and Howard Ferguson.

heurté (Fr.). Abrupt, harsh, jerky.

Hewitt, James (1770–1827). American composer (born in Great Britain), he was a leader of George III's court orchestra before coming to America in 1792. He was active in New York as a music publisher, concert violinist, director of theater orchestras, and organist of Trinity Church in Boston. Piano works: *The Battle of Trenton, Mark My Alford with Variations* (based on the tune we know as "Twinkle, Twinkle, Little Star"), and *The Fourth of July: A Grand Military Sonata,* plus other pieces.

hexachord. A six-note scale. It usually means six notes with the interval pattern tone–tone–semitone–tone–tone (e.g., C–D–E–F–G–A).

Hexameron Variations. Variations on a march by Vincenzo Bellini, Chopin, Czerny, Henri Herz, Liszt, Johann Pixis, and Thalberg, 1837. Each composer wrote one variation. Liszt also wrote the introduction, several interludes, and the finale. A grand Romantic extravaganza.

Hickenlooper, Lucy. See Samaroff, Olga.

Hiller, Ferdinand (1811–85). German pianist, conductor, and composer, he studied with Hummel. He founded the Cologne Conservatory and was the first to play Beethoven's Piano Concerto no. 5 in Paris. His piano works include three concertos and numerous smaller pieces.

Hindemith, Paul (1895–1963). German composer, he was one of the major composers of the 20th century. He approached composition through linear writing, and his expanded tonal concept is unique. He taught at Yale University from 1940 to 1953. His name is associated with the term *Gebrauchsmusik,* music written for everyday home use, especially attractive to amateurs. His piano works include *Ludus Tonalis, Suite, Tanzstücke, Variations,* three sonatas, a sonata for piano duet, and one for two pianos.

Hinson, Maurice (b. 1930). American pianist, teacher, writer, and editor, he studied at The Juilliard School, the University of Florida, and the University of Michigan. He has been a member of the faculty of the School of Church Music at the Southern Baptist Theological Seminary since 1957. He has written books on various areas of piano literature and piano pedagogy and has edited more than 150 editions of piano music. His books include *Guide to the Pianist's Repertoire, Music for Piano and Orchestra, The Piano in Chamber in Piano Ensemble, Music for More than One Piano, The*

Pianist's Bookshelf, and *The Pianist's Guide to Transcriptions, Arrangements, and Paraphrases.*

hirtlich (Ger.). Pastoral, rustic.

His (Ger.). The note B♯.

hitch pin. A small piece of metal to which the lower end of the string is attached.

Hobson, Ian (b. 1952). English-born pianist and teacher, he studied at the Royal Academy in London and with Claude Frank at Yale University. He has won many prizes and has made numerous recordings that show great technical command and high-minded musicianship. He teaches at the University of Illinois.

Hodges, Joanna. American pianist, she studied with Firkusny in Aspen and Bruno Seidlhofer in Vienna. She has won many prizes and has concertized extensively in the United States and Europe with great success. She started the Joanna Hodges International Piano Competition, which has attracted star piano talent for many years.

Hofmann, Josef (1876–1957). Polish pianist, he studied with Anton Rubinstein and Moszkowski. He toured Europe when he was nine and the United States when he was 11. One of the world's leading pianists, he lived in the United States from 1898, becoming a citizen in 1926. He was the first director of the Curtis Institute of Music and is the dedicatee of Rachmaninoff's Third Piano Concerto. Hofmann composed a few works under the pen name of Michael Dvorsky, in a fluent and florid post-Romantic style. Students include Jeanne Behrend, Abram Chasins, Cherkassky, Nadia Reisenberg, and Slenczynska.

hold. See *fermata.*

Homeless. Felix Mendelssohn, op. 102, no. 1, in E Minor, one of the *Songs without Words.*

hommage (Fr.). Respect, homage, veneration. Many composers have used the piano to compose *hommages.* A few examples are Debussy, Arthur Honegger, Liszt, Paderewski, Poulenc, Albert Roussel, Tansman, Tcherepnin, and Villa-Lobos.

Hommage à Chopin. Edvard Grieg, Study in F Minor, op. 73, no. 5, from *Moods,* 1905. *Hommage à Chopin* is the subtitle and imitates Chopin's style of his etudes so convincingly that one is left wondering what happened to Grieg's own style!

Hommage à S. Pickwick, Esq. P.P.M.P.C. Claude Debussy, *Préludes,* book 2, no. 9, 1913. This tribute to Samuel Pickwick is Debussy's impression of the pomp and humor of Charles Dickens's celebrated character from *The Pickwick Papers.* The initials in the title stand for Perpetual Vice President–Member Pickwick Club. Debussy's English is slightly wrong, but English was not his strongest suit!

honky-tonk. 1. A style of playing the piano related to ragtime. 2. A tinny-sounding, out-of-tune piano.

hopak. A Russian dance in brisk duple meter. Mussorgsky arranged a *hopak* from his opera *The Fair at Sorochinsk* for piano.

Hope. Felix Mendelssohn, op. 38, no. 4, in A Major, one of the *Songs without Words.*

Hopkinson, Francis (1737–91). Hopkinson was the first known American composer as well as a signer of the Declaration of Independence and a personal friend of George Washington. His music is couched in the conventional English style and modeled after pieces by Thomas Arne. Piano works: *7 Songs* (actually eight!) that can be performed as solo keyboard music or as songs, the first collection of secular music by a native-born American composer published in America; *Lessons,* an anthology of keyboard compositions and arrangements copied in Hopkinson's hand.

hopper. The level used to raise the hammer in a piano and to regulate the escapement.

Horowitz, Vladimir (1904–89). Russian pianist, he studied at the Kiev Conservatory until 1921. He toured Europe and made his U.S. debut in 1928; he settled in the United States and married conductor Arturo Toscanini's daughter. His career as an international virtuoso of the highest rank was interrupted by illness from 1936 to 1938. Beginning in 1953 he played only for recordings, but he returned to the concert platform in 1965. He was at his best with Scarlatti, Schumann, Liszt, and other Romantic composers.

Horszowski, Mieczyslaw (1892–1993). Polish pianist, he studied with Leschetizky. He became internationally known as soloist and ensemble player of the highest rank. He settled in the United States in 1942 and taught at the Curtis Institute of Music beginning in 1941. He played recitals through his late years. His students include Richard Goode, Steven de Groote, Seymour Lipkin, Luvisi, Perahia, Peter Serkin, and Claudette Sorel.

Hughes, Edwin (1884–1965). American pianist and teacher, he studied with Joseffy and Leschetizky and served as the latter's assistant in 1909–10. He made his European debut in Vienna in 1912 and toured Germany as a recitalist and soloist. He then settled in New York and taught at the Institute of Musical Art (1918–23) and gave many master classes. He was editor-in-chief for G. Schirmer from 1920 to 1925 and prepared an edition of J. S. Bach's *Well-Tempered Clavier.* He also played duo piano recitals with his wife, Jewel Bethany Hughes.

Hummel, Johann Nepomuk (1778–1837). Austrian pianist and composer, he studied with Mozart and received the advice of Haydn and Salieri. He was employed by a number of German courts and toured as a concert pianist. He was extremely expert at improvisation. His piano works include seven piano concertos plus a double concerto for piano and violin, much piano chamber music, etudes, preludes, nine sonatas, and variations. He wrote an important *Klavierschule* (Keyboard School, 1828); the complete title is *A Complete Theoretical and Practical Course of Instructions on the Art of Playing the Pianoforte.*

humoresque (Fr.). A light, lively (capricious) composition, with a playful or changeable character. Dvořák, Grieg, MacDowell, Carl Nielsen, Poulenc, Rachmaninoff, Schumann, Sibelius, and Jenö Takács, among others, have written examples for the piano.

humour (Fr.). Humor.

Hungarian. Edward MacDowell, op. 39, no. 12, 1890. From a set of *Twelve Studies* "for the development of technique and style," this piece focuses on dash, speed, and the ability to scamper over the keyboard quickly.

Hungarian Dances. Johannes Brahms, 21 piano duets composed between 1852 and 1869. These pieces were written in "Hungarian style," freely imitating the Hungarian *czárdás* and gypsy music rather than being based on Hungarian folk music. He orchestrated three of them and arranged some for piano solo.

Hungarian Rhapsodies. Franz Liszt, 20 piano pieces composed between 1846 and 1885. Inspired by Hungarian gypsy music, these pieces provide dazzling pianistic brilliance and have much to recommend them.

Hunting Song. Felix Mendelssohn, op. 19, no. 3, in A Major, one of the *Songs without Words.*

hurtig (Ger.). Quick, agile.

Hutcheson, Ernest (1871–1951). Australian pianist and teacher, he studied at the Leipzig Conservatory and in Vienna. He made tours of Europe and England and came to the United States in 1900 to head the piano department at the Peabody Conservatory. He joined The Juilliard School when it was founded in 1924, becoming dean in 1927 and serving as president from 1937 to 1945. He wrote two books on the piano: *The Elements of Piano Technique*, and *The Literature of the Piano*, later added to by Rudolf Ganz.

Hyde, Miriam (b. 1913). This Australian composer and pianist graduated from the Adelaide Conservatorium and then spent three years in London at the Royal College of Music. She is best known for her piano music, which is eminently pianistic. Her style is grounded on 19th-century harmonic and rhythmic use but colorfully infused with unique handling of mildly contemporary techniques. She knows how to end a piece, and no "padding" is found in her writing. Her piano works include *Magpies at Sunrise, Reflected Reeds, Valley of Rocks,* two concertos, plus numerous smaller piano pieces.

hymn. A religious or sacred song. Many composers have used this term as the title for piano works. A few examples are Alan Hovhaness, Philipp Jarnach, Liszt, Norman Lloyd, Nicolai Medtner, Milhaud, Poulenc, Stravinsky, and Tansman.

I

Ibéria. Isaac Albeniz, 1906. This pianistic marvel is Albeniz's masterpiece, 12 pieces with enormous technical demands that are evocative of Spanish scenes and landscape.

idyll. A composition with peaceful, pastoral character, eclogue. MacDowell and Smetana, among others, have composed idylls.

im Zeitmass (Ger.). Original tempo, *a tempo.*

Images (Pictures). Claude Debussy, 1905 and 1907. Two books of piano pieces, three pieces in each book. Book 1: *Reflets dans l'eau* (Reflections in the Water), *Hommage à Rameau* (Homage to Rameau), *Movement* (Movement). Book 2: *Cloches à travers les feuilles* (Bells through the Leaves), *Et la lune descend sur le temple qui fût* (And the Moon Descends on the Ruined Temple), *Poisson d'or* (Goldfish).

Images (oubliées) (Forgotten Pictures). Claude Debussy, 1894. *Lent, doux et mélancolique* (Lent), *Sarabande "Souvenir du Louvre"* (Sarabande, Souvenir of the Louvre—the first version of the future Sarabande in his *Pour le piano*), *Quelques aspects de "Nous n'irons plus au bois"* (Some Aspects of "We Go No More to the Woods" [because the weather is so unbearable]—this popular song was used by Debussy again in *Jardins sous le pluie* in *Estampes*).

immer (Ger.). Always, ever, constantly.

impalpable (Fr.). Extremely subtle; imperceptible.

impetuoso (It.). Impetuous, hasty, vehemently, forcefully.

implacable (Fr.). Relentless, unyielding.

Impressionism. Term used to describe works of painters Monet, Degas, Whistler, Renoir, et al. (late 19th century) who avoided sharp contours but tried to convey an "impression" of a subject in slightly blurred images and dashes of color. It has been used to describe the musical style of Debussy and early Ravel, which was evocative and suggestive with a dreamy character. This musical style was very popular from around 1890 to 1910.

impromptu (Fr.). 1. A short character piece of extemporaneous or capricious style. Pieces with this name were composed by Chabrier, Chopin, César Cui, Dohnányi, Fauré, Granados, Grieg, MacDowell, Schubert, Schumann, Scriabin, and Tchaikovsky, among others. 2. An extemporaneous performance.

Impromptu—Le sabbat **(Witches Dance).** Clara Wieck Schumann, op. 5, no. 1, 1835–36. Clara often played this piece at her recitals during the time she was touring as a concert pianist. Here she has the witches dancing furiously to offbeat (third beat) accents.

improvisation. Unpremeditated music, the act of creating music spontaneously. Cadenzas were improvised in concertos and sonatas in the eighteenth and early nineteenth centuries. Many composers have "written" piano improvisations, a type of free-form piece or a variation(s) on a hymn or melody. Some examples are by Pierre Max Dubois, Fauré, Gieseking, Grieg, Grant Johannesen, Nicolai Medtner, Selim Palmgren, Paul Paray, Walter Piston, Poulenc, Reger, Stig-Gustav Schönberg, Svend Tarp, and Harold Zabrack.

improvise. To play unpremeditated music, i.e., make it up as you go along.

in lontananza (Sp.). In the distance, background.

in modo di (It.). In the manner of.

in tempo (It.). In strict time.

incalcando (It.). Growing faster and stronger (louder).

incalzando (It.). Hurrying, to chase; pursue hotly, with constantly increasing vehemence, with growing warmth and fervor.

incisif (Fr.). Distinct, cutting, biting.

incisivo (It.). Incisive, sharply marked.

incolore et toujours (Fr.). Always without dynamics; colorless.

indeciso (It.). With indecision, hesitating.

Indianische Fantasie (Indian Fantasy). Ferruccio Busoni, op. 44, 1913. This work for piano and orchestra is based on American Indian themes.

Indianisches Tagebuch (Indian Diary). Ferruccio Busoni, op. 47, 1915. This "Indian Diary" consists of four short works based on American Indian themes.

indication (Fr.). Expression mark.

indifférent (Fr.). To be played equally (both hands) alike, indifferently as regards to dynamics.

ineffablement doux (Fr.). Inexpressively sweet.

infiniment lent, extatique (Fr.). Exceedingly slow, rapturous.

innig (Ger.). Sincere. A direction to play with intense feeling.

Innigkeit (Ger.). With fervor; intense feeling.

innocentemente (It.). Innocent, childlike, playful, natural, unaffected.

inquiet (Fr.). Restless, agitated.

inquieto (It.). Restless; play agitatedly, excitingly, or violently.

insensible (It.). By imperceptible degrees, gradually.

insensiblement (Fr.). Gradually, by degrees.

insistant (Fr.). Insistent, lay stress on.

insouciant (Fr.). Easy-going, carefree.

intensités (Fr.). Dynamics: *f, p, pp, mf,* etc.

interlude. Literally "between music." A short composition. Examples for piano have been written by Arthur Bliss, Cage, Irving Fine, Daniel Pinkham, Paul Pisk, Kaikhosru Sorabji, Tansman, Hidenori Tokunaga, and Joseph Wagner, among others.

intermezzo (It.). An interlude or group of short incidental pieces. Examples for piano have been written by Brahms, Alfredo Casella, Dohnányi, Dvořák, Otto Luening, MacDowell, Poulenc, Rachmaninoff, Reger, Schumann, and Richard Strauss.

interpretation. The act of performance in the manner of communicating the intentions (in part expressed by the directions) of the composer's musical work. Most composers indicate such details as dynamics, phrasing, tempo, plus other expression marks. While performing the composition, most performers consider they have musical license to interpret the work in their own individual way.

intimement doux (Fr.). Intimately gentle.

intimo (It.). Heartfelt; inward emotion.

introduction. The opening section, usually short, of a composition.

Introduction to the Art of Playing on the Pianoforte. Muzio Clementi, 1801. This work is among the earliest keyboard methods written specifically for the piano. Varied pieces by well-known composers are used instead of the usual short practice pieces written by the author. This was the most popular tutorial of its day.

invention. A name given by J. S. Bach to a set of short two and three-part contrapuntal pieces. The 15 pieces in two parts (Two-Part Inventions) were included in his *Klavierbüchlein* of 1720, while the 15 pieces in three parts (Three-Part Inventions) were called *sinfonias*. Many composers have written pieces using the name inventions: Carlos Chavez, Cowell, Paul Creston, Finney, Lucas Foss, Ulysses Kay, Otto Luening, Colin McPhee, Hermann Reutter, Halsey Stevens, and Thomson, among others.

Invitation to the Dance (Aufforderung zum Tanz). Carl Maria von Weber; Rondo Brilliant in D-flat Major, op. 65, 1819. This represents a ballroom scene, written in a rondo design with numerous thematic fragments woven into a successful whole. Exquisite when well performed.

ironique (Fr.). Ironic, mocking, sardonically.

Islamey. Mily Balakirev, 1865. Oriental fantasy and his most famous work for piano, based on Lisztian technique.

Island Spell, The. John Ireland (1879–1962), from *Decorations*, 1913. This Impressionist piece contains an evocative melody over restless figuration, builds to a climax, then subsides. The other pieces in this colorful suite are *Moon-glade* and *The Scarlet Ceremonies.*

Isle joyeuse, L' (The Island of Joy). Claude Debussy, 1904. His largest piece for solo piano, it was inspired by Watteau's painting *L'embarquement pour Cythère* (The Embarkation for Cythere), which pictures an early-18th-century scene of a party ready to leave for the island sacred to Venus. Orchestrally conceived with great animation and the least inhibited of all of his piano works, advanced pianism is required.

istesso (It.). The same. *l'istesso tempo:* the same speed (tempo); the beat remains the same even though the time signature has changed (from $\frac{3}{4}$ to $\frac{2}{4}$, for example).

Istomin, Eugene (1925–2003). American pianist, he studied at the Curtis Institute with Rudolf Serkin. He toured with the famous

Istomin-Stern-Rose Trio for many years. He won the Leventritt Award in 1943 and went on to enjoy a successful career.

"Italian" Concerto. J. S. Bach, BWV 971, 1735. Concerto for Harpsichord with two keyboards. The title was used to point out the fact that there are alternating contrasting passages and three movements that resemble those of the Italian *concerto grosso*.

Italienne (Fr.), *Italiano* (It.). In Italian style.

Iturbi, José (1895–1980). Spanish pianist and conductor, a child prodigy, he studied at the Valencia and Paris conservatories. He was head of the piano department at the Geneva Conservatory from 1919 to 1923. He had great success touring Europe and the United States and was conductor of the Rochester (N.Y.) Philharmonic Orchestra from 1935 to 1944. He also appeared in several films. He played with great dexterity and possessed superb pianistic equipment. His sister Amparo (1898–1965), with whom he often performed, was also a pianist.

Ives, Charles (1874–1954). American composer, he worked in isolation and refused to follow any rules he did not make up himself. His piano music is exceedingly complex. He would have to be considered an early *avant-garde* composer who fused elements from the Romantic vocabulary with elements of American folk music. His piano works include three sonatas, 22 studies, *Set of Five Take-offs, Three Protests, Varied Air and Variations,* and numerous individual pieces. Ives, who made his fortune in the insurance industry, stopped composing several decades before his death. Pianist Ralph Kirkpatrick was a tireless advocate to bring his works to public notice.

J

Jackson, Raymond (b. 1934). American pianist and teacher, he studied at the New England Conservatory, The Juilliard School with Gorodnitzki and Webster, and with Jeanne-Marie Darre privately. He has won many awards and fellowships. His playing exemplifies the very finest musicianship with a strong technique to back it up. He has taught at Howard University for many years.

Jacobs, Paul (1930–83). American pianist, he studied with Hutcheson and Webster. He was staff pianist of the New York Philharmonic and an outstanding musician. His strong and objective style is heard to advantage in his many recordings of Busoni, Carter, Debussy, Messiaen, Schoenberg, and Stravinsky.

***Jahr, Das* (The Year).** Fanny Mendelssohn Hensel, 1841. Twelve character pieces (kind of a 12-part suite with a postlude), one for each month of the year.

Jamaican Rumba. Arthur Benjamin (1893–1960), 1938. Suite for two pianos, also arranged by the composer for solo piano.

Janáček, Leoš (1854–1928). Czech composer, his study of his native Moravian folk music formed the character of all his thematic invention. His piano works are refreshingly far from the gigantism of much of the piano writing of the time. His piano works include

In the Mist, National Dances of Moravia, The Overgrown Path, Sonata der Strasse I–X ("In the Street" I–X), *Zedenka Variations*. For piano duet: *National Dances of Moravia, Vallachian Dances*.

Janis, Byron (Yanks, Yankelevitch) (b. 1928). American pianist, he studied with Josef and Rosina Lhévinne and later with Horowitz. Janis has made many world tours. He has had a strong affinity with Chopin but plays the repertoire from Mozart to Rachmaninoff. His technique is astonishing, plus he has a rich, expressive tone.

Janissary music. Term used for the imitation of Turkish music produced by triangle, cymbals, and bass drums as in Mozart's opera *Die Entführung aus dem Serail* (The Abduction from the Seraglio). The Janissaries were the sultan's bodyguard, disbanded in 1828, who had a band. Mozart used the term "in Turkish style" in the *Rondo alla turca* in his piano Sonata in A Major, K. 331, imitating Turkish music.

Jedliczka, Ernst (1855–1904). Russian pianist and teacher, he studied with Nikolai Rubinstein and was a student at the Moscow Conservatory in 1881–88. He then went to Berlin where he taught at the Klindworth School and later at Stern's School. His students included Samaroff.

jeu (Fr.). Game (plural: *jeux*), to play.

Jeux d'eau **(Fountains (or Play) of the Water).** Maurice Ravel, 1901. Fluid arpeggio figures and sparkling watery cadenza, showing the influence of Liszt.

Jeux d'enfants **(Children's Games).** Georges Bizet, 1871. Suite of 12 pieces for piano duet.

jig. See *gigue*.

Johannesen, Grant (b. 1921). American pianist, he studied with Casadesus at Princeton University and Petri at Cornell University. He made his New York debut in 1944 and toured Europe in 1949. He made extensive tours of Russia and Europe in 1962 and 1970. He was director of the Cleveland Institute of Music from 1974 and president from 1977 to 1984. Johannesen plays a wide repertoire but is especially known for his performance of French music. From 1963 to 1973 he was married to the cellist Zara Nelsova, with whom he often appeared in concerts and made recordings.

Johansen, Gunnar (1906–91). Danish pianist and teacher, he studied with Lamond, Fischer, and Petri. His debut was in 1924. He toured Europe for a number of years, then settled in the United States, teaching and performing at the University of Wisconsin. He recorded the complete keyboard music of J. S. Bach and made more than 60 recordings of the piano music of Liszt. He also admired Busoni and recorded his complete piano music.

joie (Fr.). Joy, gladness.

joie moderée (Fr.). Merrily.

joli, jolie (Fr.). Pretty, pleasing.

Jones, Martin (b. 1940). English pianist, he studied at the Royal Academy in London and received the Dame Myra Hess Award in 1968. He made his London and New York debuts the same year. He is a prolific recording artist; his many recordings include the complete solo piano works of Brahms, Debussy, Grainger, Mendelssohn, Stravinsky, Szymanowski, and the sonatas of Welsh composer Alun Hoddinott (b. 1929). He has performed all over the world, including performances with some of the great orchestras. He performs with intellectual power and a wide range of styles.

Joplin, Scott (1868–1917). Black American composer and ragtime pianist, he had little formal training. Some of his most famous piano rags include *The Easy Winners, The Entertainer, The Maple Leaf Rag,* and *Pine Apple Rag.* He composed 54 rags for piano and has finally been recognized as an outstanding composer in his genre.

Joseffy, Rafael (1852–1915). Hungarian pianist, teacher, and editor, he studied at the Leipzig Conservatory with Moscheles and Tausig and during the summers with Liszt at Weimar. His debut in 1870 in Berlin was an immediate success, as was his American debut in 1879. He was professor of piano at the National Conservatory in New York from 1884 to 1906 and edited the complete edition of Chopin for G. Schirmer.

jota (Sp.). A vivacious Spanish national dance in quick triple time. Examples were written by de Falla, Granados, Liszt, and Saint-Saëns, among others.

jouer (Fr.). Play, resume playing. *jouer à vue:* to sight-read.

joyeux (Fr.). Joyous.

jubiloso (It.). Jubilant, exulting.

jusqu'à (Fr.). Until, up to.

just intonation. A method of tuning by perfect fifths and thirds as opposed to equal temperament.

K

K., K.V. Abbreviation for *Köchel Verzeichnis,* the thematic catalog number for Mozart's works by Ludwig von Köchel. *K.* is also the abbreviation for Kirkpatrick (Ralph), referring to a thematic catalog of Scarlatti's keyboard sonatas.

Kabalevsky, Dmitri (1904–87). Russian composer and pianist, his writing is designed for immediate utility and popular consumption. His music for young pianists is unusually appealing. Piano works: *15 Children's Pieces, 24 Little Pieces, 6 Preludes and Fugues,* 24 preludes, four rondos, three sonatas, and eight sets of variations. For piano and orchestra: three concertos, *Rhapsody on a Theme of the Song "School Years,"* and *Prague Concerto* for young pianists.

Kabos, Ilona (1892–1973). Hungarian pianist and teacher, she studied at the Liszt Academy, taught there from 1930–36, and toured Europe extensively. She settled in England before World War II, where she taught and performed. She married Louis Kentner in 1931 (divorced 1945) and performed two-piano recitals with him. In 1965 she settled in New York and taught at The Juilliard School until her death.

Kahane, Jeffrey (b. 1956). American pianist, he studied at the San

Francisco Conservatory and The Juilliard School. He made his U.S. debut in 1978 and has won prizes at the Clara Haskil Competition in 1977, the Van Cliburn Competition in 1981, and the Arthur Rubinstein Competition in 1983. He has appeared with many American orchestras and performs a wide range of repertoire, displaying much sensitivity to various styles.

Kaiserman, David (b. 1937). American pianist and teacher, he studied at The Juilliard School and the University of Iowa; his teachers include Gorodnitzki, Vincent Persichetti, John Simms, and Robert Donnington. He won numerous piano competitions and twice won the Grand Prize in the Teachers Division of the International Piano Recording Competition sponsored by the National Guild of Piano Teachers. He is an authority on the piano music of Russian composer Sergei Liapunov (1859–1924) and taught at a number of universities, including Northwestern University for 17 years. He has given frequent recitals and master classes throughout the United States and Canada.

Kalkbrenner, Friedrich (1785–1849). German pianist, teacher, and composer, he studied at the Paris Conservatoire and joined the piano manufacturing firm of Pleyel in Paris in 1824. He established himself as a renowned teacher and was a friend of Chopin, who dedicated his E Minor Piano Concerto to him. He wrote a piano method—*Méthode pour apprendre le pianoforte à l'aide du guide-mains* (Method for Studying the Pianoforte with the Help of the Hand-Guide, op. 108, 1831)—plus 13 piano sonatas, four piano concertos, and much chamber music.

***Kamennoi ostrow* (Rocky Island).** Anton Rubinstein, op. 10, 1853–54. Twenty-four portraits (character pieces) make up this suite.

Kammermusik (Ger.). Chamber music.

Kapell, William (1922–53). America's greatest native-born pianist, he studied at the Philadelphia Conservatory and The Juilliard School with Samaroff. His New York debut took place in 1941. He toured the United States and Europe with great success and was killed in an air crash in San Francisco returning from a trip to Australia. In one decade he had won a worldwide audience. Kapell played like a master.

Karp, David (b. 1940). American pianist and teacher, he studied piano with Canin, Arthur Lloyd, and Santos Ojeda and composition with Nicholas Flagello and Norman Lockwood and holds degrees from the Manhattan School of Music and Teachers College of Columbia University. Karp has composed some significant repertoire for the young pianist plus other advanced literature. He started and is the director of the National Piano Teachers Institute, one of the finest pedagogy conferences in the world. He is also a first-rate pianist.

Katahn, Enid (b. 1932). American pianist and teacher, she studied at the Hartt College of Music, George Peabody College for Teachers, and the University of Hartford. She has concertized extensively in Europe and the United States. An outstanding soloist and highly respected teacher, she presently teaches at Vanderbilt University.

Katz, George (b. 1939). American pianist and teacher, he studied with Raieff at The Juilliard School and in Paris with Cortot and Long. A spectacular pianist, he taught for a number of years at Drake University.

Kawai. Japanese piano manufacturing firm founded in 1927 in Hamamatsu by Koichi Kawai, son of a wagon maker who as a youth had been the first person in Japan to build a complete piano action.

"Keltic" Sonata. Edward MacDowell, Sonata no. 4 in E Minor, op. 59, 1901. One of MacDowell's finest works, it involves idiomatic virtuoso writing and requires advanced pianism. The Keltic (Celtic) legend describing the beautiful Deirdre, daughter of the harper King Conchobar, inspired the subtitle, Above the dedication to Edvard Grieg, MacDowell placed the following: "Who minds now Keltic days of Yore, Dark Druid rhymes that thrall, Deidre's Song and wizard lore, of great Cuchulin's fall."

Kempff, Wilhelm (1895–1991). German pianist and composer, he studied at the Berlin Hochschule and university. His reputation grew from 1916 as a highly successful touring virtuoso. Noted for his playing of Beethoven, he also composed a piano concerto and chamber music.

Kentner, Louis (1905–87). Hungarian pianist, he studied at the Liszt Academy in Budapest. Beginning in 1935 he lived in London and toured England, Europe, and the United States extensively. He had complete command of the keyboard and played a wide range of repertoire, including the premieres of Bartók's Second Concerto, Alan Rawsthorne's First Concerto, and Tippett's Concerto. He made many delightful recordings.

key. 1. The levers that are moved on the keyboard that cause the instrument to sound. 2. The tonic name of any major or minor scale; the use of the notes of a major or minor scale that form a tonal center.

key signature. A grouping of sharps or flats usually at the beginning of the staff.

keyboard. The complete set of keys on the piano.

Khachaturian, Aram (1903–78). Armenian composer, he studied at the Moscow Conservatory, where he began teaching in 1950. His works are very successful; rhapsodic freedom and colorful textures are characteristic of his style. Piano works: *3 Marches, 7 Recitatives and Fugues, Sonatina,* a sonata, *Suite,* and a concerto.

Kilenyi, Edward (1911–2000). American pianist, he studied with Dohnányi in Budapest from 1927 and made his debut in Amsterdam in 1929. He toured Europe in 1935 and served in the U.S. Army during World War II. He had a large repertoire and recorded over 100 works. Kilenyi was instrumental in bringing his teacher, Dohnányi, to the United States to teach at Florida State University.

***Kinderszenen* (Scenes of Childhood).** Robert Schumann, op. 15, 1838. Thirteen pieces "about children," not for them (according to the composer). The most famous is no. 7, *Träumerei.*

Kinsky, Georg (1882–1951). German musicologist, he compiled a catalog of the works of Beethoven.

Kirkpatrick, John (1905–91). American pianist and scholar, he studied at Princeton University and continued his studies with Boulanger. In 1968 he was appointed curator of the Charles Ives Collection at Yale University. Kirkpatrick gave first performances of many American piano works, most notably Ives's *Concord Sonata* in 1939. He was close to the Ives family and cataloged Ives's works as well as edited the composer's *Memos.*

Kirkpatrick, Ralph (1911–84). American harpsichordist, his study of Domenico Scarlatti resulted in a catalog of Scarlatti's sonatas and the accepted standard numbering system for them.

Kissin, Evgeny (b. 1971). Russian pianist, he studied at the Gnesin Music School in Moscow and with Anna Kantor from the age of six. His debut with the Moscow Philharmonic Orchestra took place in 1983 playing both Chopin concertos. He has toured worldwide giving solo recitals and playing with orchestras. He is now one of the dozen or so pianists who enjoy a worldwide reputation of the highest caliber.

K.K. Abbreviation used to refer to entries in the catalog of Chopin's works by Polish musicologist Krystyna Kobylanska. This is the most complete and up-to-date thematic catalog of Chopin's compositions.

Klang (Ger.). Sound.

klanglich (Ger.). Sonorous.

klar (Ger.). Clear.

Klavier (Ger.). Piano; keyboard, harpsichord, clavichord.

Klavierauszug (Ger.). Arrangement for piano.

Klavierbüchlein (Little Keyboard Book). Title given by J. S. Bach to three collections of his keyboard music: 1. Instruction pieces for his oldest son, Wilhelm Friedemann Bach (1710). 2. Small collection for his wife Anna Magdalena (1722). 3. Larger collection for his wife (1725).

Klavierschule (School of Clavier Playing). Daniel Gottlob Türk (1756–1813), 1789. This well-organized "keyboard school" updates C. P. E. Bach's "Essay" on performance practices in the late 18th century.

Klavierstück (Ger.). Piano piece.

Klavierstücke I–XI (Piano Pieces 1–11). Karlheinz Stockhausen, 1952–56. Many new techniques of playing the piano are introduced in these pieces. No. 11 comes in several forms (19 sections of music) printed on one sheet of paper: the player selects at random any section with his or her own tempo, then goes to any other section, performing it according to directions contained in the preceding section. An *avant-garde* collection of pieces.

Klavierübung (Keyboard Exercises). J. S. Bach, published in four parts between 1726 and 1731. Contents: Six Partitas, BWV 825–830, 1731; Overture in the French Style, BWV 831, and Concerto in the Italian Style, BWV 971, 1735; Four Duets, BWV 802–805, 1739; and the "Goldberg" Variations, BWV 988, 1742.

Knabe. Firm of piano manufacturers. William Knabe (1803–64) established the company in 1837 in Baltimore in collaboration with

Henry Gaehle. In 1926 the Knabe piano was selected to be the official piano of the Metropolitan Opera House, an association which continues today.

Köchel, Ludwig von (1800–1877). Austrian musicologist, he compiled a chronological thematic catalog of Mozart's works and gave each work a number (e.g., K. 488).

Komachi. Alan Hovhaness (1911–2000), op. 240, 1971. Seven short descriptive pieces in a suite that honor Ono no Komachi, the great Japanese woman poet.

Konzertstück (Ger.). Concert piece; a small concerto, often in one movement with contrasting tempos, for solo instrument and orchestra, e.g., Weber's *Konzertstück* for piano and orchestra.

Korngold, Eric Wolfgang (1897–1957). Austrian composer and pianist, he was one of the most formidable composing prodigies in the history of music. By the time he was 11 he had already acquired his idiosyncratic style, which basically did not change during the rest of his life. It represents the last fling of the Romantic spirit of Vienna: big tunes with simple triads loaded with extra tones. His greatest success came in Hollywood writing music for motion pictures. Piano works: *Don Quixote* (character pieces), *7 Märchenbilder* (Fairy Tales), three piano sonatas, four waltzes, and other piano pieces. He also composed a piano concerto for left hand and orchestra.

Kowalchyk, Gayle (b. 1955). American pianist and educator, she received degrees from Ohio University, Northwestern University, and Teachers College of Columbia University. She is the author of over 100 educational publications for students—preschool through adults—and has taught at Eastern Illinois University, the University of Oklahoma, and Oklahoma Baptist University. She is recognized as a specialist in piano pedagogy, group teaching, and supplementary piano teaching music. She is currently a senior keyboard editor of the Alfred Publishing Company.

kräftig (Ger.). Energetically, powerful, strong, vigorously.

krakowiak, cracovienne (Pol.). Early-19th-century Polish dance (named after the city of Kraków) in lively duple meter, with distinctive syncopation; it is often a type of simple polonaise. Chopin wrote a *krakowiak:* the Grand Concert Rondo in F major, for piano and orchestra, op. 14, 1824.

Kraus, Lili (1903–86). Hungarian pianist, she studied at the Franz

Liszt Academy with Bartók and Zoltán Kodály and privately with Schnabel. She had very successful world tours and was imprisoned by the Japanese during World War II for four years. She had a special affinity with the music of Mozart and Schubert and published a complete set of cadenzas for the Mozart piano concertos. She taught at Texas Christian University during her later years.

Kreisleriana. Robert Schumann, op. 16, 1838. Eight untitled pieces comprise this eccentric masterpiece. The title refers to Kapellmeister Kreisler, a character in several of the tales by E. T. A. Hoffmann. Schumann dedicated this set to Chopin.

"Kulawy" Mazurka. Frédéric Chopin, Mazurka in G Major, BI 16, no. 1, 1826. The title comes from the style of the dance: *kulawy* means "lame." It was improvised by Chopin during dance entertainments in the home of Dr. Samuel Lindl, the director of the Warsaw Lyceum. Friends wrote down the mazurka.

"Kurfürsten" Sonatas. Ludwig van Beethoven, Sonatas in E-flat Major, F Minor, and D Major, WoO 47, 1782–83. Beethoven composed these for the Kurfürst (Elector) of Cologne, Archbishop Maximilian Frederick, when the composer was 13 years old.

kurz (Ger.). Short, detached, staccato.

L

L. Abbreviation for left, as in *L.H.*, left hand.

la (It.) The sixth degree of the scale, or the note or tonality (key) A; e.g., Stravinsky's *Serenade en la.*

Labèque, Katia and Marielle (b. 1953/1956). French pianists, these sisters studied at the Paris Conservatoire, and their debut as duo-pianists was in 1961. They have been highly successful with a diverse repertoire including jazz, Luciano Berio, Boulez, and Messiaen and have collaborated with a guitarist.

lâcher (Fr.). To release, to loosen, let go.

lâchez et tenez avec les pédales (Fr.). Release, and hold down with the pedals.

lâchez la main gauche seulement (Fr.). Release the left hand only.

lacrimoso, lagrimoso (It.). Tearful, mournful, sad.

Laires, Fernando (b. 1925). This American pianist (born in Portugal) and teacher studied piano in Lisbon and with Philipp, Friskin, and Hutcheson in New York. Solo performer in recitals and with orchestras on five continents, he was decorated in 1984 with the highest honor given to a civilian by the Portuguese government. He has also been presented with the Liszt Commemorative Medal by the government of Hungary. He has concertized widely with great success and performed the Beethoven cycle of sonatas. Laires has been praised for the vitality and freshness of his performances and the flexibility of his technique. He has taught at the Peabody Conservatory of Music and is presently teaching at the Eastman School of Music.

l'aise (Fr.). With ease.

laisser vibrer (Fr.). Allow to vibrate; let the sound keep ringing by keeping the damper pedal depressed.

lament. A piece of elegiac music expressing grief.

Lamond, Frederic (1868–1945). Scottish pianist, he studied with von Bülow and Liszt. He was noted for his performances of Beethoven and Liszt and taught for a time in the Netherlands and the United States.

Lancaster, E. L. (b. 1948). American pianist and educator, he received degrees from Murray State University, the University of Illinois, and Northwestern University. He founded the graduate program in piano pedagogy at the University of Oklahoma and has presented workshops for teachers throughout the United States, China, Malaysia, Norway, Singapore, and Thailand. Lancaster is recognized as a specialist in piano pedagogy, group teaching, and educational piano instructional materials. He is currently the vice president and Keyboard Editor-in-Chief of the Alfred Publishing Company.

lancer le mouvement (Fr.). Plunge into the tempo.

Ländler (Ger.). A slow Austrian rural waltz in triple meter. Beethoven, Dohnányi, Liszt, Joseph Raff, and Schubert, among others, composed *Ländler. ländlich:* country-like.

Landowska, Wanda (1877–1959). Polish pianist and harpsichordist, she studied at the Warsaw Conservatory and in Berlin. She settled in Paris in 1900 and toured Europe and the United States. She was a major influence in reviving the harpsichord in the 20th century and was noted for her interpretation of Baroque keyboard composers. Both de Falla and Poulenc wrote harpsichord concertos for her.

langsam (Ger.). Slow.

langueur (Fr.). Lingering, less animated.

Laredo, Ruth (b. 1937). American pianist, she studied with Rudolf Serkin at the Curtis Institute of Music, and her formal concert debut took place in 1949. She became internationally known after her recordings of the complete works of Scriabin and Rachmaninoff. Laredo's performances always combine power and gentleness with infectious enthusiasm—she is a joy to hear.

largamente (It.). Broadly, dignified, stately, with no change of tempo.

large (Fr.). Broad, liberal, lax; *largo.*

largement (Fr.). *Sostenuto*, broadly, fully, grandly.

largement chanté (Fr.). Generously singing.

larghetto (It.). Faster than *largo,* slower than *lento;* rather slow.

larghezza (It.). Breadth, largeness, freedom.

larmoyant (Fr.). Weeping, whining.

largo (It.). Very slow and stately, broad.

largo andante (It.). Slow, distinct, exact.

Larrocha, Alicia de (b. 1923). Spanish pianist whose first public appearance was at age five and her concert debut in 1935. She has an international reputation and is the greatest interpreter of Spanish piano music.

las (Fr.). Weary, relaxed, and unhurried.

Lateiner, Jacob (b. 1928). Cuban-born American pianist and teacher, he studied at the Curtis Institute. He made his U.S. debut in 1945 with the Philadelphia Orchestra and made tours of Australia and Europe. He is often associated with the repertoire of Beethoven and contemporary American music. He commissioned Carter's Piano Concerto and gave the first performance of Roger Session's Sonata no. 3. He has taught at The Juilliard School since 1966.

launig (Ger.). Humorous, capricious.

Lebewohl, Das (The Farewell). See *Adieux, Les.*

lebhaft (Ger.). Lively, quick.

leçon (Fr.). Lesson or study (etude), exercise.

Lees, Benjamin (b. 1924). Born in China, this American composer studied at the University of Southern California and in Europe on a Guggenheim Fellowship. His style mixes polyphonic texture with classic forms in a thoroughly contemporary idiom. Piano works: *Fantasy, Fantasy Variations, Kaleidoscopes, Odyssey, Six Ornamental Etudes, Sonata Breve, Three Preludes, Toccata,* four sonatas. For piano and orchestra: two concertos, *Declamations, Five Etudes.*

legatissimo (It.). 1. Hold notes longer than written, the "prolonged" touch, in the 18th century. 2. A super legato; keep finger in touch with key, do not lift finger from key, extremely smooth and fluent, in the 19th century.

legato (It.). Smooth, with no pause between notes; bound together. The opposite of *staccato.*

légende (Fr.). Legend, a piece in Romantic or narrative style. Halfdan Cleve, Liszt, Prokofiev, Franz Reizenstein, and Fartein Valen, among others, have composed *légends.*

léger (Fr.). Light, nimble, buoyant, airy.

légèrement (Fr.). Lightly, nimbly, swiftly.

leggiero, leggere (It.). Light, delicate. *leggeramente:* lightly *leggerissimo:* as light as possible.

Leginska, Ethel (1886–1970). English pianist and conductor, she studied with Leschetizky for three years. She gave her debut in 1907 followed by tours of Europe and the United States. She took up conducting in 1926 and became one of the first female conductors to conduct major symphony orchestras. In 1940 she moved to Los Angeles, where she taught piano for a number of years.

leicht (Ger.). Light, easy, facile, nimble.

leidenschaftlich (Ger.). Passionately.

leise (Ger.). Low, softly, gently, lightly.

lejano (Sp.). In the distance, far away.

lent (Fr.), **lento** (It.). Slow, slowly, sluggish.

lent et détaché sans sécheresse (Fr.). Slow and short and dry (played without pedal).

lentement (Fr.), **lentamente** (It.). Very slowly.

lenteur (Fr.). With slowness; delay.

Leschetizky, Theodor (1830–1915). Polish pianist, teacher, and composer, he studied with Czerny and made his public debut at 10 and was in demand as a teacher at 14. He taught at the St. Petersburg Conservatory from 1862 to 1878 then moved to Vienna, where he established his own school and attracted students from around the world. Some of his outstanding students included Ossip Gabrilowitsch (1878–1936), Benno Moisewitsch (1890–1963), Paderewski, and Schnabel. He composed two operas and numerous piano pieces. Malwine Bree, one of Leschetizky's students, wrote a book, *The Groundwork of the Leschetizky Method,* that purports to be a technical manual of his system of teaching.

Lesghinka. Sergei Liapunoff (1859–1924), no. 10 of *Twelve Transcen-*

dental Etudes, op. 11, 1897–1905. "A *lesghinka* is a courtship dance of the Lesghians, a Mohammedan tribe of the Caucasus mountains, in which the woman moves with graceful ease while the man dances wildly about her. It is similar in rhythm to a tarantella. The music is of an oriental character" (Kaiserman, p. 97).

lestamente (It.). Quickly, lively, freely, flippantly, briskly.

lesto (It.). Lively, nimble, gay, quick.

levez peu à peu (Fr.). Lift (the pedal) gradually.

Levitzki, Mischa (1898–1941). Ukrainian pianist, he studied in Warsaw and with Dohnányi in Berlin. He became an American citizen and toured extensively in Europe. He was known for his virtuosic performances of the Romantic repertoire, but he personally preferred the works of Mozart. Levitzki composed a few salon pieces written in an ingratiating style.

Lewenthal, Raymond (1926–88). American pianist, he studied with Samaroff at The Juilliard School and with Cortot in Paris. He began touring and established a fine reputation. He specialized in numerous neglected 19th-century composers, especially Alkan. He edited a collection of piano works by Alkan as well as wore period costumes at his performances.

Lhévinne, Josef (1874–1944). Russian pianist, he studied at the Moscow Conservatory under Vassily Sofonov and was a fellow student with Rachmaninoff and Scriabin. He made his debut in 1899 with Anton Rubinstein conducting. In 1919 he and his wife Rosina moved to the United States, where they taught at The Juilliard School and toured solo and together. He was one of the world's greatest pianists. His students included Gorodnitzki, Marcus, Stell Andersen, Vera Brodsky, Lillian Freundlich, and Arthur Gold.

Lhévinne, Rosina (1880–1976). Russian pianist and teacher, she studied at the Kiev Conservatory. She made her debut in Moscow in 1895 and toured Europe. After her marriage to Josef Lhévinne, she taught at The Juilliard School. She was a great teacher who had many famous students including Cliburn, Dichter, Oppens, and Daniel Pollack.

libertad (Sp.). Freedom, liberty, license, freedom from restraint.

librement (Fr.). Freely, easily, without restraint. *librement rhythmé*: freely rhythmical.

licence (Fr.). Deviation from the rules, freedom of tempo or rhythm; permission.

lié (Fr.). Tied, bound, connected, *legato*.

Liebestraum (Dream of Love). Franz Liszt, S. 541, ca. 1850. The melody of this piece has made Liszt's name universally famous. In 1847 he published a song entitled *O Lieb, so lang du lieben kannst,* which he transcribed for piano and subsequently became known the world over. There are two other *Liebesträume,* songs composed about 1849; all three were transcribed for piano and published under this name.

Lieder ohne Worte **(Songs without Words)** (Ger.). See *Songs without Words.*

ligado (Sp.). *Legato.*

ligne mélodique en dehors (Fr.). Bring out the melodic line.

Lindaraja. Claude Debussy, 1901. This tone poem for two pianos exhibits Spanish influence, winsome colors, and habanera rhythms. Ideas from this early suite turn up in later works such as *Soirée dans Grenade* and the *Prélude* in *Pour le piano.*

linke (Ger.). Left; left hand.

Lipatti, Dinu (1917–50). Romanian pianist, he studied with Cortot in Paris. He toured Europe and settled in Switzerland, where he gave master classes at the Geneva Conservatory. His early death cut short the career of one of the great pianists of his day. For piano: *Symphonie Concertante* for two pianos and strings, works for solo and two pianos, and works for left hand alone.

lisse (Fr.). Smooth, flowing.

List, Eugene (1918–85). American pianist, he studied with Samaroff at The Juilliard School and made his debut in 1934 with the Philadelphia Orchestra. He served in the U.S. army for four years and gave a concert in Potsdam in 1945 at the meetings of Truman, Churchill, and Stalin. He toured with his wife Carroll Glen, a violinist, from 1946. He featured Gottschalk on his programs and did much to restore this American composer's music to the repertoire. He taught at the Eastman School of Music from 1964 to 1975 and then at New York University.

l'istesso tempo (It.). See *istesso.*

Liszt, Franz (1811–86). Hungarian pianist, composer, and teacher, he studied piano with Czerny and composition with Antonio Salieri. He toured Europe with great success and was considered the greatest pianist in the world, his only competition coming from Chopin and Thalberg. Liszt became a celebrated teacher, and most of the major (and many minor) pianists played for him in master classes. His works for piano include three piano concertos and other works for piano and orchestra, three volumes of *Années de pèlerinage,* several sets of *études,* 19 *Hungarian Rhapsodies,* the Sonata in B minor, 12 books of *Technical Studies,* many transcriptions, and numerous other pieces. Liszt probably had more influence on the musical life and style of the 19th century than any other composer and led the way for developments in the 20th century.

loco (It.). 1. Place. 2. A direction to play as written, used after the sign *8va.*

Loesser, Arthur (1894–1969). American pianist and writer on music, he studied at the City College of New York, Columbia University, and the Institute of Musical Art. His debut was made in Berlin in 1913 followed by a world tour with frequent performances in the United States. He taught at the Cleveland Institute from 1926 until his death. He was the author of *Men, Women and Pianos: A Social History.*

loin (Fr.). Far away.

lointain (Fr.). Distance, in the distance, remote.

"London Bach." See Bach, Johann Christian.

London Pianoforte School 1770–1860, The. This 20-volume set includes over 400 individual pieces by 44 composers, including the complete works for piano solo by Clementi, Irish composer Philip Cogan (1748–1833), Field, George Frederick Pinto, and Sir William Sterndale Bennett (1816–75). It is edited by Nicholas Temperley and published by Garland Publishing.

Long, Marguérite (1874–1966). French pianist, she studied at the Paris Conservatoire. She became a well-known interpreter of the music of Debussy, Fauré, Milhaud, and Ravel and wrote three books about her memories of her work with Debussy, Fauré, and Ravel.

long appoggiatura. Written as a small note slurred to the main note: . The small note is played on the beat, taking its time from the main note.

Longo, Alessandro (1864–1945). Italian pianist and composer, he compiled a catalog of the keyboard works of Scarlatti. The works were identified by the Longo or "L" number. This catalog has been replaced by the more up-to-date Ralph Kirkpatrick catalog.

lontano (It). Far away, in the distance.

Loriod, Yvonne (b. 1924). French pianist, she studied with Messiaen at the Paris Conservatoire and married him. She became internationally famous and has given first performances of works by Bartók, Messiaen, and others. The solo piano part of Messiaen's *Turangalila* symphony was composed for her.

l'ornement avant le temps (Fr.). (Play) the ornament (grace) before the beat.

Lost Happiness. Felix Mendelssohn, op. 38, no. 2, in C Minor, one of the *Songs without Words.*

Lost Illusions. Felix Mendelssohn, op. 67, no. 2, in F-sharp Minor, one of the *Songs without Words.*

loud pedal. The piano pedal which lifts the dampers (more appropriately the "damper" pedal), the right pedal.

lourd (Fr.). Heavy, thick.

Lowenthal, Jerome (b. 1932). American pianist and teacher, he studied with Samaroff at the Philadelphia Conservatory, privately with Kapell, with Steuermann at The Juilliard School, and with Cortot in Paris. He has won many prizes at world competitions and has toured extensively in Europe and the Far East. His reputation is based on his solid performance and recordings of the Romantic repertoire.

Lucktenberg, George (b. 1930). American pianist, harpsichordist, and teacher, he studied piano with Soulima Stravinsky and Kilenyi at the University of Illinois and Florida State University, and harpsichord with Eta Harich-Schneider. He also holds an Artist's Diploma in Harpsichord from the State Academy in Vienna. He toured with his wife Jerrie Cadek, violinist, as the Lucktenberg Duo for many years as well as founded the South East Historical Keyboard Society. He coauthored, with Edward Kottick, the book *Early Keyboard Instruments in European Museums,* taught for many years at Converse College, and presently teaches at Reinhardt College. Lucktenberg performs with gusto, combining emotional involvement with a superb sense of rhetorical clarity.

Ludus Tonalis **(Play of Tonalities [Notes]).** Paul Hindemith, 1942. A piano work consisting of 12 fugues in different keys, connected by 11 interludes in free lyric and dance forms preceded by a Prelude in C that serves, in retrograde inversion, as a Postlude.

A cyclical whole arranged in a key sequence based on Hindemith's ranking of tonalities.

loure (Fr.). A slow and majestic French gigue with heavy accents, usually in $^6_4$ meter. J. S. Bach's Fifth French Suite in G contains a *loure*.

Luftpause (Ger.). A slight break in the musical line indicated by an apostrophe above the staff. For a pianist, this indicates the end of a phrase.

lugubre (Fr.). Dismal, mournful, gloomy.

luisant (Fr.). Bright, sheen, gloss.

lullaby. A cradle song filled with tranquility. See also *berceuse.* Composers who have composed piano pieces with this title include Bax, Debussy, Frederick Delius, Percy Faith, Irving Fine, Alan Hovhaness, Martinů, Andrés Sás, and Harry Somers, among others.

Lullaby. Felix Mendelssohn, op. 67, no. 6, in E Major, one of the *Songs without Words.*

lumineux (Fr.). Luminous, bright.

Lunde, Solveig (b. 1920). American pianist and teacher, she studied with Johansen and Harold Logan at the University of California–Berkeley and Samaroff at the Juilliard Graduate School. Following her critically acclaimed New York debut in Town Hall, and under Columbia Artists Management, she toured extensively as recitalist and soloist with orchestras throughout the United States, Canada, Mexico, and Scandinavia. Her performances drew critical praise for their "poetic" insight and "all-around technical mastery." After her marriage and residence in Europe and the Middle East for 15 years, she returned to the United States to live in Salt Lake City, where she has been active as performer, lecturer, adjudicator, and teacher. She has taught at Brigham Young University and the University of Utah in addition to her private studio.

lunga pausa (It.). Long pause or rest.

Lupu, Radu (b. 1945). Romanian pianist, he studied at the Moscow Conservatory. He won first prize in the Van Cliburn Competition in 1966 and has had an international career ever since. He is well known for his performances of the Classical and Romantic repertoire.

lusingando (It.). Performing in a coaxing, intimate manner; in a tender fashion.

lustig (Ger.). Merry, cheerful, to play in a happy and joyful style.

luttuoso (It.). Sorrowful, mournful.

Luvisi, Lee (b. 1937). American pianist, he studied with Dwight Anderson and at the Curtis Institute with Rudolf Serkin and Horszowski. He joined the Curtis faculty upon his graduation. His New York debut took place in 1957, and in 1963 he became artist-in-residence at the University of Louisville. He has continued to concertize as soloist and chamber music player. He became an artist member of the Chamber Music Society of Lincoln Center in 1983. Luvisi plays the standard repertoire with great technical precision, stylistic expertise, and superb power, but he has a special place in his heart for Mozart and Schubert, which always shows when he performs these two great composers.

Lyra piano. An upright piano from the early 19th century with the case shaped like a Greek lyre.

lyric. A short poem. Grieg used the title for his *Lyric Pieces.*

Lyric Pieces. Edvard Grieg, 73 pieces in 10 books, 1867–1901. They encompass all of Grieg's styles of writing for the piano. Many have descriptive titles, and many are fairly substantial pieces.

M

M. Abbreviation for *mano* or *main*, hand.

ma (It.). But. *ma non troppo:* but not too much.

Ma mère l'oye (Mother Goose). Maurice Ravel, 1908–10. A five-movement suite depicting characters in fairy tales, originally written for piano duet: *Pavane de la belle au bois dormant* (Pavane for a Sleeping Princess), *Petit poucet* (Tom Thumb), *Laideronnette, impératrice des pagodes* (Laideronnette, Empress of the Pagodas), *Les entretiens de la belle et de la bête* (Conversations between Beauty and the Beast), *Le jardin féerique* (The Fairy Garden). Solo version transcribed by Jacques Charlot.

MacDowell, Edward (1860–1908). American composer and pianist considered by many to be the United States' first truly professional composer. He studied in Germany, where he met Liszt, who recommended him strongly to publishers. MacDowell left his finest writing in his 160 piano character piece miniatures. His piano works include numerous sets of character pieces (*Fireside Tales, First and Second Modern Suites, Forgotten Fairy Tales, Six Fancies, Woodland Sketches,* etc.), four sonatas, *12 Virtuoso Studies,* and two piano concertos.

Mach, Elyse (b. 1941). American pianist, teacher, and writer, she studied with Newman Powell and Louis Crowder and received degrees from Valparaiso University and Northwestern University. She has authored *Great Pianists Speak for Themselves,* and coauthored *Great Contemporary Pianists Speak for Themselves* and *Contemporary Class Piano.* She has toured the United States and Europe giving concerts and has taught at Northeastern Illinois University since 1964.

Madsen, Solveig. See Lunde, Solveig.

Maelzel, Johann Nepomuk (1772–1838). German inventor of the metronome in 1816.

maestoso (It.). Majestic, stately, in a dignified manner.

Magrath, Jane (b. 1949). American pianist and teacher, she studied at Wesleyan College, the University of North Carolina, and Northwestern University. She received the first doctorate in piano performance and pedagogy awarded by Northwestern. Her teachers have included Marvin Blickenstaff, Donald Issak, Frances Larimer, and Michael Zenge. She has taught at the University of Oklahoma for a number of years. She has written *The Pianist's Guide to Standard Teaching and Performance Literature* and has edited more than 30 volumes for the Alfred Publishing Company.

Maier, Guy (1892–1956). American pianist and teacher, he studied at the New England Conservatory and with Schnabel in Berlin. He made his U.S. debut in Boston in 1914 and formed a duo-piano team with Lee Pattison (1890–1966) in 1916. He gave many seminars for teachers and numerous master classes. He taught at the University of Michigan (1924–31), The Juilliard School (1935–42), and UCLA (1946–56).

main (Fr.). Hand.

Main, Der **(The Main).** Paul Hindemith, Sonata no. 1, 1936. Inspired by Friedrich Hölderlin's poem *Der Main,* this large-scale work is in five movements and requires textural clarity and solid chord playing.

main droit (Fr.). Right hand.

main gauche (Fr.). Left hand.

majestätisch (Ger.). Majestically.

majestueusement (Fr.). Majestically.

Makrokosmos. George Crumb, "24 Pieces after the Zodiac for Amplified Piano," 1973 and 1974. Two books of 12 fantasy pieces each for amplified piano, written in a highly eclectic style including the performer singing, whistling, speaking, and groaning as well as playing both inside the piano and on the keyboard. Each of the pieces in each volume is associated with a different sign of the Zodiac and with the initials of one of Crumb's friends born under that sign. Crumb said that he had Bartók's *Mikrokosmos* and Debussy's 24 preludes in mind when he wrote his cycle.

malagueña (Sp.). A Spanish dance from the province of Málaga, a fandango in quick triple time, with the music frequently beginning and ending on the dominant. Albeniz, Chabrier, and Ernesto Lecuona, among others, have composed *malagueñas* for the piano.

malinconico (It.). Melancholy, in a melancholy style.

mancando (It.). Decreasing, dying away in dynamics and speed.

mani (It.). Both hands.

manière (Fr.). Manner, style.

mano destra (It.). Right hand, abbreviated *m.d.*

mano destra sopre (It.). Right hand over.

mano sinistra (It.). Left hand, abbreviated *m.s.*

mano sinistra sopre (It.). Left hand over.

Manus, Iris (b. 1932). American music publisher, she has worked side by side with her husband Morton Manus as executive producer of the Alfred Publishing Company. Together they have built the company into one of the world's leading publishers of piano music (among other publications). Iris and Morton were later joined by two of their three sons, Ron and Steve. Alfred is currently a family business owned by Morton, Iris, Ron, and Steve.

Manus, Morton (b. 1926). American music publisher, he graduated from the City College of New York in 1949. He joined the Alfred Publishing Company and began publishing educational music books in 1952 and in the process edited and coauthored several major music publications: *Alfred's Basic Piano Library* and *Alfred's Basic Adult Piano Course* (with Amanda Vick Lethco and Willard A. Palmer) and *Essentials of Music Theory* (with Karen and Andrew Surmani). The Alfred Company today is a leading publisher of piano music.

marcando (It.). Strongly marked.

marcato (It.). Marked, accented, with emphasis, often regarding a melody that is to be brought out.

march. A piece with strongly marked rhythm usually in $\frac{4}{4}$, $\frac{2}{4}$, or $\frac{6}{8}$ meter, suitable for accompanying troops while walking. Many composers have written marches including Bartók, Byrd, Chabrier, Chopin (a funeral march), Dohnányi, Grieg, Liszt, Mozart, and Schubert.

Marche militaire (Military March). Franz Schubert, op. 51, no. 3, 1826. Originally for piano duet, it has been arranged for solo piano and many other instruments. It was originally the third of three marches, op. 51, by Schubert and is best known by its nickname.

marcia (It.). March.

Marcus, Adele (1906–95). American pianist and teacher, she studied at The Juilliard School with Josef Lhévinne and in Berlin with Schnabel. She made her New York debut in 1929 as winner of the Naumberg Prize. She was Lhévinne's assistant for seven years before joining the Juilliard faculty. She performed both in recitals and with orchestras and gave many master classes. Some of her outstanding students were Janis, Agustin Anievas, Horacio Gutierrez, Tedd Joselson, and Thomas Schumacher.

marionettes. Name used by several composers (e.g., César Cui, Mac-Dowell, and Martinů) for character pieces or dances describing the movements of marionettes (puppets or dolls in the toy box).

markiert (Ger.). Strongly accented, marked.

marqué (Fr.). Marked, evident, accented.

marquer la main gauche (Fr.). Stress the left hand.

martelé (Fr.). Very strongly accented, very distinct.

martellato (It.). Hammered, strongly marked, forceful.

Martinů, Bohuslav (1890–1959). Czech composer and violinist, he studied at the Prague Conservatory. Czech folksongs, French clarity, modality, exactness, and rhythmic zest are all fused in Martinů's music. His piano works include dances, numerous short character pieces, a sonata, and five concertos.

Marvin, Frederick (b. 1923). American pianist and musicologist, he studied at the Curtis Institute and with Arrau. He has toured throughout the United States, Central America, India, and Europe. Marvin has an extensive repertoire and has worked to revive interest in the Spanish composer Antonio Soler (1724–83). He has edited 65 of Soler's sonatas for keyboard, and his system for numbering Soler's works has been widely adopted.

marziale (It.). Martial, marchlike, warlike.

Mason and Hamlin. American piano manufacturing firm, founded in Boston in 1854 by Henry Mason (1831–90).

Mason, William (1829–1908). American composer and educator, his compositions are Classical in form and refined in style and treatment. Considered the "father of piano pedagogy" in the United States, he wrote a number of books on piano pedagogy. Mason composed over 50 works for solo piano and works for piano duet and chamber music.

Masselos, William (1920–92). American pianist, he studied with Carl Friedberg at The Juilliard School and privately with Saperton. He made his New York debut in 1939 and began touring. He identified with the contemporary scene and gave the first performance of Ives's Sonata no. 1 and of Copland's Piano Fantasy and recorded both works. He had a very strong technique and was one of the most interesting pianists among American performers. He taught at the Catholic University of America (from 1976) and The Juilliard School.

Massengale, Donald (b. 1945). American pianist and teacher, he holds degrees from the University of Mississippi and Arkansas Tech University; his teachers include Desmond Kincade and Raymond Liebau. He has taught at Mount Aloysius College, the University of Arkansas at Monticello, and since 1992 at Southern Utah University. He has been active as performer and competition director and is the founder and director of the Maurice Hinson Solo Piano Competition.

mässig (Ger.). Moderate, moderato.

master class. A form of teaching where a celebrated performer instructs a group of students (or one student) in front of other students or a paying audience.

Mastroianni, Thomas (b. 1934). American pianist, he studied with Webster at The Juilliard School and at Indiana University with Sydney Foster and Béla Nagy. He has played numerous concerts and appeared with orchestras throughout the United States, Europe, and Mexico. He is the president of the American Liszt Society and teaches at the Catholic University of America. In recent years he has been involved in research regarding the physical makeup of the pianist.

Mathias, Georges (1826–1910). French pianist, he studied at the Paris Conservatoire and with Chopin and Kalkbrenner. He was professor of piano at the Paris Conservatoire from 1862 to 1893 and passed on to his students ideas and technique acquired from Chopin. He was also a composer who composed two piano concertos, studies, and other pieces, as well as songs and chamber music. His students included Teresa Carreño, Paul Dukas, Philipp, Raoul Pugno, Satie, and Ernest Schelling.

Matthay, Tobias (1858–1945). English pianist, he was a teacher at the Royal Academy of Music from 1880 and founded his own school. He was one of the best-known teachers of his time and wrote books on how to play the piano. One of his books still highly regarded is *Musical Interpretation, Its Laws and Principles, and Their Application in Teaching and Performing* (1913). His students included Harriet Cohen, Genhart, Hess, Moura Lympany, and Fanny Waterman.

May Breezes. Felix Mendelssohn, op. 62, no. 1, in G Major, one of the *Songs without Words.*

Mazeppa. Franz Liszt, S. 138, no. 4 of his *Transcendental Etudes,* based on Victor Hugo's story. According to legend, Mazeppa was a Cossack chief whose enemies tied him to a wild horse, which galloped across plains, rivers, and mountains until it finally collapsed from exhaustion. He was eventually released by the Cossacks and led them in a great uprising.

mazurka (Pol.). Polish national dance in triple meter, first used as a stylized piece for the piano by Chopin. Many composers have composed mazurkas, among them Albeniz, Balakirev, Lennox Berkeley, Alexander Borodin, Cramer, César Cui, Debussy, Frederick Delius, Fauré, Liszt, Prokofiev, and Scriabin.

m.d. Abbreviation for *main droite* or *mano destra,* right hand.

m.d. au second plan (Fr.). Right hand in the background.

m.d. en dehors (Fr.). Right hand in the foreground.

mécanisme (Fr.). Technique.

Meditation. Felix Mendelssohn, op. 67, no. 1, in E-flat Major, one of the *Songs without Words.*

medley. A succession of well-known melodies loosely connected to one another. Finney composed his *Medley* based on the songs *Red River Valley* and *Dinah, Won't You Blow Your Horn.*

mehr (Ger.). More.

mélancolique (Fr.). Melancholy, sad, mournful.

mélodie (Fr.). A songlike or lyrical piece. Composers writing piano pieces with this name include Samuel Coleridge-Taylor, Arthur Farwell, Jean Françaix, Grieg, Liszt, MacDowell, and Paderewski.

melopiano. An instrument, invented in 1873, by converting a piano into a sustaining instrument. The device, which could be installed in a conventional piano, contained metal springs that caused small hammers to bounce repeatedly against the strings, producing a tremolo effect.

même (Fr.). Same, even, also.

même Mouv'. un peu plus las (Fr.). Same tempo, a little more relaxed.

Mendelssohn, Felix (1809–47). German composer, pianist, conductor, and organist. A child prodigy, Mendelssohn was composing masterpieces by the time he was 17. He was one of the finest pianists of his time and was probably one of the greatest improvisers. The embodiment of the Universal Genius, he also became the greatest conductor in Europe. He was the conductor of the Leipzig Gewandhaus Orchestra and founded the Leipzig Conservatory. His piano works include *3 Caprices, 3 Fantasies,* Fantasia in F-sharp Minor, *6 Preludes and Fugues,* three sonatas, variations, *Variations Sérieuses,* and two piano concertos plus other works for piano and orchestra.

meno (It.). Less.

meno mosso (It.). Less movement, to play a little slower.

menuet (Fr.). A slow graceful dance in triple meter. It often occurs between the Sarabande and the Gigue (as an optional dance) in Baroque keyboard suites. The name comes from the French word *menu* (small steps). Same as minuet.

Mephisto Waltzes. Franz Liszt. There are four waltzes with this title (Mephisto is short for Mephistopheles, or the Devil): no. 1, S. 110, 1860; no. 2, S. 111, 1881; no. 3, S. 216, 1883; and no. 4, S. 696, 1885. No. 1 is the most famous (often heard in its orchestrated version), a virtuoso's delight.

Messiaen, Olivier (1908–92). French composer, teacher, and organist. Messiaen has had much influence on other 20th-century composers, especially on his students Boulez and Stockhausen. He is counted among the more Romantic and expansive of 20th-century French composers. Modes and rhythms of Hindu music, Gregorian chant, bird calls, and Impressionistic music are reflected in his style. He taught at the Paris Conservatoire from 1942. His piano works include *Catalogue d'oiseaux* (Catalog of Birds), *Fantaisie burlesque* (Burlesque Fantasy), *8 Preludes, Quatre études de rythme* (Four Rhythmic Etudes), *Vingt regards sur l'enfant Jésus* (20

Contemplations of Looking at the Christ Child), works for two pianos, and a number of works for piano and orchestra.

mesto (It.). Gloomy, sad.

metronome. An instrument introduced by Maelzel in 1816 to indicate the exact speed or tempo from 40 to 208 beats per minute at which a composition should be played. Beethoven adopted Maelzel's metronome but later changed his mind about its usefulness. Whether performers should pay heed to Beethoven's metronome indications is a subject of much musicological controversy. The abbreviation M.M. at the beginning of a work indicates the rate of speed: M.M. ♩ = 132 means 132 beats (quarter notes) are to be played in one minute.

mettez (ôtez) les sourdines (Fr.). Put on/use (take off) mutes or dampers.

mettre beaucoup de pédale (Fr.). Use much pedal.

mf. Abbreviation for *mezzo forte,* moderately (half) loud.

m.g. à plat (Fr.). Left hand flat (as for a cluster).

m.g. par dessus (Fr.). The left hand crosses over.

mi (It.) The third degree of the scale, or the note or tonality (key) E; $mi\flat = E\flat$.

Michelangeli, Arturo Benedetti (1920–95). Italian pianist, as a child prodigy he studied with his father and at the Milan Conservatory. He won first prize at the Geneva International Competition in 1939, and after World War II he began touring. With the release of some remarkable recordings he established himself as one of the world's great pianists. His flair for the music of Debussy, Mozart, Ravel, and Scarlatti was especially remarkable.

Midi. See *Twelve O'Clock (Midi).*

Mikrokosmos (The Universe Is Small). Béla Bartók, 1926–39. A set of 153 "progressive" pieces for piano, many using folk tunes, published in six volumes. Arranged gradually from easiest to more difficult, it is full of exquisite miniature masterpieces.

Milchmeyer, Johann Peter (1750–1813). German theorist, he wrote a keyboard method book entitled *Die Wahr Art das Pianoforte zu Spielen* (The True Art of Playing the Pianoforte, 1787).

Milhaud, Darius (1892–1974). French composer who used a variety of techniques, both old and new. Polytonality, contrapuntal textures, folksong, and jazz are all utilized generously. He composed three piano sonatas and numerous smaller pieces.

militaire (Fr.). Military.

"Military" Polonaise. Frédéric Chopin, Polonaise in A Major, op. 40, no. 1, 1838. This is a sonorous piece with powerful rhythms and suggests military style in all its glory.

mimoso (Port.). Delicately.

min. Abbreviation for minor.

minacciando (It.). Threateningly, menacing.

Miniatures. A name for a short piece. Many composers have written miniatures, including César Cui, Percy Faith, Glazunov, Alexander Gretchaninov, Ingvar Lidholm, Achille Philipp, Karol Rathaus, Stig Gustav Schönberg, Turina, and David Ward-Steinman.

Minstrels. Claude Debussy, *Préludes,* book 1, no. 12, 1910. Sarcastic music hall parody that anticipates Stravinsky.

minuet. See *menuet.*

"Minute" Waltz. Frédéric Chopin, op. 64, no. 1, in D-flat Major, 1846–47. This piece bears an erroneous nickname since the story long associated with this nickname presumes the pianist is supposed to play the piece in one minute. The word "minute" means small or little waltz. The origin of the alternate nickname, the "Dog" Waltz, is attributed to Chopin's lover George Sand (pseudonym of the author Amandine Dudevant). She suggested to Chopin that he improvise a piece with the right-hand part imitating her dog chasing his tail.

Miroirs **(Mirrors).** Maurice Ravel, 1905. A set of five impressionistic pieces with titles: *Noctuelles* (Moths), *Oiseaux tristes* (Sad Birds), *Une barque sur l'océan* (A Boat on the Ocean), *Alborado del gracioso* (Morning Song of the Clown), *La vallée des cloches* (The Valley of the Bells).

misterioso (It.). Mysteriously.

misura (It.). With measure: a direction to play in strict tempo.

mit (Ger.). With.

mit Dämpfer (Ger.). With dampers, muted.

mit freiem Vortrag (Ger.). In a free style.

M.M. Abbreviation for Maelzel's metronome. See metronome.

moderato (It.). Moderate tempo.

modéré (Fr.). Moderate.

modéré et très ennuyé (Fr.). Moderate and very restless.

modestement (Fr.). Modestly, simply.

moins (Fr.). Less.

moins animé (Fr.). Less animated, less brisk.

moins possible de pédale, le (Fr.). The least pedal possible.

moins rigoureux (Fr.). Less strict, freer.

Moisewitsch, Benno (1890–1963). Russian pianist, he studied with Leschetizky. He made his debut in England in 1908 and toured extensively throughout the world. He was an expert in Classical repertoire but was widely hailed for his interpretation of the music of Rachmaninoff.

moll (Ger.). Minor (key), e.g., G moll: G minor.

mollement (Fr.). Softly.

molto (It.). Very, much, extremely, a great deal.

Moment musical (Musical Moment) (Fr.). A popular title in the 19th century for short character pieces, such as Schubert's *6 Moments musicaux*. Rachmaninoff also composed a set of *6 Moments musicaux*.

Mompou, Federico (1893–1987). Spanish composer, his miniature Impressionist tone poems are steeped in the folk music of his native Catalonia. His piano music requires extensive yet subtle pedal usage. Piano works: *Canción y Danza* (Songs and Dances: 12 pieces), *Cants Magics* (Magic Melodies), *Charmes, Fêtes lointaines* (Far-Away Festivals), *Música Callade* (Quiet Music), *Suburbia, Variations on a Theme of Chopin,* and numerous other pieces.

"Moonlight" Sonata. Ludwig van Beethoven, Sonata in C-sharp Minor, op. 27, no. 2, 1800–1801. The origin of the nickname can be traced to a critic (Ludwig Rellstab) who said the first movement made him think of a boat drifting by moonlight on Lake Lucerne in Switzerland. Beethoven never visited this lake!

moquer (Fr.). To mock, make fun of.

Moravec, Ivan (b. 1930). This Czech pianist studied with Ilona Kurz and Michelangeli. He gave his United States debut in 1964 and has made many recordings. He is a great Chopin interpreter who overflows with aristocratic and polished playing that is supported by a tremendous technique. He has plenty of temperament, and his Beethoven is full of natural elegance. A player of the first rank.

morceau (Fr.). A piece, tidbit; a short composition. Many composers have used this title, among them Anton Arensky, César Cui, Glazunov, Reinhold Glière, Charles Gounod, Sergei Liapunov, Selim Palmgren, and Reger.

mordent (It.). 1. Biting, piercing. 2. A musical ornament consisting of the alternation of the written note with the note immediately below it.

morendo (It.). Dying away gradually, getting quieter.

morne (Fr.). Gloomy, dismal.

Morning Song. Felix Mendelssohn, op. 62, no. 4, in G Major, one of the *Songs without Words.*

Moscheles, Ignaz (1794–1870). Bohemian pianist and composer, he studied in Vienna and became a touring virtuoso. He became a friend of Beethoven as well as a piano rival of Hummel. He settled in London in 1826, and in 1846 he joined Mendelssohn in founding the Leipzig Conservatory. His piano output included 50 preludes, four sonatas, 24 studies, and for piano duet *50 Daily Studies* and two sonatas.

mosso (It.). Moving, lively; stirred, troubled, agitated.

Moszkowski, Moritz (1854–1925). German/Polish pianist and composer, he is best known for his lighter salon-style piano pieces. His piano works include *20 Short Studies, 15 Virtuoso Etudes,* and his *Spanish Dances* for piano duet.

Mother Goose Suite. See *Ma mère l'oye.*

motif (Fr.), **motiv** (Ger.), **motive** (Eng.). A short melodic or rhythmic figure that occurs from time to time throughout the composition.

moto (It.). Motion. *moto perpetual:* perpetual motion, continuous fast notes.

Moura Castro, Luiz de (b. 1941). Brazilian-American pianist, he studied at the Brazilian National School of Music, Lorenzo Fernandez Academy of Music, and Liszt Academy in Budapest. He has concertized in the United States, Canada, Europe, South America, and most of the rest of the world. His recitals have established him as a master of the piano. He has made recordings and teaches at the Hartt School of Music of the University of Hartford. His performances are clear and direct with rhythmic spontaneity and infused with rich tone color.

mourant (Fr.). Dying.

mouvement (Fr.). 1. Tempo. 2. Movement or division of a larger work. 3. Animation, sparkle. 4. *a tempo* (following instruction such as *cedez, rit.,* etc.).

mouvementé (Fr.). With animation.

movement. A formal division of a larger work.

movido (Sp.). Moving.

Mozart, Wolfgang Amadeus (1756–91). Austrian composer and pianist, he excelled in a greater number of musical forms than any other composer. His music is the epitome of Classical aristocracy. Mozart toured Europe as a child prodigy and later served the Prince Archbishop of Salzburg. When he was 25 he moved to Vienna, established himself, and got married. He produced a number of brilliant works (concertos and operas) while in Vienna, but he died when he was only 35. He was one of the world's greatest composers. His piano works include 19 sonatas, 15 sets of variations, many shorter works, and 29 concertos, plus a concerto for two pianos and one for three pianos, and a sonata for two pianos in addition to two sonatas for piano duet.

m.s. (It.). Abbreviation for *mano sinistra,* left hand.

Mulliner Book. A collection of 131 pieces, most for keyboard, compiled around 1560 by Thomas Mulliner. An important source for early English keyboard music.

munter (Ger.). Lively.

Munz, Mieczyslaw (1900–76). Polish pianist and teacher, he studied at the Akademie für Musik in Vienna and at the Hochscule für Musik in Berlin, and privately with Busoni. He toured the world for many years with great success. He taught at the Curtis Institute, Peabody Conservatory, and The Juilliard School.

murmuré (Fr.). Murmured.

musette (Fr.). 1. A dancelike composition with a drone, often a part of suites in the optional dances. 2. A 17th- and 18th-century French bagpipe.

musique concrète (Fr.). Music of sounds (artificial, such as electronic or real) other than normally used instruments. Examples: waves breaking, bird calls, wind blowing, a door slamming. Luciano Berio, Boulez, Cage, Messiaen, and Stockhausen are a few composers who have used this type of electro-acoustic music.

Mussorgsky, Modest (1839–81). Russian composer, he studied with Balakirev and a member of the "Mighty Five." His best-known piano work is *Pictures at an Exhibition* 1874, a set of impressions in music on paintings by his friend Victor Hartmann; the *Pictures* are linked by a Promenade. He also composed several smaller works for piano.

mute. On the piano the sound can be muted by using the left pedal, the *una corda* (sometimes called the "soft" pedal).

mutig (Ger.). Spirited, bold.

muy (Sp.). Very, greatly. *muy mucho:* Very much.

mysterieux (Fr.). Mysterious, uncanny.

mystic chord. A chord devised by Alexander Scriabin consisting of fourths: C–F♯–B–E–A–D would form such a chord.

N

---

nach (Ger.). After, to, according to.

nach Belieben (Ger.). At pleasure, *ad libitum.*

nach jeden Stück ausgiebige Pause; die Stücke nicht ineinander übergehen! (Ger.). Long pause after each piece; the pieces must not run together!

nach und nach (Ger.). By degrees, little by little.

nachdrücklich (Ger.). Emphatic, play with emphasis, forcibly. *nachdrücksvoll:* full of emphasis.

nachlassend (Ger.). Retarding, relaxing, literally "leaving behind." A direction to play slower and slower.

Nachtstück (Ger.). Night music, nocturne. Robert Schumann composed four *Nachtstücke,* op. 23.

Nagel, Louis (b. 1943). American pianist and teacher, he studied with Dwight Anderson in Louisville and at The Juilliard School with Raieff, Lhévinne, and Bloch. He has won several awards and has concertized in Australia, Canada, Europe, and the United States. He has taught at the University of Michigan since 1969 and often gives two-piano recitals with his wife Julie. Nagel plays a broad range of repertoire from the Baroque period to the 20th century.

He is a pianist who plays with freshness, superb technique, and an infectious enthusiasm.

naïf, naïve (Fr.). Simple, natural.

Napoli Suite (Naples Suite). Francis Poulenc, 1922–25. Three movements: *Barcarole, Nocturne, Caprice Italien.* This is one of Poulenc's finest piano works.

Nat, Yves (1890–1956). French pianist, he studied at the Paris Conservatoire and taught there from 1934 to his death. He studied with Louis Diémer (1843–1919) and won first prize for piano playing. Some of his students include Yuri Boukoff, Theo Bruins, Jörg Demus, Geneviève Joy, Jacques Loussier, and Roy Hamlin Johnson.

nationalism. Stylistic traits found in the music of one certain country, distinguishing it from that of other countries. The nationality of many composers can be identified by hearing their music: it sounds Spanish, or Russian, or American, etc. Folk materials from different countries play a large part in the nationalistic identity.

natural. The sign ♮, which restores a note to its original position, canceling a sharp or flat.

Nazareth, Ernesto (1863–1934). Brazilian composer and pianist, he played with Villa-Lobos at the Odeon Cinema in Rio de Janeiro from 1920 to 1924. Nazareth composed around 200 polkas, tangos, waltzes, and other dance compositions for piano. He was a pioneer in helping develop a national Brazilian style, writing pieces in European forms that featured Brazilian rhythms.

ne garder la pédale que sur la 1ʳᵉ moitié de la mesure (Fr.). Hold the pedal only through the first half of the measure.

ne . . . pas (Fr.). Not.

ne pas presser (Fr.). With no accelerando.

ne pas ralentir (Fr.). Do not slow down.

Neeley, Marilyn (b. 1941). American pianist, she studied with Leginska. She has given recitals throughout the United States and Europe and has received accolades from the press. Neeley is a powerful technician who also knows how to infuse beauty and poetry in her playing. She teaches at The Catholic University of America.

négligente (It.). Carelessly, play carelessly, in an easy-going manner.

Negro Melodies, Twenty-four. Samuel Coleridge-Taylor (1875–1912), op. 59, 1904. Folk elements predominant (spirituals). Uses the theme of each of these pieces like a motto so that it can be quickly recognized.

neoclassicism. A 20th-century stylistic movement (especially in the 1920s) that denotes new compositions adapted to the revival of older musical forms, especially those from between 1600 and 1800. Stravinsky's *Serenade en la* (Serenade in A) is a four-movement work written in the spirit of the 18th century and is thus neo-(newly) Classical. Satie wrote a *Sonatine bureaucratique* (Bureaucratic Sonatina) in 1917 that parodies a sonatina by Clementi, another example of neoclassical influence.

nerveux (Fr.). Nervous, excitable, vigorous.

net (Fr.). Clear, distinct, natural.

nettement (Fr.). Distinctly, clearly, neatly.

Neuhaus, Heinrich (1888–1964). Russian pianist and teacher. He toured Europe at an early age and studied composition in Berlin and piano with Godowsky in Vienna. He taught at the Kiev Conservatory from 1918 to 1922 and then at the Moscow Conservatory until his death. He wrote *The Art of Piano Playing* in 1958. His students include Gilels, Lupu, and Richter.

Newman, William (1912–2000). American pianist and teacher, he studied with Loesser and gave recitals and appeared with various orchestras. He became an outstanding teacher and taught at the University of North Carolina for many years. He wrote *The Pianist's Problems, A History of the Sonata Idea* (three volumes), and *Beethoven on Beethoven—Playing His Piano Music His Way.*

nicht (Ger.). Not.

niente (It.). Nothing.

Night Fantasies. Elliott Carter, 1979–80. A major piano work of the 20th century. It is an elaborate, episodic score with deliberate virtuosic intent. Carter has likened this work to the visions of an insomniac trying vainly to sleep.

Nights in the Gardens of Spain. See *Noches en los jardines de España.*

Nikolaeva, Tatiana (1924–93). Russian pianist and composer, she was a renowned pianist who played the premiere of Shostakovich's *24 Preludes,* dedicated to her. She has composed *24 Concert Etudes* and two children's albums.

Nine Bagatelles. William Bolcom (b. 1938). This was the commissioned piece for the 1997 Van Cliburn Piano Competition.

Ninety Plus (90+). Elliott Carter, 1994. Written in honor of Italian composer Goffredo Petrassi's 90th birthday. The composer wrote in the score that the work "is built around 90 short, accented notes played in a slow regular beat. Against these the content changes character continually."

nobile (It.). Noble, grand; in a noble, refined, lofty style.

noch (Ger.). Still, yet.

noch schneller (Ger.). Still faster.

Noches en los jardines de España (Nights in the Gardens of Spain). Manuel de Falla, 1911–15. Three symphonic impressions for piano and orchestra: *En el Generalife* (In the Generalife), *Danza lejana* (Distant Dance), *En los jardines de la Sierra de Córdoba* (In the Gardens of the Sierra de Córdoba).

nocturne (Fr.). Night piece; a piece dealing with the atmosphere of night, especially a dreamlike pensive composition. Field first used the term for this genre, and it was later taken up by Chopin. Many other composers have composed nocturnes, including Balakirev, Barber, Benjamin Britten, Cramer, Debussy, Fauré, Grieg, Liszt, Paderewski, Poulenc, and Rachmaninoff.

noël (Fr.), **nowell** (Eng.). A Christmas carol or song derived from *nouvelles,* meaning "tidings." Bartók composed 20 *Rumanian Christmas Songs* for piano in two series, 10 in each, to be played as connected cycles.

non (It., Fr.). Not.

non troppo allegro (It.). Not too fast.

Norma Fantasy. Franz Liszt, S. 394, 1841. Transcription of themes from Bellini's opera, also called *Réminiscences de Norma.* This is not only an effective concert piece, but it gives an outstanding summary of the musical themes of the opera.

"Norse" Sonata. Edward MacDowell, op. 57, 1900. MacDowell was always interested in his Scottish ancestry, and he had a strong interest in Celtic and Nordic legends. These interests appear in his music as atmospheric suggestions rather than programmatically. He outlines a Nordic saga at the beginning of this sonata, hence the subtitle "Norse."

nostalgique (Fr.). Nostalgic, pining; sad, weary.

notes coulées (Fr.). Slurred notes.

notes marquées du signe—expressives et un peu en dehors, les (Fr.). Bring out the marked notes—with expression.

notes martelées (Fr.). Accented or very distinct notes.

nourri (Fr.). Full, rich; sustained.

Nouvelle Études, Trois (Three New Etudes). Frédéric Chopin, Etudes in F minor, A-flat Major, and D-flat Major, BI 130, 1839. Three new etudes composed for the instruction book of Moscheles and Fétis. They have no opus number, and each focuses on a specific technical problem.

Novaês, Guiomar (1895–1979). Brazilian pianist, she studied under Philipp at the Paris Conservatoire. Her Paris debut was in 1911 followed by tours of Europe and the United States. She had a fluent, swift, and accurate technique and a keen rapport with the Romantic composers. She made many recordings.

novelette (Fr.). Name given to a set of character pieces by Robert Schumann, *Noveletten,* op. 21. Schumann described these eight untitled pieces as "longish connected tales of adventure." Other composers writing *novelettes* include Balakirev, York Bowen, MacDowell, Poulenc, Nicolai Rimsky-Korsakov, Tansman, and Tcherepnin.

novelty piano. A term, popular in the 1920s, that referred to a variety of piano music based on ragtime. Characteristic of it was the "novelty break," an interruption of the melody and harmony. Some fine examples are Joplin's *Euphonic Sounds: A Syncopated Novelty* and Zez Confrey's *My Pet* and *Kitten on the Keys.* The term "novelty ragtime" is sometimes used with the music of Confrey and Roy Bargy.

nuage (Fr.). Cloud, mist, gloom, shadow.

nuage de pédale (Fr.). Literally "film of pedal," covered with pedal; use much pedal.

nuovo (It.). New.

nuance (Fr.). Subtle variety in the expression of shading, dynamics, tone colors, tempo, touch, etc.

O

o (It.). Or, as, either.

oberek (Pol.). A round dance for couples, in fast triple meter and related to the mazurka. Chopin's Mazurka, op. 56, no. 2, is a good example.

Obertasten (Ger.). Upper keys.

Oborin, Lev (1907–73). This Russian teacher, composer, and pianist taught at the Moscow Conservatory and was a distinguished pedagogue. He also had a fine career as a concert pianist. His compositional style is a mixture of Scriabin and Shostakovich. His piano works include *Quatre morceaux* (Four Pieces) and the Sonata in E-flat Minor.

"Ocean" Etude. Frédéric Chopin, Etude in C Minor, op. 25, no. 12, 1836. Arpeggios sweep up and down the keyboard, suggesting the enormous surge of the ocean tides.

oct. aiguës (Fr.). An octave higher.

"Octaves" Etude. Frédéric Chopin, Etude in B Minor, op. 25, no. 10, 1832–34. This nickname is appropriate because of all the octaves in the piece.

oder (Ger.). Or.

œuvre (Fr.). Work or opus; used to refer to a composer's total body of works.

Ogdon, John (1937–89). English pianist, he studied at the Manchester College of Music. In 1962 he won (jointly with Ashkenazy) the Tchaikovsky Competition in Moscow, which helped launch an international career. He had a large repertoire that included many 20th-century works. He taught at Indiana University for a time in the 1970s. He married Brenda Lucas, a pianist, and they gave joint performances. His career was cut short by illness.

Ohlsson, Garrick (b. 1948). American pianist, he studied at The Juilliard School and won the Warsaw International Chopin Competition in 1970. He is known as a Chopin player, but his interests range from Thomas Tomkins to Scriabin. He is six feet four inches tall, with large hands to match. He produces a large tone that is nonpercussive. He has made many recordings and in 1984 premiered Charles Wuorinen's Third Piano Concerto.

ohne (Ger.). Without. Some composers' works without opus numbers, notably Beethoven's, are listed with the abbreviation WoO (+ number), which means *Werk ohne Opuszahl* (work without opus number).

ohne ped. (Ger.). Without pedal.

Oiseaux exotiques **(Exotic Birds).** Olivier Messiaen, 1955–56. This work for piano and chamber orchestra conjures up in sophisticated idealization the tweets, warbles, twitters, and trills of 40 polychromatic birds of Asia and America. These are combined with involved rhythmic patterns. Messiaen was an avid collector of bird song.

on (Fr.). One, you, they, we.

On the Departure of a Beloved Brother. See *Capriccio on the Departure of a Beloved Brother.*

On the Proper Performance of All Beethoven's Works for the Piano. Carl Czerny, 1839. An important documentation of Czerny's study of the master's piano works with the composer.

On the Seashore. Felix Mendelssohn, op. 53, no. 1, in A-flat Major, one of the *Songs without Words.*

ondes martenot (Fr.). A melodic electronic keyboard with quarter-tone scale possibilities and a great variety of glissando, timbre, and vibrato effects, invented in 1928 by Maurice Martenot. Boulez,

Arthur Honegger, Messiaen, Milhaud, and Edgard Varèse have written for it.

Ondine. Claude Debussy, *Préludes,* book 2, no. 8, 1913. This title is probably inspired by an illustrated book by Arthur Rackham, *Undine,* the legendary water sprite. Fast, fragmented phrases suggest the quick, darting movements of a fish. It has an atmosphere of unreality.

ondoyant (Fr.). Tremolo, wavering, undulating, flowing like the tide.

Op. posth. (Lat.). Posthumous opus or work (published after composer's death).

open pedal. Dampers raised. Clementi used this direction.

Oppens, Ursula (b. 1944). American pianist, she studied at The Juilliard School with Rosina Lhévinne. Her debut came in 1969 in New York. She has been an advocate for contemporary music and has toured extensively throughout the United States and Europe. She has given premieres of works by Elliott Carter (*Night Fantasies*) and Frederic Rzewski (*The People United Will Never Be Defeated*).

opus (Lat.). Work; used by composers (or their publishers) to number the order in which their works are composed. Abbreviated as *op.,* e.g., op. 111.

Orage (The Storm). Franz Liszt, *Années de pèlerinage,* book 1 (*Swiss*), no. 5, 1848–54. As its title implies, this piece is a graphic description of a mountain storm scene. It is typical of Liszt in his more violent mood.

orageux (Fr.). Stormy.

ordre (Fr.). Used by composers in the 17th and 18th centuries to indicate a keyboard suite. See suite.

ornament. A conventional melodic embellishment. In early music some ornaments (trills, turns, grace notes, mordents, etc.) were indicated in the score, while at other times the performer was expected to add them. An accepted system of signs was used to indicate ornaments.

Ornstein, Leo (1892–2002). American pianist and composer, born in Russia and a musical prodigy, he studied at the Petrograd Conservatory. In 1907 he came to New York and studied at the Institute of Musical Art. He made a New York debut in 1911 and made tours of Europe in 1913–14, where he was recognized as an outstanding pianist. He became well known for his experimental piano music such as *Dwarf Suite* and *Wild Men's Dance.* His concerts caused an uproar between conservative and forward-thinking musicians as being "too advanced" for the time. He taught at the Philadelphia Academy of Music and directed his own school of music. He also composed *A la chinoise, Impressions of Notre Dame, 3 Moods, Poems of 1917, Some New York Scenes,* four sonatas, *Tarantelle,* and over 100 other piano pieces.

ossia (It.). Or, or else; it may be. A term used to indicate an alternative (frequently easier) version of a passage, if necessary.

ostentation. Show, flamboyance.

ostinato (It.). 1. Obstinate, continual, unceasing, stubborn. 2. *Basso ostinato* is a term given to a frequently repeated bass (often called a "ground bass") throughout a passage or composition with a continuous varied melody or counterpoint over it.

Ott, Margaret Saunders (b. 1920). American teacher and pianist, she studied at Eastern Washington University, the University of Washington, Mills College, and The Juilliard School. At Juilliard she studied with Gorodnitzky, Rosenthal, and Samaroff. Ott has taught piano since she was 11 years old. Some of her students include Stephen Drury, Colette Valentine, Rick Nobis, and Donald Manildi. Ott has taught at Lebanon Valley Conservatory, Gonzaga University, and Whitworth College along with years of teaching privately in her Spokane studio. She was awarded the 2003 Teacher of the Year by the Music Teachers National Association.

Ousset, Cécile (b. 1936). French pianist, she studied with Marcel Ciampi at the Paris Conservatoire. She won many prizes before beginning a concert career. She has made many recordings that display a facile technique plus poetic understanding.

Out of Doors. Béla Bartók, 1926. A five-movement suite: *Avec tambours et fifres* (With Drums and Pipes),*Barcarolla, Musettes, Musiques nocturnes* (Night Musics),*La Chasse*(The Chase). The pieces are more concerned with color than structure.

overstring. Arranging the strings of a piano in such a way that one set of strings crosses the rest diagonally.

overture. An introductory movement. Composers writing overtures for the piano include J. S. Bach, Benjamin Carr, P. M. Dubois, Handel, and Mozart, among others.

P

P. Abbreviation for *pedal.*

p. Abbreviation for *piano* (It.), quiet, soft.

pacato (It.). Calm, quiet.

Pachmann, Vladimir de (1848–1933). Russian pianist, he studied at the Vienna Conservatory and made his debut in 1869. He continued to study and returned to his career in 1882 touring Europe and the United States. He was a celebrated interpreter of Chopin and was renowned for his sensitive touch and talking to his audiences

Paderewski, Ignace Jan (1860–1941). Polish pianist and composer, he studied composition in Berlin and piano with Leschetizky in Vienna. He toured Europe and the United States with great success. During World War I he became involved with politics and served as prime minister of a free Poland for a time. At age 63 he left politics and returned to his concert work. He was internationally famous. His piano works include a sonata, Theme and Variations, the famous Menuet in G, a piano concerto and the *Polish Fantasy* for piano and orchestra plus other smaller pieces.

"Paganini" Etudes. 1. Six concert etudes (*Études d'exécution tran-*

scendante d'après Paganini) by Franz Liszt (1838). Based on Paganini's *Capricci* for solo violin, op. 1 (except no. 3, *La campanella,* which is after Paganini's *Rondo alla campanella*). 2. Two sets of six etudes for piano by Robert Schumann, op. 3 (1832) and op. 10 (1833), on themes from Paganini's *Capricci.*

"Paganini" Variations. A number of composers have written variations on the well-known theme from Paganini's 24th Caprice in A Minor: Johannes Brahms, two books of *Variations on a Theme of Paganini,* op. 35; Luigi Dallapiccola, *Sonatina Canonica on Paganini Caprices* (on the 24th and other caprices); Witold Lutoslawski, *Variations on a Theme of Paganini* for two pianos; and Sergei Rachmaninoff, *Rhapsody on a Theme of Paganini* for piano and orchestra.

palettes (Fr.). The white keys of a keyboard.

Palmer, Willard (1917–96). American musicologist and pianist, he studied at the Leipzig Conservatory, Millsaps College, and the University of Houston. His extensive research and editorial expertise for the Alfred Publishing Company placed him in the highest esteem throughout the music profession and especially the piano world.

pandiatonicism. This term or "white-note harmony" is used to describe the free use of dissonant diatonic notes in otherwise tonal-centered harmony. It was coined by the prolific writer and musicologist Nicolas Slonimsky. Stravinsky, Kabalevsky, Prokofiev, and Shostakovich are some of the composers who use this "wrong note" technique.

Papillons **(Butterflies).** Robert Schumann, op. 2, 1829–31. A cycle of 12 imaginative dance movements, it employs chromatic weaving of inner parts and canonic devices. The piece ends with the clock striking 12 and the dancers dispersing.

paraphrase. Freely modifying, excerpting, or changing an original work's musical content for another instrument or instruments: for example, Franz Liszt's operatic paraphrases for piano, where he takes material from an opera (e.g., Bellini's *Norma* or Verdi's *Rigoletto*) and uses the themes to create an entirely new composition, usually virtuosic in nature. A paraphrase can also stay closer to the original form of a piece, as in Liszt's paraphrases of Schubert *Lieder.*

paresseux (Fr.). Lazy, sluggish.

parlando (It.). In a speaking style. Sometimes the pianist has to literally speak, for example, in Crumb's *Makrokosmos.*

part. The music used by the performer in ensemble playing.

Parthenia. Title of the first keyboard book of music printed in England in 1611. It contains 21 pieces by Bull, Byrd, and Orlando Gibbons.

partita (It.), **Partien** (Ger.). 1. Variations. 2. Suite. J. S. Bach's six Partitas are suites. See suite.

Partitur (Ger.). A full score that shows the parts for all instruments in an ensemble.

pas si vite (Fr.). Not so fast.

pas trop lent (Fr.). Not too slow.

pas vite (Fr.). Not fast.

passacaglia (It.), **passacaille** (Fr.). 1. A stately dance form in triple meter. 2. More generally, a piece in triple meter with a recurring harmonic pattern over which variations of the melody occur, similar to a *chaconne. Passacaglias* for piano have been written by Copland, Dohnányi, Godowsky, Handel, Walter Piston, Satie, Kaikhosru Sorabji, and Louise Talma, among others.

passage work. Figuration, often of technical difficulty, intended to display the performer's technique; usually without special musical substance.

passepied (Fr.). A lively French dance in $\frac{3}{8}$ or $\frac{6}{8}$ meter, normally beginning with an upbeat. It was one of the optional dances incorporated into the Baroque suites, somewhat similar to the *menuet.* Claude Debussy included one in his *Suite bergamasque.*

passer (Fr.). Go on.

Passion. Felix Mendelssohn, op. 38, no. 5, in A Minor, one of the *Songs without Words.*

pasticcio (It.). A musical medley. A work put together with pieces (parts) written by different composers, for example, the *Hexameron Variations* by Liszt et al.

pastiche (Fr.). Imitation. One composer mimics the style of another composer; e.g., Ravel's *A la manière de Chabrier* (In the Style of Chabrier).

pastorale (Fr.). Rustic. A piece depicting a rural or rustic scene in a flowing $\frac{6}{8}$ or $\frac{12}{8}$ meter, frequently with a drone-bass imitating a shepherd's tune. Composers who have written *pastorales* include

Georges Auric, Dohnányi, Alan Hovhaness, Liszt, Nicolai Medtner, Poulenc, Prokofiev, Gabriel Pierné, Joaquin Rodrigo, Scott, and Tansman.

"Pastorale" Sonata. 1. Ludwig van Beethoven, Sonata in D Major, op. 28, 1801. When the publisher Cranz of Hamburg published this sonata in 1838 he gave it this nickname. Perhaps the overall sunny character of the music suggested it. 2. Scarlatti, Sonata in C Major, K. 513. "The bagpipes of the southern Italian *zampognari* with the droning basses and lilting Christmas tunes of the *pifferari* are always to be heard in those pieces to which Scarlatti himself gives the subtitle 'Pastorale' " (Kirkpatrick, p. 203).

patetico (It.). Pathetic, with great emotion or suffering, touching to a very high degree; with a certain greatness.

Pathétique **Sonata.** Ludwig van Beethoven, Sonata in C Minor, op. 13, 1798–99. We are not sure if Beethoven or the first publisher gave the name *Pathétique* (meaning compassion, suffering, tragic passion, pathetic) to this piece. Beethoven at least sanctioned the name.

pauroso (It.). Timid, fearful.

Pause (Ger.). Pause, stop, rest, interval.

pavane, pavan (Eng.), *pavana* (It.). *pavane* (Fr.). A stately Italian dance in $\frac{4}{4}$ meter apparently derived from the *paduana,* a dance from Padua. It was usually followed by the more lively *galliard* in triple meter. Composers who have written *pavanes* include Albeniz, H. and J. Andriessen, Bull, Byrd, Giles Farnaby, Orlando Gibbons, Morton Gould, Christopher Morley, Peter Philips, Ravel, and Soulima Stravinsky.

Pavane pour une infante défunte **(Pavane for a Dead Princess).** Maurice Ravel, 1899. This piano piece requires a steady tempo (not too slow) and is not easy to project on the piano.

paventato (It.). Fearfully.

Paysage (Fr.). A term used for character pieces. It literally means bustling, stirring. Ernest Chausson, Mompou, and Prokofiev have written pieces with this title.

paysage allant (Fr.). Moving ahead.

ped. Abbreviation for pedal. This indication means to depress the right pedal (damper) and hold until told to release it, often via the sign ＊.

ped. à chaque accord (Fr.). Change pedal on each chord.

131

ped. à chaque mesure (Fr.). Change pedal at each measure.

ped. par mesure (Fr.). Pedal each measure.

pedal. One of two or three foot levers on a piano that alters the timber or acts as a string damper.

pedal movement. The moving parts operated by a foot lever.

pédale à moitié enforcée (Fr.). Pedal half depressed, half pedal.

pédale enforcée (Fr.). Pedal deeply (depressed).

pédale jusqu'à la fin (Fr.). Pedal to the end.

pédale non obligée (Fr.). Optional use of the pedal.

pédale obligée (Fr.). Use pedal.

peine (Fr.). Scarcely, barely.

pendant (Fr.). During, while.

pendelnd (Ger.). Softly swaying unrhythmic motion.

pénétrant (Fr.). Keen, acute, penetrating.

Pennario, Leonard (b. 1924). American pianist, he studied with Maier and Vengerova. He has performed throughout the world as soloist and in chamber ensemble with violinists Jascha Heifetz, violist William Primrose, and cellist Gregor Piatigorsky from 1961 and in 1967 gave the premiere of Miklos Rozsa's Piano Concerto, op. 31, which is dedicated to him. He has more recently specialized in the music of Gottschalk. He has recorded with various companies.

pentatonic scale. A scale of five tones, in particular the *tonal pentatonic* scale corresponding to the intervals of the five black keys of the piano. It is used in much of the folk music of the world. A few composers who have used it include Bartók, Debussy, Liszt, and Ravel.

Perahia, Murray (b. 1947). American pianist, he studied at the Mannes School and with Horszowski. He made his New York debut in 1972 and settled in London in 1973. He won the Leeds International Competition in 1972, which helped to launch an international career. He is a highly sensitive virtuoso who is closely associated with the music of Mozart, Beethoven, and Schumann.

percuté (Fr.). Percussive.

percuté, en laissant résonner (Fr.). Struck, allowing to sound.

perdendo, perdendosi (It.). Decreasing in power and tempo, dying away to nothing; quieter and quieter, slower and slower.

perlé (Fr.). Pearly, delicate, brilliant.

Perlemuter, Vlado (1904–2002). Lithuanian pianist, he studied at the

Paris Conservatoire. He studied with Cortot and taught at the Conservatoire until 1977. He was world renowned and spent months with Ravel learning his music. Perlemuter worked to give his interpretations an orchestral sound and would endlessly try out new fingerings in search of musical colors. He was considered the keeper of Ravel's musical traditions for the piano. His students included Timbrell and Ilana Vered.

perpetuum mobile. Perpetual motion. A rapid piece with notes of equal value throughout. The last movement of Weber's sonata, op. 24, is an excellent example.

Perry, John (b. 1935). American pianist and teacher, he studied with Genhart at the Eastman School of Music. He has won several international competitions and has performed worldwide extensively. Perry has taught at a number of schools and presently is a member of the music faculty at the University of Southern California. He is a pianist with a formidable technique that can glow, be suave, and sometimes be lighthearted. Perry is also a superb teacher in master class situations. He has had prize-winning students in many competitions and has made numerous recordings.

pesante (Fr.). Heavy, weighty, strong, forceful.

Peters. German firm of music publishers established by Carl Friedrich Peters (1779–1827). The company has achieved a worldwide reputation for quality under the name C. F. Peters publishing works by Bach, Beethoven, Brahms, Grieg, Wagner, and others.

petit (Fr.). Small.

petit pédale (Fr.). *Una corda,* soft pedal.

petitement (Fr.). Diminutively.

petites notes s'exécutent sur le temps, les (Fr.). Play the grace notes on the beat.

Petrarch Sonnets. Franz Liszt, S. 161, after 1846. Originally composed as songs in 1839–49, Liszt transcribed them for his second volume (*Italie*) of the *Années de Pèlerinage.* They are admirable examples of Liszt's power to translate music from one medium to another without any loss of feeling. They were originally settings of poems by the Italian Renaissance poet Petrarch, nos. 47, 104, and 123, respectively.

Petri, Egon (1881–1962). German pianist of Dutch parentage, he studied with Teresa Carreño from the age of three and later with Busoni. In 1902 he made his debut and showed that he liked to present long recitals that made intellectual demands on his audience. He was a marvelous technician and musician and a virtuoso of the highest order. He taught in Basle, Berlin, Manchester, and the United States. In 1940 he settled in the United States and continued playing recitals till late in life. He prepared a 25-volume edition of the keyboard works of J. S. Bach.

***Petrouchka, Trois Mouvements de* (Three Movements from Petrouchka).** Igor Stravinsky, 1921. Virtuoso paraphrases of three scenes from his ballet of the same name arranged for piano by the composer: *Danse russe* (Russian Dance), *Chez Petrouchka* (At Petrouchka's), and *La semaine grasse* (The Shrove-Tide Fair).

peu (Fr.). Little, a little.

peu à peu (Fr.). Little by little, gradually.

peu à peu sortant de la brume (Fr.). Gradually emerging from the mist.

peureux (Fr.). Timid.

pezzo (It.). Piece

Pf. 1. Abbreviation of pianoforte. 2. Soft then loud. 3. *più forte:* louder.

phantasie (Fr.). Fantasy.

Phantasiestück (Ger.). Fantasy piece. See *Fantasiestücke.*

Philipp, Isidore (1863–1958). Hungarian pianist, teacher, and editor, he studied at the Paris Conservatoire. He made many solo tours and performed with orchestras and in chamber music throughout Europe and the United States. He became a French citizen and professor of piano at the Paris Conservatoire in 1903. He was a famous piano teacher and wrote books on the instrument. Philipp settled in the United States in 1940. He edited works by Debussy, Fauré, Kabalevsky, MacDowell, Mozart, and Rachmaninoff and wrote a booklet entitled *Some Reflections on Piano Playing.* His students included Kenneth Amada, Stell Andersen, Jeanne-Marie Darré, Dorfman, Kirkpatrick, Laires, Nikita Magaloff, Guiomar Novaes, Slenczynska, Soulima Stravinsky, and Webster.

phrase. A complete short musical idea, usually ending with a cadence: larger than a motive, a unit of a musical sentence or a period.

phrase mark. A curved line connecting the notes of a phrase.

phrasing. The art of properly interpreting each phrase of a composition. This involves complete articulation, application of dynamics, varieties of touch, and the ability to bring out the greatest musical effect.

piacere (It.). Pleasure.

piacevole (It.). Pleasantly, gracefully, with charm.

pianette (Fr.), **pianino** (It.). A small piano, an upright piano.

piangendo, piangente (It.). Crying, sad, mournful.

pianissimo (It.). Very quiet, soft; abbreviated *pp* or *ppp*.

piano (It.). 1. Quiet, soft. 2. Abbreviation for pianoforte. This keyboard instrument was invented by Cristofori around the beginning of the 18th century. The sound is produced by hammers striking the strings operated by a keyboard of 88 keys (some models have a few extra keys at the lower end of the keyboard). In the upright piano the strings are arranged vertically; in the grand piano they are horizontal. The name *pianoforte* was given to it because it could play soft (*piano*) and loud (*forte*).

piano à queue (Fr.). A grand piano, concert grand.

piano à pilastres (Fr.). An upright piano.

piano droit (Fr.). An upright piano.

piano arrangement. See arrangement.

piano de boudoir (Fr.). A smaller grand piano called a baby grand or parlor grand.

piano duet. 1. Two pianists at one piano. 2. Music composed for two pianists, sometimes marked "for four hands." There is a large body of works for this medium.

piano quartet. A chamber ensemble for piano, violin, viola, and cello. Rarely a quartet of four pianos ("The First Piano Quartet" was popular in the United States during the 1950s and '60s).

piano quintet. A chamber ensemble for piano plus string quartet (two violins, viola and cello).

piano roll. For the player piano, a paper roll with perforations that correspond to the length and pitch of the notes to be produced.

piano trio. A chamber ensemble for piano, violin, and cello.

pianola. A player piano.

Pictures at an Exhibition. Modest Mussorgsky, 1874. A suite of 10 descriptive pieces for piano of drawings and paintings by Victor Hartmann (1834–73), a friend of the composer. This is his most important work for piano. Often heard in an orchestral arrangement by Ravel.

piece. A composition, piece, *morceau*.

Pièces froides (Cold Pieces). Erik Satie, 1897. Set 1: *Airs à faire fuir* (Airs That Scare You Away), *D'une manière particuliere* (In a

Very Unusual Manner), *Modestement* (Simply), *S'inviter* (Invitingly). Set 2: *Danses de travers* (Crooked Dances), *En y regardant par deux fois* (Taking a Second Look [at Things]), *Passer* (Go On), *Encore* (Again). Written in barless notation.

pietoso (It.). Compassionate, sympathetic; a direction to play tenderly and with compassion.

pincé (Fr.). Bitten, compressed, plucked.

più (It.). More.

più lento (It.). Slower.

più mosso (It.). Faster.

più moto (It.). Swiftly.

pizzicato (It.). Plucked; abbreviated *pizz.* Sometimes used in scores where the pianist is to play on the strings. *alla pizzicato:* Like a quickly struck and released key (*staccatissimo*).

placido (It.). Placid, smooth, calm.

plainté (Fr.). Elegy, lament.

plaintif (Fr.). Simple, doleful, plaintive.

plaisant (Fr.). Pleasantly, merry, humorous.

plaisantant (Fr.). Joking, *giocoso.*

plaisir (Fr.). Pleasure, pleasantness.

plaqué (Fr.). Not arpeggiated.

player piano. A piano with a mechanical apparatus (often using a paper roll with the music "punched" into it) or electro-mechanical apparatus that plays back prerecorded performances.

plein (Fr.). Lively.

pleureux (Fr.). Weeping.

Pleyel, Ignaz (1757–1831). Austrian pianist, composer, and piano manufacturer, he studied with Haydn. He settled in Paris in 1795 and began his piano company in 1807. His piano works include sonatas, a piano method with Dussek entitled *Méthode pour le piano forte* (Pianoforte Method, 1797), two concertos, approximately 50 piano trios, and numerous individual pieces.

plus (Fr.). More.

plus chaleureux (Fr.). More ardor, warmth.

plus détendu (Fr.). More relaxed.

plus en plus (Fr.). More and more.

plus lent et en retenant jusqu'à la fin (Fr.). Still slower and slowing down to the end.

plus lourd (Fr.). Weighty.

plus rein (Fr.). Nothing more.

plus retenu (Fr.). More held back: slow down further.

plutôt (Fr.). Rather.

plutôt retenu (Fr.). Rather held back.

poco (It.). Little. *pochetto:* very little. *pochissimo:* the least possible.

poco a poco (It.). Little by little.

poco mosso (It.). Somewhat more rapidly.

poem. A single short movement in rhapsodic style. Many composers have composed poems, including Bax, Ernst Bloch, Brahms (ballades), Frank Bridge, Claudio Carneyro, Theodore Dubois, Dvořák, Percy Faith, Zdenko Fibich, Mikhail Glinka, Grieg, Granados, Griffes, Liszt, and MacDowell.

Poème de l'extase (Poem of Ecstasy). Alexander Scriabin, Sonata no. 5 in F-sharp Major, op. 53, 1908. Written soon after Scriabin had finished his Symphony no. 4, the *Poème de l'extase.* Scriabin said he saw Sonata no. 5 in a flash of inspiration and struggled to write it down as quickly as possible. This is why he subtitled the sonata with the title of his symphony.

Poet's Harp, The. Felix Mendelssohn, op. 38, no. 3, in E Major, one of the *Songs without Words.*

Pogorelich, Ivo (b. 1958). Croatian pianist, he studied in Moscow and won the Montreal International Competition in 1980. He had great success in tours of the United States, Russia, and Europe. His London debut took place in 1981. He was eliminated from the Chopin Competition in 1980 and thereby caused a furor that brought him much publicity. He is a world-class artist.

poi (It.). Then, after that, next; *p poi f:* soft (quiet) then loud.

point de repos (Fr.). A hold, fermata.

point d'orgue (Fr.). Fermata; concerto cadenza.

pointillism. This term is borrowed from painting and used for a musical texture in which notes are presented in isolation rather than in linear sequence, as in some post–Webern music of the 1950s and 1960s. Crumb uses this technique most effectively.

polacca. A Polish dance in $\frac{3}{4}$ meter; in the style of a polonaise. Composers writing *polaccas* include C. P. E. Bach, Hummel, and Weber.

polichinelle (Fr.). A dance suggesting the comic antics of Punch, the clown. Joseph Jongen, Rachmaninoff, and Villa-Lobos wrote pieces with this title.

"Polish" Ballade. Frédéric Chopin, Ballade no. 1 in G Minor, op.

23, 1831, 1835. According to Brown's thematic index, this work is often referred to with this title (p. 73).

polka. A dance in $\frac{2}{4}$ meter that originated among the peasants of Bohemia. Many composers have composed polkas for the piano, including Balakirev, Lenox Berkeley, J. J. Castro, Dvořák, Jacobo Ficher, Mikhail Glinka, Gottschalk, Martinů, Joachim Raff, Anton Rubinstein, Shostakovich, Smetana, Stravinsky, and Tchaikovsky.

Pollack, Daniel (b. 1935). American pianist, he was a child prodigy and later studied with Leginsky. His Los Angeles (where he was born) debut took place in 1942. He continued study with Rosina Lhévinne at The Juilliard School, and his New York debut was in 1957. He later studied with Kempff in Europe. Pollack was one of the winners of the 1958 Tchaikovsky Piano Competition in Moscow. He has toured Europe, the United States, and most of the world and has taught at the University of Southern California for many years.

Pollei, Paul (b. 1936). American pianist and teacher, he holds degrees from Florida State University and was chairman and coordinator of the piano pedagogy program at that school. He taught at Brigham Young University for many years and has been Founder-Artistic Director of the Gina Bachauer International Piano Foundation since 1976. He is also a founding member of the American Piano Quartet, a group of four pianists dedicated to the performance of music for two pianos/eight hands. He has presented master classes, workshops, and concerts worldwide as well as adjudicated international competitions. He has written *Pedagogical Tips for Piano Teaching* and *Essential Technique for the Pianist.*

Pollini, Maurizio (b. 1942). Italian pianist, he studied at the Milan Conservatory and with Michelangeli. He won first prize at the Chopin Competition in 1960 and commands a formidable technique. His repertoire ranges from the classics to the contemporary, and some 20th-century composers have written works for him. Pollini is a genius at the keyboard.

polonaise (Fr., Ger.). A stately Polish dance in $\frac{3}{4}$ meter dating from the 17th century. This dance represents the true Polish spirit; the polonaises of Chopin are the supreme examples. Other composers writing polonaises include J. S. Bach, W. F. Bach, Beethoven, John Alden Carpenter, César Cui, Godowsky, Liszt, MacDowell, Moszkowski, Scriabin, Szymanowski, and Weber.

Polonaise héroïque **(Heroic Polonaise).** Frédéric Chopin, Polonaise in A-flat Major, op. 53, 1842. The strong, martial rhythm may be the character that has given this piece its nickname.

polytonality. Several keys or tonal centers used simultaneously in a piece.

pompeux (Fr.), *pomposo* (It.). Stately, majestic, pompous, solemn, grand (play in a grand manner or style).

port de main (Fr.). Hand position, carriage of the hand.

portable keyboard. An electronic keyboard, with enclosed speakers, that can be easily transported. See dummy keyboard.

portamento (It.). Carrying. In piano music it means *portato*.

portato (It.). A direction to play half-way between *legato* and *staccato*, a non-*legato* tone but not as short as *staccato*, indicated by a dot with a curved line over or under the note(s):

posato (It.). Sedate, quietly.

portrait. A character piece; some composers actually have their subject sit while they compose a musical portrait. Composers using this title include Paul Bowles, Jean Francaix, Robert Helps, Liszt, Paul Paray, Sam Raphling, Thomson, and Turina.

postlude. "Closing music"; play after. The opposite of *prelude*, "opening music," and related to *interlude*, "between music." Sometimes the terms *epilogue, benediction,* or *finale* are used to indicate a closing movement. Some composers who have written postludes are Dohnányi, George Fiala, Daniel Lesure, Liszt, Poulenc, Prokofiev, Saint-Saëns, and Charles Widor.

pouce (Fr.). Thumb.

Poudre d'or **(Gold Dust).** Erik Satie, c. 1901. A charming waltz.

Poulenc, Francis (1899–1963). French composer and pianist whose music may prove to be the most durable of any of the group known as "Les Six" (The Six). His music is characterized by unpretentiousness, wit, freshness, and accessibility. His piano works include *14 Improvisations,* impromptus, *Mouvements perpétuels, Napoli Suite, Nocturnes, Promenades, Suite in C, Suite française;* a sonata for piano duet and one for two pianos, *Aubade* for piano and chamber orchestra, concerto for two pianos and orchestra, and a concerto for piano and orchestra.

pour (Fr.). For, in order to.

pour finir (Fr.). Final ending (after first or second endings).

pour reprendre au commencement (Fr.). To go back to the beginning.

pp. Abbreviation for *pianissimo* (It.), very quiet, very soft.

Praeludium (Ger.). Prelude.

praembulum (Lat.). Prelude.

Pralltriller (Ger.). Upper (inverted) mordent.

préambule (Fr.). Prelude.

precipitato, precipitando, precipitoso (It.). Impetuously, hurriedly.

précipité (Fr.). With precipitation, impetuously.

preciso (It.). Exact, precise. *precisione:* precision, exactness.

Pre-Classical. That period in music history immediately preceding the Classical period, sometimes referred to as the Rococo. It includes composers like C. P. E. Bach (or all of the Bach sons) who are considered to be later than the Baroque and leading to the Classical style of Haydn and Mozart.

prelude. 1. Opening music; play before. 2. A short introductory piece, as in "Prelude and Fugue," such as those in Bach's "Forty-eight" that make up the *Well-Tempered Clavier.* 3. Short independent character pieces, such as those by Chopin, Debussy, Rachmaninoff, and Shostakovich.

Prélude de la porte héroïque du ciel **(Prelude to the Heroic Gate of Heaven).** Erik Satie, 1894. "I dedicated this work to myself. E. S." Characterized by a calm and profoundly tender feeling, unresolved floating chords, no dynamics, and barless notation.

prepared piano. A piano whose sound has been changed by the insertion of foreign material such as nuts, bolts, paper, wire, rubber, cloth, or thumbtacks pressed into the hammers. The prepared piano was introduced by Cage around 1938, who composed works for it. Other composers who have written for the prepared piano are Crumb, Lou Harrison, and Christian Wolff.

presque (Fr.). Nearly, almost, as if.

presque lent (Fr.). Almost slow.

presque lent—dans un sentiment intime (Fr.). Almost slow—with an intimate feeling.

presque plus rien (Fr.). Almost nothing more, hardly anything left.

pressando (It.). Pressing; increase speed.

pressez (Fr.). Press ahead, get faster, hurry, rush. *pressez un peu:* accelerate a little.

Pressler, Menaham (b. 1928). Israeli pianist born in Germany, he has had an international career as a soloist and has appeared with many major orchestras. He has made many recordings and is a member of the famous Beaux Arts Trio. He has taught at Indiana University for many years.

prestissimo (It.). Extremely fast. In the 18th century, a little slower than extremely fast. Türk says "very rapid" (p. 106).

presto (It.). Quick, swift, nimble, very rapidly. In the 18th century, a little slower than quick, swift, or very rapidly.

prima, primo (It.). First. In piano duet writing, the *primo* refers to the part (or player) on the upper register of the keyboard; the second or lower part (player) is the *secondo*.

prima volta (It.). First time.

Probestücke **(Example Pieces).** C. P. E. Bach, W. 63, 1753. Eighteen example pieces organized into six sonatas, each sonata in three movements. Bach wrote these pieces to help explain his *Essay on the True Manner of Playing Keyboard Instruments*.

procession. A character piece, frequently with a marchlike quality. Some composers who have written processions are Herbert Elwell, John Lessard, Douglas Moore, Felix Petyrek, Andrés Sás, and Halsey Stevens.

profond (Fr.). Profound, deep.

profondément calm (Fr.). Profoundly calm.

program music. Music designed to tell a story or illustrate some action, idea, scene, or event, sometimes accompanied by an explanatory text or based on literature. Liszt included a quotation from Byron in his *Eclogue,* S. 160, which characterizes the basic mood of the piece. Program music is the opposite of *absolute music,* which is composed without extra-musical inspiration.

progressivement le mouvement du début (Fr.). Gradually return to the opening tempo.

Prokofiev, Sergei (1891–1953). Russian composer and pianist, he developed an individual percussive style which was probably the most significant innovation in piano technique since Chopin and Liszt. His nine sonatas and approximately 100 smaller pieces constitute a treasured contribution to 20th-century piano literature. In addition, he composed five concertos for piano and orchestra, as well as transcriptions of music from his ballets.

prolonged style. This style of playing consists of holding notes longer than they were indicated. A kind of finger pedaling. See finger pedaling and *tenuto* touch.

prolongement (Fr.). The middle pedal (*sostenuto*) of the piano, which prolongs certain notes, as distinguished from the left pedal (*una corda*) and the right pedal (*tre corda*) or damper pedal.

prolonger jusqu'à extinction du son (Fr.). Hold until the sound dies.

promenade. A character piece, usually in a moderate tempo to suggest someone strolling or promenading. Composers who have written *promenades* include Ruy Coelho, Karl Panzera, Poulenc, Prokofiev, Albert Roussel, Arthur Shepherd, and Yngve Sköld.

pronto (It.). Prompt, strict.

"Prussian" Sonatas. C. P. E. Bach, W. 48, 1742. Six sonatas, each with three movements, dedicated to Frederick the Great of Prussia. These sonatas are among the musical high points between J. S. Bach and Haydn and firmly established this Bach son as a major composer.

P.T.O. Please turn over (the page).

Puerta del Vino, La (The Wine Gate). Claude Debussy, *Préludes*, book 2, no. 3, 1913. One of the gates to the Alhambra Palace in Grenada. A superb Spanish piece.

Pugno, Raoul (1852–1914). French pianist, he studied at the Paris Conservatoire, where he later became a faculty member. He quickly established an international reputation as an outstanding pianist by touring Europe and the United States. He also gave duo recitals with other artists of the day. He edited a complete edition of the works of Chopin, and Saint-Saëns dedicated his *Etude*, op. 116, no. 6 (the famous Toccata) to Pugno.

puissant (Fr.). Powerful, strong.

pulse. A beat; the underlying beat over which rhythm is superimposed.

puntato (It.). Pointed, staccato.

pyramid piano. An upright piano made in the shape of a truncated pyramid. First made during the first half of the 18th century, they lost their popularity around 1825.

Q

Quadrat (Ger.). A sign for a natural: ♮

quadruple meter. A time signature of $\frac{4}{4}$ or $\frac{12}{8}$ four beats to the measure.

quadruplet. A group of four notes of equal time played in the same time of three or six of the same value.

Qual (Ger.). Agony. *qualvoll:* agonized.

quartal harmony. Harmony based on combinations of the interval of a fourth, as distinct from tertian harmony, which is based on combinations of thirds. Scriabin experimented with quartal harmony in some of his piano music. See mystic chord.

quarter tone. An interval one-half of a half step. Ives wrote *Three Quarter-Tone Pieces* for two pianos. Piano 2 is tuned a quarter tone higher than normal pitch.

quartet (Eng.), **Quartett** (Ger.), **quartetto** (It.), **quatuor** (Fr.). A composition for four solo performers. A piano quartet consists of violin, viola, cello, and piano, a form of chamber music. The First Piano Quartet, which consisted of four pianists, were very popular in the United States during the 1950s and 1960s.

quasi (It.). Almost, nearly, approximately, as if, in the style of, like, as. *quasi sonata:* resembling a sonata. Beethoven's title for his

143

"Moonlight" Sonata, *Sonata quasi una fantasia,* means "Sonata in the style of a fantasia."

quasi niente (It.). Almost nothing, extremely soft.

quatre mains (Fr.), ***quattro mani*** (It.). (For) four hands.

quaver. In British terminology, an eighth note. A sixteenth note is a semiquaver, a thirty-second note a demisemiquaver, etc.

queue (Fr.). A nickname for the concert grand piano.

quintet. A composition for five solo performers. The piano quintet consists of a string quartet plus piano.

quintuple meter. A meter with five beats to the measure: $\frac{5}{4}$, $\frac{5}{8}$.

quintuplet. A group of five notes to be performed in the time of four of the same value.

quitter (Fr.). To leave, release.

quittez en laissant vibrer (Fr.). Release and allow to vibrate.

quodlibet (Lat.). "What you please!" A composition made up of popular tunes or fragments of tunes that are put together for humorous results or for technical virtuosity. The finale of J. S. Bach's "Goldberg" Variations is a *quodlibet.*

R

R. 1. Abbreviation for right. *R.H.:* right hand. 2. (Fr.). Abbreviation for *ritard:* gradually slowing.

Race, William (1923–99). American pianist, he studied at the University of Colorado with Storm Bull and at the University of Michigan with Dexter. Race gave many recitals and workshops throughout the United States and appeared with his wife Kay (who is an outstanding pianist) and daughter Susan (a superb pianist) in two-piano recitals. He was professor and coordinator of piano at the University of Texas from 1968 until his death. Race's playing was sensitive, fresh, and accurate, and his technique was superb.

Rachmaninoff, Sergei (1873–1943). Russian pianist, he studied at the Saint Petersburg and Moscow conservatories. He became the greatest pianist-composer of the 20th century and an outstanding conductor. He settled in the United States in 1917, where he achieved great success as a concert pianist. His piano music is written in an individual eclectic style derived from Brahms, Chopin, Liszt, Schumann, and Tchaikovsky and is flavored with Russian nationalism. His piano works include *17 Études tableaux, Four Improvisations,* three nocturnes, *Five Pieces, Seven Pieces,* 24 preludes, *Six movements musicaux,* two sets of variations on themes of

Chopin and Corelli, four piano concertos, and the *Rhapsody on a Theme of Paganini* for piano and orchestra and two suites plus *Symphonic Dances* for two pianos.

raddolcendo (It.). Becoming softer, sweeter.

radieux, radieuse (Fr.). Radiant.

raffrenando (It.). Slowing down.

Rage over the Lost Penny, The. Ludwig van Beethoven, *Rondo a Capriccio* in G Major, op. 129, 1795–98. "The Rage over the lost penny, given vent in a caprice." Robert Schumann says of this composition: "It would be difficult to find anything merrier than this whim. This was a moment for Beethoven to use his favorite expression when he was inwardly merry. 'Today I feel altogether unbuttoned' and then he laughed like a lion and beat about him, for he was always untamable. 'But with this Capriccio I'll get you' " (Schumann, p. 105; Berkowitz, p. 125).

rageur (Fr.). With anger, angry.

ragtime. Mainly for piano with a syncopated ragged beat over an "oom-pah" bass, started around the 1890s by African American piano players in the southern part of the United States. Ragtime was the forerunner of jazz. Joplin, James Scott (1886–1938), and Joseph Lamb (1887–1960) were three of the most famous rag composers. Other composers using ragtime in piano pieces include William Albright, William Bolcom, Rosenthal, Stravinsky, and Thomson.

Raieff, Josef (1906–2002). Russian pianist, he studied at the American Conservatory, the Juilliard Graduate School, and with Steuermann in Vienna and Schnabel in Berlin. He became an American citizen in 1938 and served in the army during World War II. He influenced the lives and careers of many students he taught at The Juilliard School from 1926 until 2001.

"Raindrop" Prelude. Frédéric Chopin, Prelude in D-flat Major, op. 28, no. 15, 1839. This prelude and no. 6 in B minor have been claimed for this nickname. George Sand wrote about a rainstorm that took place in Valldemosa, Majorca, where she and Chopin were living when he composed this piece. The rain dripping from the roof is suggested by the repeated A♭'s (and the G♯'s in the middle section).

Rákóczi March. A Hungarian national tune notated ca. 1810 by János Bihari in homage to Prince Ferenc Rákóczi (1676–1735), who led the Hungarian revolt against Austria. Liszt used the melody in his *Hungarian Rhapsody* no. 15.

ralentir (Fr.). To slow down.

ralentir en pasant sur la main droit: clair mais p (Fr.). Slowing down while stressing the right hand: clear but piano.

ralentir en s'effaçant (Fr.). Slowing down and fading away.

ralentissant (Fr.). Lessening, slowing.

rallentando (It.). Gradually getting slower. This term usually refers to a longer space (four to eight measures, etc.) than *ritardando*.

Rameau, Jean-Philippe (1683–1764). French composer, harpsichordist, and organist. His 53 pieces for keyboard comprising three books of suites come off well on the piano because they have a sustained quality about them. Rameau uses some or all of the four basic movements to the suite and adds other movements with illustrative titles. He also wrote an important treatise on harmony and a treatise on technique: *Méthode sur la mecanique des doigts sur le clavessin* (Method for Finger Mechanics at the Harpsichord, 1724).

rapidamente (It.). Rapidly, quickly.

rapide (Fr.). Fast, quick, rapid.

rapide et fuyant (Fr.). Quick and fleeting.

rapido (It.). Rapid, quick.

rapsodie (Fr.). See rhapsody.

rasch (Ger.). Spirited, quickly, lively, swift, fast.

rasch, aber leicht (Ger.). Fast, but light.

rattenuto (It.). Hold back, restrain.

Rauscher (Ger.). A repeated note on the piano.

Ravel, Maurice (1875–1937). French composer and pianist, he studied at the Paris Conservatoire and became one of the most outstanding composers of the 20th century. Ravel extended the pianistic traditions of Liszt and had a profound influence on the piano writing of Debussy. His piano works (see the individual entries for more information) include *À la manière de* (1) *Borodin* and (2) *Chabrier* (In the Style of Borodin and Chabrier), *Gaspard de la nuit, Jeux d'eau, Menuet antique* (Menuet in Antique Style), *Menuet sur le nom de Haydn* (Menuet on the Name of Haydn), *Miroirs, Pavane pour une infanté défunte, Prelude, Sérénade grotesque* (Grotesque Serenade), *Sonatine, Le tombeau de Couperin, La Valse, Valses nobles et sentimentales;* a piano concerto and a concerto for the left hand; for piano duet *Ma mère l'oye* and *Frontespice* for five hands; for two pianos *Sites auriculaires.* This last piece is one of the strangest in all of Ravel's works and shows Satie's influence. Ravel apparently envisioned two places (sites) that were to be visited, or comprehended by means of the ear (*auriculaires*). The first piece, *Habanera,* suggests a Spanish landscape; the second piece, an epigraph, focuses upon the sensuous exoticism found in the music.

ravviando (It.). Quickening.

re (It.). The second degree of the scale, or the note or tonality (key) D.

realization. The pianist may be required to add material to the score to "realize" the composer's intentions and give musical life to a piece. A realization may need ornaments or the filling in of material to an incomplete or sketchy score to achieve a convincing musical performance.

recapitulation. That section of a composition written in sonata-allegro form in which the themes and tonal centers heard in the exposition are repeated, closer to their original form and usually more in the original order of appearance than one finds in a development section.

recht (Ger.). Right, right hand.

recital. A concert presented by one or more soloists performing solo works. This term originally referred only to singers but ca. 1840 it was applied to Liszt's concert performances.

recitative. This title has been used by composers of piano pieces such as Richard Arnell, Angelo Corradini, Meyer Kupferman, Hans Poser, Mel Powell, and Richard Yardumian.

recueilli (Fr.). Meditative, contemplative.

redite (Fr.), **redita** (It.). A repeat.

redoublé (Fr.). A turn.

reduction. 1. A small version of the original. 2. A reduction or arrangement for piano, usually from orchestral score, for example, a reduction of a piano concerto for two pianos.

réduire (Fr.). To reduce, arrange, transcribe. *réduit:* reduced.

reel. A lively dance from Ireland and Scotland. Douglas Moore has composed a "Reel" for piano as part of his *Suite for Piano.* Lou Harrison has written a *Reel, Homage to Henry Cowell* for piano where the Irish-like tune is treated with all black-key clusters in the right hand and white-key clusters in the left hand, except where indicated. Their textures contrast with thick clusters. In the United States the reel is known as the Virginia reel.

reflection. The mirror effect or the reflected inverted image seen when music is placed against a mirror. Vincent Persichetti (1915–87) has composed for piano *Reflective Keyboard Studies,* 48 miniature studies to obtain simultaneous development of both hands. The pieces use symmetrical inversion, or, as Persichetti calls it, mirror music: exact intervals duplicated in each hand. These are preparatory studies for his *Mirror Etudes.* One hand mirrors the actions of the other by repeating the same intervals and patterns in inversions. He has also written a *Little Mirror Book,* in which one hand plays exactly what the other hand plays, in contrary motion and at the same time.

Reger, Max (1873–1916). German composer, pianist, and organist, he was a master of contrapuntal writing. Bach and Brahms highly influenced his compositional style. He taught at the Leipzig and Munich conservatories and toured as a concert pianist. Reger composed many complex works. The piano pieces range from short one-page sketches to 50-page fugues. For piano he wrote four sonatinas and a large number of smaller works, preludes and fugues, two sonatas, two suites, and sets of variations on themes of Bach and Telemann.

register. A section of the range or compass of an instrument (upper or lower register).

regret (Fr.). Regret, sorrow.

Regrets. Felix Mendelssohn, op. 19, no. 2, in A Minor, one of the *Songs without Words.*

Reich, Steve (b. 1936). American composer, he studied at The Juilliard School and Mills College. He became interested in Balinese and African music and has developed a compositional style that uses gradually changing repeated patterns that move out of phase, with staggered repetition, thus creating shimmering effects that can be hypnotic and spellbinding. His piano music is for two or more pianos and includes *Piano Phase* for two pianos or two marimbas that uses time-space notation and *Six Pianos.*

Reinagle, Alexander (1756–1809). English-American composer and pianist, he studied in Edinburgh and London and settled in the United States. He met C. P. E. Bach during a visit to the Continent.

Reinagle came to Philadelphia in 1786 and became a major influence in shaping the musical life of the city. He was probably the most important composer in America during the early life of the nation. His piano works include four sonatas (written in the United States), two sets of *Twenty-four Short and Easy Pieces, Theme with Variation,* and shorter pieces.

Reinecke, Carl (1824–1910). German composer, pianist, conductor, and teacher, he was a prolific composer, influenced to some extent by Schumann and Mendelssohn. He taught at a number of schools before settling in Leipzig, where he taught piano at the conservatory and conducted the Gewandhaus Orchestra from 1860 to 1892. His piano works included three concertos, piano pieces (many were of a pedagogic nature), sonatas, and over 40 cadenzas for piano concertos by other composers.

relever (Fr.). To pick up, raise up, hold up.

relever la pédale lentement sans enliver le main (Fr.). Raise the pedal slowly without lifting the hand.

religioso (It.). In a devotional style.

"Religious Meditation." Louis Moreau Gottschalk, *The Last Hope,* op. 16. This work has borne this subtitle because the main melody can be found in various hymnals. Gottschalk called this piece "Evening Prayer," having played it every evening to the memory of a Cuban lady whose last moments he had eased with its improvisation (Berkowitz, p. 130).

"Remembrance" Waltz. John Field, Waltz in E Major, sometimes applied to his Nocturne no. 12, Hopkinson no. 51A (e). The composer's title was *Sehnsuchts Waltzer* (The Yearning Waltz), but when the publisher made an English edition of these waltzes, the E-major one was called "Remembrance" (Berkowitz, p. 130).

"Reminiscence" Nocturne. Frédéric Chopin, Nocturne in C-sharp Minor, BI 49, 1830. In Poland this work is given this name because of its self-quotations from Chopin's Second Concerto in F Minor and from the song "The Wish" (*Zycenie*).

renforcer (Fr.). To increase, reinforce.

renforcer sans attaquer, et lâcher la pédale (Fr.). Press without striking and release the pedal.

renvoi (Fr.). The repeat or return sign.

repeat signs. A sign signifying the music between ‖: and :‖ is to be repeated. The first double bar is sometimes omitted at the beginning of a composition. If the dots are on both sides :‖: it means that the parts before and after the double bar are to be repeated.

répéter (Fr.). To repeat, rehearse.

repetition action. The mechanical portions which provide for double escapement, so that the hammer can strike again before falling to its dead level.

réponse (Fr.). A pause, caesura, answer.

reprendre avec la m.d. sans refrapper (Fr.). Play again with the right hand without sounding.

reprendre du début et passer la 1ʳᵉ reprise (Fr.). Return to the beginning and skip the first repeat.

reprendre la note rivement sans la rejouer (Fr.). Catch the note quickly without replaying.

reprendre le cluster avec les 2 avant-bras (Fr.). Take the cluster with the two forearms.

reprendre les accords dans la pédale, sans frapper (Fr.). Sustain the chords with the pedal without restriking.

reprendre un peu en dessus de la nuance (Fr.). Start again, a little quieter (softer).

reprise. 1. Resuming or resumption; to play again. 2. A repeat of the material of the first section in a composition after an episode or contrasting section. 3. In 18th-century French keyboard music, the second section of a piece in two-part form. 4. The recapitulation in sonata-allegro form.

resonance. A prolongation of an original sound by means of a sympathetic vibration.

résonner (Fr.). To reverberate, be sonorous.

respecter strictement le jeu des pédales (Fr.). Pay strict attention to the pedaling.

ressortir (Fr.). To emphasize, bring out.

rest. A symbol used to indicate relative periods of silence. The values correspond to note values (whole, half, quarter, eighth, etc.).

rester, restez (Fr.). Remain (linger) on a note without hurrying off it.

Restlessness. Felix Mendelssohn, op. 19, no. 5, in F-sharp Minor, one of the *Songs without Words*.

restringendo (It.). Becoming faster.

retarder, retardez (Fr.). Hold back, to *ritard;* slower.

retenant (Fr.). Holding back, retarding, restrained.

retenu (Fr.). Held back.

Retrospection. Felix Mendelssohn, op. 102, no. 3, in D Major, one of the *Songs without Words*.

retrouver le mouvement (Fr.). *A tempo*.

Return, The. Felix Mendelssohn, op. 85, no. 5, in A Major, one of the *Songs without Words*.

rêve (Fr.). A dream, illusion.

revenez au 1er movement (Fr.). Return to the first tempo.

rêverie (Fr.). Dreaming or a dreamy composition. A term used by many composers of character pieces. Composers who used it include Balakirev, Debussy, Dvořák, Sergei Liapunov, Poulenc, Vladimir Rebikov, Scriabin, Sibelius, Tausig, and Tcherepnin.

Reverie. Felix Mendelssohn, op. 85, no. 1, in F Major, one of the *Songs without Words*.

rêveur (Fr.). Dreaming, musing.

rêveusement lent (Fr.). Dreamily slow.

"Revolutionary" Etude. Frédéric Chopin, Etude in C Minor, op. 10, no. 12, 1831?, so called because of the fall of Warsaw in September 1831, the news of which reached Chopin at Stuttgart. Sometimes this etude is referred to as the "Fall of Warsaw." There is no documentary evidence that Chopin was inspired to compose it by the events in his native land or gave it either nickname.

Rezits, Joseph (b. 1925). American pianist and teacher, he studied at the Curtis Institute with Vengerova. He pursued a concert career that included playing in many U.S. cities and with some of the major orchestras. He taught at Indiana University from 1962 until his retirement. He is the author of *The Pianist's Resource Guide* and *Beloved Tyranna: The Legend and Legacy of Isabelle Vengerova*.

rhapsody. A one-movement work in free or irregular form, often improvised pieces that are later notated. Examples include Liszt's *Hungarian Rhapsody*, inspired by gypsy tunes; Gershwin's *Rhapsody in Blue*, inspired by jazz; Rachmaninoff's *Rhapsody on a Theme of Paganini* for piano and orchestra, a set of variations on Paganini's famous theme also incorporating the *Dies irae* chant from the Catholic liturgical music for the dead. Brahms also used the term for some of his works for solo piano. Many composers have written rhapsodies.

Rhodes piano. An electronic piano designed by Harold Rhodes (1910–2000).

ricecar, ricercare (It.). To seek out. A term used in Baroque music to indicate somewhat contrapuntal style with several motives. Composers from the Baroque to the present have written *ricercars* for piano including Alfredo Casella, Mario Castelnuovo-Tedesco, Lockrem Johnson, Gian Carlo Menotti, and Marcel Mihalovici.

Richter, Sviatoslav (1914–97). Russian pianist, he studied at the Moscow Conservatory with Neuhaus. Through his recordings his reputation preceded his tours in Western Europe and the United States. Prokofiev dedicated his ninth piano sonata to Richter. He is considered to be one of the most outstanding pianists of the 20th century.

richtig (Ger.). Correct, precise.

ridicoloso (It.). Absurd, preposterous.

rien (Fr.). Nothing.

rigaudon (Fr.), **rigadoon** (Eng.). A lively 17th-century dance in duple meter, usually having a pick-up beat. Composers writing *rigaudons* include Couperin, Johann Pachelbel, Purcell, Rameau, Ravel, and Scott.

rigoroso (It.). In strict time.

rigueur (Fr.). Exactness, severity, rigor.

rilasciando (It.). Slowing down.

rinforzando, rinforzato (It.). Reinforced, stressed, accented. Abbreviated to *rf* or *rfz*. A definite increase in power extending through a phrase or passage.

riprendere (It.). To resume the original tempo.

risoluto (It.). Resolute, energetic, boldly.

ritardando, ritard, rit. (It.). Retarding, holding back; gradually slowing down, get slower and slower. This term usually covers a short area (one, two, or three measures).

ritenuto (It.). Hold back immediately; a sudden reduction in tempo and play on in the slower tempo.

ritmico (It.). Rhythmic.

Ritual Fire Dance (Danza ritual del fuego). Manuel de Falla, 1914–15. This piece is from the ballet *El amor brujo* (Love, the Sorcerer). De Falla made this highly effective arrangement for solo piano from the orchestral score.

Robert, Walter (1908–2000). Austrian-American pianist, he studied in Vienna and gave recitals throughout Europe, South America, and the United States. He performed much chamber music and was accompanist for well-known singers and instrumentalists. He taught at Indiana University for many years until his retirement. He wrote *From Bach to Brahms: A Musician's Journey through Keyboard Literature.*

robuste (Fr.). Hardy.

Rococo. A term used to describe style characteristics (decorative and delicately ornamental) of the transitional period between the Baroque and Classical periods from around 1720 to 1765. Another term for this period is "pre-Classical." The works of the Bach sons, Scarlatti, and early Haydn fall into this period.

Rodriguez, Santiago (b. 1952). Cuban pianist, he studied at the University of Texas with Race and at The Juilliard School with Marcus. He has won many honors in international competition and has made numerous orchestral and recital appearances in the United States. He has toured most of the world receiving high praise. A number of recordings have been made by Rodriguez, who teaches at the University of Maryland.

rolled chord. A chord in which the pitches are played consecutively, rather than played simultaneously; an *arpeggio*.

Roman Sketches, Four. Charles Griffes, op. 7, 1915–19. Four impressionistic pieces: *The White Peacock, Nightfall, The Fountains of the Acqua Paola, Clouds.*

romance (Fr., Eng.), *romanza*(It.), **Romanze** (Ger.). A piece with a tender, sentimental, or reflective character. Many composers have used this term, including Jéhan Alain, Bartók, Alfredo Casella, Louis Durey, Fauré, Liszt, MacDowell, Nicolai Medtner, Milhaud, Rachmaninoff, and Clara and Robert Schumann.

Romantic. A term used to describe the type of music literature composed during most of the 19th century through the beginning of the 20th century. "Romantic" has to do with romance and the idealization of beauty and the past; it features strong emphasis on individuality and subjective style, the distant, the exotic, and the unattainable. Romanticism mixes fantasy with beauty. Many character pieces were composed during this period.

rondo (It.), **rondeau** (Fr.). Round. A composition in which the theme (first section) returns repeatedly (goes around) after the presentation of contrasting sections. A frequently found form (where A is the principal theme or section) is ABACABA. It frequently formed the last movement of the classical sonata, concerto, or symphony, but many composers wrote *rondos* as independent pieces, for example, Chopin.

Rose, Jerome (b. 1938). American pianist, he studied at the Mannes College of Music with Shure and at The Juilliard School. He has received many honors and has played all over the world receiving high acclaim. He taught at Bowling Green (Ohio) State University for many years and has made numerous recordings.

Rosen, Charles (b. 1927). American pianist, he studied at The Juilliard School and Princeton University and with Rosenthal. His New York debut was in 1951, and he has since performed solo and with leading orchestras throughout the United States and Europe. He has written books on music including *The Classical Style: Haydn, Mozart, Beethoven* and a book on sonata form. His repertoire includes Beethoven to contemporary composers. He currently teaches at the University of Chicago.

Rosenthal, Moritz (1862–1946). Polish pianist, a student of Karl Mikuli (pupil of Chopin), Joseffy, and Liszt. He made his U.S. debut in 1888, and critics praised his perfect performance and style. He was appointed court pianist to the Austrian emperor Franz Josef. His repertoire ranged from Scarlatti to Debussy with special notice of his exquisite Chopin performances.

roulade (Fr.). A brilliant run; ornamental florid passage.

row. See twelve-tone music.

rubato (It.). Robbed, stolen. A free playing style where one or more notes may be extended at the expense of another for purposes of expression. Another manifestation is varying the tempo of a passage for expressive purposes. Often employed in performing works from the Romantic repertoire.

Rubinstein, Anton (1829–94). Russian pianist and composer. He founded the St. Petersburg Conservatory. Rubinstein was one of the keyboard giants of the 19th century. He wrote with a powerful, crazy lyricism: he sings like Mendelssohn, thunders like Liszt, but always remains himself. His piano works include three piano sonatas, numerous smaller works, and four piano concertos.

Rubinstein, Arthur (1887–1982). Polish pianist. He played throughout Europe and the United States with great success, finally settling in America in 1939. He was one of the greatest performers of the

20th century. His repertoire was broad, Beethoven and Brahms to works of the 20th century, but his interpretation of the works of his compatriot Chopin were recognized as coming from the greatest performer of Chopin of the 20th century.

Rubinstein, Beryl (1898–1952). American pianist, composer, and teacher. He toured the United States as a prodigy and studied in Europe from 1911–16 with Busoni, then with José Vianna da Motta. He was head of the piano department at the Cleveland Institute of Music, dean of the faculty, and finally director. He was a remarkable pianist who composed for the piano a sonatina, studies, smaller pieces, two concertos, and a suite for two pianos. He wrote *Outline of Piano Pedagogy*. His students included Ward Davenny and Lionel Nowak.

rude (Fr.). Rough, harsh, boisterous.

Ruggles, Carl (1876–1971). American composer, he worked out his own particular method of composing a unique form of atonal music. His piano works include *Evocations, Four Chants* for solo piano, and *Polyphonic Composition* for three pianos.

ruhig (Ger.). Quiet, peaceful, calm, play with tranquility.

Rumanian Rhapsody. Franz Liszt. Arranged, edited, and published by Busoni as the *Hungarian Rhapsody* no. 20. The work has all the tuneful verve and exotic moodiness of Liszt's most popular *Hungarian Rhapsodies*. A Bartókian element can be detected in the oriental-sounding main section.

rumba. An Afro-Cuban dance in rapid duple meter with strongly percussive syncopated and broken rhythms. It became popular in the United States during the 1930s. A *Jamaican Rumba* for piano was composed by Arthur Benjamin (1893–1960).

Rummel, Walter (1887–1953). German pianist, he studied with Godowsky in Berlin between 1904 and 1909. He became a close friend of Debussy and championed his and other 20th-century music. He enjoyed a major career in Europe during the 1920s and 1930s. He made transcriptions of Bach and of earlier composers' works as well as making a number of recordings.

rumor (Sp.). Murmur.

run. A fast scale passage.

Ruralia hungarica. Ernst von Dohnányi, op. 32a, 1924. Seven pieces for piano based on old Hungarian folk songs.

rustico (It.). Rustic, rural; a rural or country-like feeling.

Rustle of Spring. Christian Sinding, op. 32, no. 3, 1909. Probably
the most famous piece describing this season.

rythme libre (Fr.). Rhythmically free.

rythmer (Fr.). To punctuate, to make rhythmical.

rythmique (Fr.). Rhythmical.

S

S. (Ger.). The note E flat. Abbreviation for *segno, senza, sinistra, solo, subito,* (Wolfgang) Schmieder's catalog of the works of J. S. Bach.

saccade (Fr.). Staccato, jerky, abrupt.

sacred piano music. Music appropriate for church use. Liszt composed the most music in this category, but many other composers have contributed to it including Alkan, J. S. Bach, Bartók, Alexander Borodin, Brahms, Busoni, Mario Castelnuovo-Tedesco, Dussek, Johann Fischer, Mikhail Glinka, Gottschalk, Adolph von Henselt, Henri Herz, Gustav Holst, Johann Kuhnau, Mendelssohn, Messiaen, Reger, Satie, Ronald Stevenson, Georg Philipp Telemann, and Ralph Vaughan Williams.

Sadness of Soul. Felix Mendelssohn, op. 53, no. 4, in F Major, one of the *Songs without Words.*

sagement (Fr.). Wisely, steadily, discreetly.

s'agrandissant. (Fr.). Expanding.

Saint Anthony Variations. Johannes Brahms, Variations for Two Pianos, op. 56b, 1873, also known as *Variations on a Theme of Haydn.* This is one of the masterpieces in the two-piano repertoire. Although better known in its orchestral form, it was originally written for two pianos. Brahms frequently played this work with Clara Schumann.

Saint-Saëns, Camille (1835–1921). French composer and pianist, he studied at the Paris Conservatoire. He was a brilliant pianist with a fine sense of style and an excellent craftsman—facile, elegant, and well grounded. He has been called the "French Mendelssohn." His piano works include *Allegro appassionata, Six Bagatelles,* 12 Etudes, suite, five concertos, and works for two pianos: *Caprice arabe* (Arab Caprice), *Caprice héroïque* (Heroic Caprice), and *Variations on a Theme of Beethoven.* One of his most famous works is for two pianos and chamber orchestra, *Carnaval des Animaux.*

Salón Mexico, El. Aaron Copland, 1943. Based on Mexican folksongs and originally for orchestra, Leonard Bernstein made a highly effective arrangement for two pianos. El Salón Mexico was the name of a dancehall in Mexico City.

Samaroff, Olga (1880–1948). American pianist and teacher. She was born Lucy Hickenlooper but changed it when she went on the concert stage. She studied with Constantin Sternberg in Philadelphia, then at the Paris Conservatoire and with Hutcheson back in the United States for further study. Her New York debut in 1905 opened doors for touring Europe and the United States plus appearances with orchestras. She married the conductor Leopold Stokowski in 1911. She taught at the Philadelphia Conservatory and The Juilliard School, and she later added newspaper criticism to her activities. She played at the White House in 1911 and 1927. She was one of the most important teachers of piano in the United States during the first half of the 20th century. Pupils included Hinson, Kapell, List, Lunde, Ott, Vincent Persichetti, Tureck, and Weissenberg.

samba. An African-Brazilian dance in duple meter with highly syncopated melodies and accompaniments, introduced in the United States ca. 1940. The third movement, *Brazileira,* of Milhaud's *Scaramouche* for two pianos is a stunning "knock-out" based on a lively samba.

sämtlich (Ger.). Complete. *Sämtliche Werke:* the complete works of a composer.

Sandor, György (b. 1912). Hungarian pianist, he studied piano with

Bartók at the Liszt Academy in Budapest. He toured Europe before World War II and then settled in the United States. Sandor gave the world premiere of Bartók's Third Piano Concerto in 1946. He has recorded the complete piano works of Bartók plus many other works. He wrote *On Piano Playing,* which depends greatly on the weight doctrine. Sandor has taught at the University of Michigan and The Juilliard School.

sanft (Ger.). Soft, mild.

sanglotant. (Fr.). Sobbing.

Sanlúcar de Barrameda (Sonata pintoresca). Joaquin Turina, op. 24, 1922. Sanlúcar de Barrameda is a fortified seaport near Cádiz made picturesque by its ancient Moorish citadel and colorful fishing fleets. This work, one of Turina's most ambitious, describes the atmosphere of the town. Cyclical form is used in this four-movement work.

sans (Fr.). Without, but for.

sans aucun (Fr.). Without any.

sans aucune nuance (Fr.). With no expression.

sans céder (Fr.). Without *ritard.*

sans dureté—très lié (Fr.). Very *legato,* without harshness.

sans élargir (Fr.). Without slowing down, no broadening.

sans faire vibrer (Fr.). Without allowing to vibrate.

sans frapper (Fr.). Without striking forcibly.

sans hâte et noblement (Fr.). Nobly and without haste.

sans heurts (Fr.). Smoothly.

sans jamais presser (Fr.). Without ever hurrying.

sans les clés (Fr.). Without (using) the keys.

sans lourdeur (Fr.). Without heaviness.

sans mesure (Fr.). In free meter.

sans nuances (Fr.). Without shadings.

sans presser (Fr.). Without rushing.

sans presser les petites notes (Fr.). Without rushing the grace notes.

sans raideur (Fr.). Without stiffness; flexible.

sans ralentir du tout (Fr.). With no *ritard* at all.

sans répéter (Fr.). Without repeating.

sans retarder (Fr.). Without holding back.

sans rigueur (Fr.). Without rigidity or strictness; freely.

sans sourdine (Fr.). Without mute or damper. In playing Beethoven's piano music, this means using the damper pedal to raise the dampers off the strings so they can vibrate.

sans sourdine ni Péd. forte (Fr.). Without *una corda* or *tre corda:* with neither pedal.

sans traîner (Fr.). Without dragging.

sans trop (Fr.). Without too much.

s'apaiser (Fr.). To grow quiet, to subside.

sapateado (Port.). The sound of tap dancing.

Saperton, David (1889–1970). American pianist and teacher, he studied with Arthur Shattuck and Godowsky. He toured Europe and concertized extensively in the United States. He married Godowsky's daughter and played and recorded many of Godowsky's compositions and transcriptions. He taught at the Curtis Institute and later taught privately in New York. Some of his students included Bolet, Cherkassky, Sidney Foster, Julius Katchen, and Simon.

sarabande (Fr.), **saraband, sarabande** (Eng.). A majestic slow Baroque dance in triple meter, often with a prolonged second beat. It originated in Spain and became a standard movement in the Baroque suite. This dance survived into the 20th century with Debussy using it as the second movement in his suite *Pour le piano* and in his first book of *Images*.

Satie, Erik (1866–1925). French composer, he was one of music's greatest originals. His influence on other composers was more important than his music, but his music is unique in many ways. He parodied styles of well-known composers, quoted from their works, and deliberately attached comical names to his pieces. Fun seemed to be the essence of his aesthetic. He added text to his piano music that was not to be read during performance. See entries on individual titles for more information. His piano works include *Embryones desséchés* (Dried-Up Embryos), *3 Gnossoiennes, 3 Gymnopédies, Pièces froides* (Cold Pieces), *4 Préludes, Sonatine bureaucratique* (Bureaucratic Sonatina), *Sports et divertissements* (Sports and Divertissements), *Vexations* (play it 840 times in succession), *Véritables préludes flasque* (Four Flabby Preludes), and many more pieces plus works for piano duet.

Satz (Ger.). Movement.

Saudadoes do Brazil (Recollections [or Souvenirs] of Brazil). Darius Milhaud, 1920–21. This suite of 12 dances is written in popular Brazilian style employing bitonality, tango and habanera rhythms, changing sonorities, and varied figuration. The titles are names of different neighborhoods in Rio de Janeiro.

Sauer, Emil von (1863–1942). German pianist, he studied with Nikolai Rubinstein and Liszt and became an internationally famous virtuoso and teacher. Sauer composed two piano concertos and many pieces including studies. He edited the works of Brahms and Liszt for Peters, as well as some other works.

sauvage (Fr.). Wild, fierce.

scande (Fr.). Stressing.

Scaramouche (Clown). Darius Milhaud, Suite for Two Pianos, 1937. This is one of the most famous two-piano works. The three movements show us three moods of the Clown: *Vif, Modéré, Brazileira.* The suite is a delight, spontaneously lyrical, rhythmically vigorous, gaily discordant, and poignantly nostalgic in its Brazilian evocation.

Scarlatti, Domenico (1685–1757). Italian composer and harpsichordist, he composed more than 550 keyboard sonatas for the musically gifted Portuguese princess Maria Barbara. For nearly 10 years he served as her music teacher, and upon her marriage in 1729 to the heir of the Spanish throne, he moved with her court to Spain, where he spent the rest of his life. Scarlatti gave the binary form a variety and expressive range that has never been surpassed by any other composer. Many of his sonatas have a strong Spanish flavor, and their originality and emotional range span every mood and temperament.

Schall (Ger.). Sound.

Schein, Ann (b. 1939). American pianist, she studied at the Peabody Conservatory with Munz and privately with Arthur Rubinstein. She has performed throughout the world with great success, both solo and with orchestras. Schein has made a number of recordings and taught at the Peabody Conservatory for many years.

scherzando, scherzoso (It.). Playfully, jestingly, a light, playful style of performance.

scherzino, scherzetto (It.). A small scherzo.

scherzo (It.). A joke, jest; a quick light-hearted movement. During the late 18th century the *scherzo* gradually displaced the older *menuet* and trio as the third movement of a larger work, such as sonata, string quartet, or symphony. In the 19th century *scherzos* were composed as independent works. Chopin composed four, as did other composers such as Balakirev, Alexander Borodin, Brahms, Copland, Dohnányi, Grieg, and Liszt.

Schiff, András (b. 1953). Hungarian pianist, he studied at the Liszt Academy in Budapest. He gave his debut in Budapest in 1972 and has since toured Europe, the United States, and Asia. He is a remarkable pianist who plays a wide range of repertoire, but he is especially known for his interpretation of Bach.

schleppen (Ger.). To drag.

Schlummerlied (Ger.). Lullaby.

Schlüssel (Ger.). Clef.

schmachtend (Ger.). Languishing, pining.

schmeichend (Ger.). Flattering, coaxing.

schmerzlich (Ger.). Sad, painful.

Schnabel, Artur (1881–1951). Austrian pianist, he studied with Leschetizky. At the age of 12 he met Johannes Brahms, from which came his interest in that master's compositions. He settled in the United States in 1939. He recorded all of the Beethoven piano sonatas in 1931, and specialized in the repertoire of Mozart, Beethoven, Schubert, and Brahms. Schnabel taught at the University of Michigan during his last summers. He is considered one of the greatest pianists of the 20th century. His students included Webster Aiken, Brinkman, Curzon, Firkusny, Fleischer, Claude Frank, Kraus, Maier, Marcus, Shure, Slenczynska, Aube Tzerko, Wolff, and Carlo Zecchi.

schnell (Ger.). Quick, rapid; *schneller,* faster; *so schnell wie möglich,* as fast as possible.

Schoenberg, Arnold (1874–1951). Austrian composer, he became a United States citizen in 1941. Works from his early period follow Brahms and Richard Strauss and are written in a late Romantic style. He began taking private students, and Alban Berg and Anton von Webern studied with him. Gradually Schoenberg developed a new style and eventually arrived at 12-tone music. When he was forced by the Nazis to leave Germany where he was teaching, he came to the United States, where he taught and composed until the end of his life. He was also an Expressionist painter. His piano works are among the most significant contributions to the repertoire. His piano works include *Piano Pieces, Five Piano Pieces* (his first 12-tone pieces for piano), *Six Little Piano Pieces,* two sets of *Three Piano Pieces,* and *Suite for Piano.*

Schonberg, Harold (1915–2003). American music critic, he studied at Brooklyn College and New York University. He was on the staff of the *New York Sun* from 1946 to 1950 and in 1950 joined the music staff of the *New York Times,* where he was chief music critic for many years. His book *The Great Pianists* contains much authoritative information about the piano profession.

School of Velocity. A set of piano exercises by Carl Czerny, op. 299.

schrittmässig (Ger.). Measured, *andante.*

Schub, André-Michel (b. 1953). French pianist, he studied with Jascha Zayde and Rudolf Serkin. He made his New York debut in 1974 and won the 1981 Van Cliburn Competition. He is a solid pianist with great technical facility and expressive good taste. He has made a number of recordings.

Schubert, Franz (1797–1828). Austrian composer, he was one of the great Viennese masters of the early 19th century. Great lyric beauty, bold harmonic vocabulary, natural spontaneity, and intimate writing, sometimes coupled with large spatial design, characterize Schubert's unique keyboard style. His piano works include 21 sonatas (some not completed), 11 impromptus, six *Moments musicaux, Wanderer Fantasy,* 452 short dances (*menuets,* German Dances, *Ländler,* waltzes, *écossaises,* and *galops*), and a set of variations. He also added to the piano duet medium with a considerable amount of repertoire.

Schule der Geläufigkeit. See *School of Velocity.*

Schumacher, Thomas (b. 1937). American pianist and teacher, he studied at the Manhattan School of Music with Goldsand and at The Juilliard School with Marcus and Webster. He won a number of awards and made a Town Hall debut. Schumacher has concertized the world over and played with major orchestras, receiving superb reviews. He teaches at the Eastman School of Music.

Schumann, Clara Wieck (1819–96). German pianist and composer, she was taught by her father Friedrich Wieck and was a child prodigy. She toured at an early age and married Schumann in 1840. Her euphuistic compositions have been overshadowed by her husband's works and her own pianistic virtuosity. Her piano works display a variety of emotions including enthusiasm, melancholy, passion, and sometimes sparkle. Her piano works include *Four Characteristic Pieces, Four Pièces fugitives* (Fugitive Pieces), *Four Polonaises, Three Romances, Scherzo, Six Soirées musicales* (Musical Soirées), *Sonata in G minor, Souvenir de Vienne* (Souvenir of Vienna), *Three Preludes and Fugues, Variations de concert sur la Cavatina du Pirate, de Bellini* (Concert Variations on the Cavatina from Bellini's *Pirata*), *Variations on a Theme by Robert Schumann,* She also wrote a piano concerto and chamber music with piano.

Schumann, Robert (1810–56). German composer, pianist, and critic, his early training was as a pianist, but he had to give it up after injuring his hand. He composed and worked as a critic and married Clara Wieck in 1840, the daughter of his piano teacher. Schumann worked as a conductor and teacher in Leipzig and Düsseldorf for a time. He was the Romantic composer par excellence. His creative and fresh output for piano has provided some of the most imaginative and touching music in the pianist's repertoire. His creative energy flourished early and then decreased, due in part to his mental illness. Most of his works for piano were written for his wife, who premiered most of them. Piano works: *Abegg Variations, Album Blätter, Album for the Young, Arabesque, Blumenstück, Carnaval, Davidsbündlertanze, Éttudes symphoniques, Faschingschwank aus Wien, Fantasie, Fantasiestücke, Forest Scenes, Humoresque, Impromptus on a Theme of Clara Wieck, Kinderszenen, Kreisleriana, Noveletten, Papillons, Seven Pieces in Fughetta Form, Six Intermezzi,* three sonatas, *Three Romances, Toccata, Twelve Studies after Caprices of Paganini,* as well as a piano concerto and two pieces for two pianos. Schumann's metronome indications should be questioned by the pianist.

schwach (Ger.). Weak, soft.

schwer (Ger.). Heavy, difficult, ponderous, grave.

schwindend (Ger.). Dying away, becoming softer (quieter).

schwungvoll (Ger.). Spirited, energetic.

scintillant (Fr.). Brilliant, sparkling.

sciolto, scioltamente (It.). Loosely, that is, in a free and easy manner; with freedom, fluency.

Scionti, Silvio (1882–1973). Italian pianist, he studied at the Palermo Conservatory and at the Royal Conservatory in Naples. After his debut in Naples he came to the United States and soon became a recitalist and soloist with orchestras. He taught at the American Conservatory and the Chicago Musical College. He gave very successful two-piano recitals with his wife and former student, Isabel Scionti. They both taught at North Texas State College, now the University of North Texas.

scorrendo, scorrevole (It.). Flowing.

Scotch snap. A sixteenth note followed by a dotted eighth note. It is characteristic of Scottish folk music and was used by Haydn, Beethoven, and Mendelssohn.

Scott, Cyril (1879–1970). English composer and pianist. Scott's originality earned him the title "the English Debussy." He was also an internationally known pianist. For piano: *Egypt* (five impressions), *Indian Suite,* three sonatas, and his most famous work for piano, *Lotus Land* (pseudo-oriental).

"Scottish" Sonata. Felix Mendelssohn, Fantasia in F-sharp Minor, op. 28, 1833. Mendelssohn referred to this work as his "Scottish" Sonata (*Sonata écossaise* has become affixed as a subtitle). Mendelssohn visited Scotland in 1829, and it could be that he collected ideas at that time that he later used in the Fantasia.

Scriabin, Alexander (1872–1915). Russian composer and outstanding pianist, he studied at the Moscow Conservatory and had a fluent and spontaneous style of playing. His early works owe much to Chopin and Liszt. His chromatic harmonic vocabulary later evolved into a highly individual style. His piano works include: 10 sonatas, 24 *études,* 85 preludes, impromptus, mazurkas, and waltzes, a *Concert Allegro,* plus a piano concerto.

scucito (It.). Detached, non-*legato.*

sdegno (It.). Scorn, disdain.

se perdant (Fr.). Dying.

Sebök, György (1922–99). Hungarian-American pianist, he studied at the Liszt Academy in Budapest. He won a number of prizes and toured Europe with great success. He made numerous recordings and taught at Indiana University from 1963 until his death.

sec (Fr.). Crisp, dry, plain, staccato.

sec et musclé (Fr.). Dry and muscular.

sec les arpèges (Fr.). Perform the broken chords crisply.

sec les arpèges très serrés (Fr.). Dry, the arpeggios very taut.

secco (It.). Dry, perform in a recitative style.

sécheresse (Fr.). Dryness, shortness. In piano playing this usually refers to without pedaling.

secondo (It.). The lower part in a piano duet.

seelenvoll (Ger.). Soulful.

segno (It.). The sign 𝄋.

segue (It.). Follows; a direction to proceed to the next section without a break or pause; see *attacca*.

seguidilla (Sp.). A vivacious Spanish dance in ¾ or ⅜ meter. Albeniz wrote one for the seventh movement of his *Suite espagnole*. The most famous example is the aria from Bizet's *Carmen*.

Sehnsucht (Ger.). Longing. *sehnsuchtvoll:* filled with longing.

sehr (Ger.). Very.

sehr langsam (Ger.). Very slow.

sehr schnell (Ger.). Very fast.

Seixas, Carlos (1704–42). Portuguese composer, harpsichordist, and organist, he was a colleague of Scarlatti at the Lisbon Royal Chapel. He composed around 100 sonatas and toccatas for keyboard that have survived.

semplice (It.). Simple, unaffected.

semplicità (It.). With simplicity, naturalness.

sempre (It.). Always, continuously.

sempre forte (It.). Always loud.

sempre piano (It.). Always quiet (soft).

sensibile (It.). Expressive.

sensibilità (It.). With feeling.

sensible (Fr.). With feeling, sensitive.

senti, sentie (Fr.). Deeply felt, very expressive.

sentimento (It.). With feeling—not sentimental!

sentito (It.). Felt, expressive.

senza (It.). Without.

senza misura (It.) In free time, without a steady beat.

senza sordino (It.). Without mute or damper.

senza trascinare (It.). Without dragging.

septuplet. A group of seven notes of equal time value performed in a time allotted to a different number of notes.

serein (Fr.). Serene, calm.

serenade, serenata (Fr., It.). A term used by 19th- and 20th-century composers for character pieces usually addressed to a lover, friend, or person of rank. Composers using these terms for piano pieces include Albeniz, Alfredo Casella, Debussy, Dvořák, Grieg, Mendelssohn, Vincent Persichetti, Rachmaninoff, Ravel, Anton Rubinstein, Sinding, Stravinsky, and Szymanowski.

Sérénade interrompue, La (The Interrupted Serenade). Claude Debussy, *Préludes,* book 1, no. 9, 1910. This is an effective Spanish piece with a trace of gypsy influence.

serialism, serial music. Often applied to 12-tone music, but more strictly describing developments in music after World War II when composers like Boulez, Messiaen, Milton Babbitt, and Hans Werner Henze strictly ordered other elements of a piece, in addition to the notes themselves, like dynamics, rhythm, and even tone colors.

series. See 12-tone music.

serieux (Fr.). Dignified, serious.

serioso (It.). Seriously.

Serkin, Peter (b. 1947). American pianist, he studied with his father, Rudolf Serkin. His United States debut was at age 10, and his London debut took place in 1965. He is associated with contemporary music and has commissioned works, but he plays the repertoire from Bach to Messiaen.

Serkin, Rudolf (1903–91). Czech pianist of Russian parentage, he studied in Vienna. His Vienna debut took place in 1915, and he began touring as a concert artist in 1920. He settled in the United States, where he became associated with the Curtis Institute of Music, becoming its director in 1968. He was especially well known for his performance of the classical repertoire (Beethoven in particular), but he also gave the premiere of the Martinů piano sonata and the U.S. premiere of Prokofiev's Fourth Piano Concerto (for the left hand). Serkin was an outstanding teacher, and his pupils include Graffman, Laredo, Luvisi, and his son Peter.

serrant (Fr.). Becoming faster, pressing ahead, hastening.

serrer (Fr.). To press, push (ahead).

seul (Fr.). Alone, solo; one, only one.

seulement (Fr.). Only; but.

s'évanouissant (Fr.). Fading out.

Severac, Deodat de (1872–1921). French composer, he studied with Vincent d'Indy and Albéniz at the Schola Cantorum in Paris. He spent most of his life in southern France. His piano music is descriptive, mainly of events and local places, in his native Langue-doc. His piano works include *Baigneuses au soleil* (Sunbathers), *Cerdaña, Chant de la terre* (Song of the Earth), *En Languedoc* (In Lenguedoc), *En vacances* (On Vacation), *Peppermint-Get*, his best known piano piece, and a sonata.

sfogato (It.). Let loose; vented, unburdened, unrestrained; in a light, easy style.

sforzando, sforzato (It.). Forced. A sign (*sf*, *sfz*) meaning a strong accent or emphasis on a note or chords, with respect to the pre-vailing dynamic; sometimes it means simply loud. In Haydn, Mozart, and early Beethoven it means hardly more than an accent (<) over or under a note. This produced more of a "bite" than a *forte* or *fortissimo* on an 18th-century fortepiano.

sfp. Abbreviation for *sforzando* followed immediately by *piano*, a sud-den accent (often loud) followed immediately by a soft (quiet) sound(s).

sfz. Abbreviation for *sforzando* and *sforzato*.

shake. See trill.

"Shepherd Boy" Etude. Frédéric Chopin, Etude in A-flat Major, op. 25, no. 1, 1836. Chopin is supposed to have told a student that while composing this piece he thought of a shepherd boy taking cover in a grotto during a storm, and to make the time go more quickly the shepherd boy played this melody on his flute (Berkowitz, p. 3). Also called the "Aeolian Harp" Etude.

Shepherd's Complaint, The. Felix Mendelssohn, op. 67, no. 5, in B Minor, one of the *Songs without Words*.

Sherman, Russell (b. 1930). American pianist, he studied with Steuermann and made his debut at Town Hall when he was 15. He has performed with major orchestras and given recitals throughout Europe and the United States. He is presently chair of the piano department at the New England Conservatory and is one of the major piano talents in the United States.

shimmy. A dance popular in the United States in the 1910s and 1920s that is applied to various styles of dancing, most involving vigorous movement of the dancer's body. It started with African Americans and became a national sensation when it was introduced in the revue *Ziegfield Follies* of 1922. Hindemith included the shimmy as the second movement of his *Suite "1922."*

Shostakovich, Dmitri (1906–75). Russian composer and pianist, his early works show traces of urban folk music and of Bartók's general approach to folk music. His compositions contain sarcasm, pastiche, the grotesque, and the imitation of natural sounds. The piano music is never bombastic or overloaded. Piano works: *10 Aphorisms, Six Children's Pieces, Seven Doll's Dances, Three Fantastic Dances, 24 Preludes, 24 Preludes and Fugues* (Baroque inspired), two sonatas, plus two concertos.

Shure, Leonard (1910–95). This American pianist studied in Los Angeles, his hometown, and later with Schnabel in Berlin. From 1933 he taught successively at the New England Conservatory and the University of Texas (Austin) while continuing a concert career.

si (It.) The seventh degree of the scale, or the note or tonality (key) B; *si♭* = B♭.

Sibelius, Jean (1865–1957). Finnish composer, he studied in Helsinki and Vienna. His piano style is always definitely conceived for the piano, although most of his 117 piano pieces are insignificant when compared with the rest of his output. Piano works: *Bagatelles, Six Impromptus, Kylikki, Lyric Pieces,* a sonata, three sonatinas, and many character pieces.

siciliano (It.),

sicilienne (Fr.). Sicilian. A moderately slow dance of pastoral character in $\frac{6}{8}$ or $\frac{12}{8}$ meter, with lilting rhythms, simple melodies, and clear harmonies, much the same as the *pastorale.* Composers who have written *sicilianos* for piano include Richard Arnell, Alfredo Casella, Anis Fuleihan, Alexandre Guilmant, Madeleine Panzera, Scarlatti, Germaine Tailleferre, and Svend Tarp.

Sighing Wind. Felix Mendelssohn, op. 102, no. 4, in G Minor, one of the *Songs without Words.*

sight-reading. Reading a piece of music without rehearsal or specific preparation; playing music the first time it is set before a performer.

signe (Fr.). Sign.

Siki, Béla (b. 1923). Hungarian pianist and teacher, he was trained at the Liszt Academy in Budapest, where he made his debut. He performed throughout Europe. He taught for many years at the University of Washington and wrote the book *Piano Repertoire—A Guide to Interpretation and Performance.*

Silbermann, Gottfried (1683–1753). German maker of organs, clavichords, and fortepianos. J. S. Bach did not like his fortepianos of the 1730s but approved of one he played in 1747 at the court of Frederick the Great. Bach conceived the three-part *ricercar* from the *Musical Offering* on this instrument.

silence (Fr.), **silenzio** (It.). A rest, pause.

Siloti, Alexander (1863–1945). Russian pianist, he studied at the Moscow Conservatory with Nicolai Rubinstein and with Liszt between 1883 and 1886. He taught at the Moscow Conservatory, and later settled in the United States and taught at The Juilliard School for many years. He was an older cousin of Sergei Rachmaninoff and the dedicatee of Rachmaninoff's First Piano Concerto and of his *10 Preludes*. Siloti made wonderful transcriptions and composed a few original compositions. His students included composer Marc Blitzstein, Dexter, Alexander Goldenweiser, and Rachmaninoff.

simile, sim. (It.). Similarly, in the same way; play as before.

Simon, Abbey (b. 1921). American pianist and teacher, he studied with Saperton at the Curtis Institute. After winning many prizes, including the Naumberg Competition in 1941, he began concertizing and has played all over the world. He teaches at The Juilliard School and has made many recordings. His main repertoire is from the Romantic period, but he branches out to 20th century from time to time. His approach to the music is always full of taste plus great imagination.

sin' (It.). Abbreviation of *sino:* To, up to, until. *sin' al fine* (or *al segno*): a direction to repeat the preceding section up to the place marked *fine* (or to the sign).

Sinding, Christian (1856–1941). Norwegian composer and pianist, he studied at the Leipzig Conservatory and enjoyed wide fame in his lifetime. His most famous piano piece is *Rustle of Spring*, op. 32, no. 3.

sinfonia (It.). Symphony. J. S. Bach used this term for his Three-Part Inventions as well as the opening movement of his *Partita* no. 2 in C Minor. Other composers writing *sinfonias* for piano are Alfredo Casella and Vivian Fine, among others.

singend (Ger.). In a singing style.

singhiozzando (It.). Sobbing.

sinistra (It.). Left (hand).

s'inviter (Fr.). Invitingly.

Six, Les. French group of composers: Georges Auric, Louis Durey,

Arthur Honegger, Milhaud, Poulenc, and Germaine Tailleferre. Poulenc was the most important. They were influenced by Satie and author Jean Cocteau's anti-Romantic aesthetic.

"Sixths" Etude (or Study). Frédéric Chopin, Etude in D-flat Major, op. 25, no. 8, 1832–34. So nicknamed because of the extensive use of sixths in the piece.

sketch, *Skizze* (Ger.), ***esquisse*** (Fr.). 1. A composer's preliminary jottings of their ideas for a work. Beethoven's sketchbooks show the many stages he went through before he arrived at the final form of a piece. 2. Short piece, usually for piano. Composers who wrote piano pieces with this title include Alkan, Anton Arensky, Balakirev, Bartók, Ernest Bloch, Frank Bridge, Debussy, Grieg, Ives, MacDowell, Martinů, Nikolai Medtner, Milhaud, Mompou, Prokofiev, Rachmaninoff, Schumann, and Smetana.

slargando (It.). Becoming gradually slower.

Slavonic Dances. Antonin Dvořák, opp. 46 and 72, 1878 and 1886. Two sets of dances (16) in folk styles for piano duet, later orchestrated.

Slenczynska, Ruth (b. 1925). American pianist and teacher, she studied with her father and various teachers. As a child prodigy she was exploited; her autobiography *Forbidden Childhood* tells this story. Her other book, *Music at Your Fingertips,* deals with developing a piano technique. She taught at Southern Illinois University at Edwardsville for many years. Her playing has great spontaneity and stylistic precision.

slentando (It.). Becoming gradually slower.

slur. A curved line over (or under) two notes indicating they are to be played *legato,* with slightly more emphasis placed on the first one and less on the second one as the hand lifts off.

Smetana, Bedřich (1824–84). Czech composer and pianist, he was the first major nationalist composer of Bohemia. He explored the Czech national dance form (the polka) the way Chopin investigated the mazurka. All of Smetana's polkas are an important and too much neglected part of the nationalistic piano repertoire. Piano works: *Bagatelles and Impromptus, Concert Study "On the Seashore," Czech Dances* (two books), *Six Bohemian Dances, Six Characteristic Pieces, Six Dreams, Three Poetic Polkas, 10 Polkas, Sketches,* a sonata, *Three Wedding Scenes.*

sminuendo (It.). *Diminuendo.*

smorzando (It.). Smothered; dying away, fading, *morendo.* The direction affects dynamics, not tempo.

soave (It.). Gentle, suave, smooth, sweet.

soft pedal. See *una corda.*

sognando (It.). Dreaming, dreamily.

sol (It.) The fifth degree of the scale, or the note or tonality (key) G.

solenne (It.), **solennel** (Fr.). Solemn.

Soler, Padre Antonio (1729–83). Spanish composer, organist and harpsichordist who was active at the monastery at El Escorial. He composed many one-movement sonatas like Scarlatti. Later he wrote sonatas in three and four movements, or around 200 sonatas altogether. He also composed a most colorful *fandango* for keyboard, plus he wrote a treatise on modulation.

solfegietto, solfeggio, solfeggieto (It.). A short etude-like piece. An excellent example is that in C minor by C. P. E. Bach, who composed four *solfegiettos.*

solide (Fr.). Strong, stable.

Soliloquy. David del Tredici (b. 1937), 1956. Great cohesion achieved through close motivic control and Debussy-like sonorities. A major contribution to the repertoire.

Solomon (Solomon Cutner) (1902–88). English pianist, child prodigy, and student of Cortot. He made his debut at age eight in London playing the Tchaikovsky First Piano Concerto. He had a superb concert career that was cut short by a stroke he had in his fifties.

somber (Fr.). Gloomy, dull, heavy, somber.

sombrio (Sp.). Gloomy, hazy, dark.

son (Fr.). Sound.

sonata (It.). 1. A sound(ing) piece. 2. An instrumental composition, usually for a solo instrument, in two to five contrasting movements. At least one of the movements often uses sonata-allegro form.

Sonata Fantasy. Alexander Scriabin, Sonata no. 2 in G-sharp Minor, op. 19, 1892–97. This was subtitled by the composer. He said about this work: "The second sonata reflects the influence of the sea. The first movement represents a warm quiet night on a seashore. The development section is the dark agitation of the deep, deep ocean. The E major middle section shows caressing moonlight on the water coming after the first darkness of night. The second movement represents the vast expanse of the ocean when it is stormy and agitated" (Bowers, *Scriabin*, vol. 1, p. 226).

"Sonata of Insects." See "Trill" Sonata.

Sonatas and Interludes. John Cage, 1946–48. For prepared piano, this 70-minute work includes a kit to prepare 45 tones. Sonatas are one page in length. This set of pieces is Cage's "Well Tampered Piano"!

sonata-allegro form. A ternary form usually applied in the first movement of a sonata. It usually treats two or three themes set in the form of exposition, development, recapitulation, and sometimes coda. See entries for each of these terms.

sonata-rondo form. A combination of sonata and rondo forms. It is a ternary form: exposition, middle section, and recapitulation. The middle section may be an episode in a related key, or a development may take place.

Sonate écossaise. See "Scottish" Sonata.

***Sonate facile* (Easy Sonata).** This name was given by its earliest publishers to Mozart's Sonata in C Major, K. 545. Mozart himself described it as "for beginners."

sonatina (It.). A little, short, undeveloped (i.e., without a proper development section) sonata. Usually in two or three movements, sometimes written as one longer movement. This form flourished in the Classical period, but during the 20th-century composers like Busoni, Luigi Dallapiccola, and Ravel have written difficult *sonatinas.*

song. Usually for voice but many piano composers have composed "songs" for the piano; the pieces are usually melodically oriented. These composers include Albéniz, Balakirev, Bartók, Beethoven, Marcel Dupré, Percy Faith, Franck, Niels Gade, Grieg, Alexandre Guilmant, Reynaldo Hahn, Alan Hovhaness, Vincent d'Indy, André Jolivet, Charles Jones, Liszt, MacDowell, Mendelssohn, Peter Mennin, Mompou, Paderewski, Saint-Saëns, Sibelius, and Tchaikovsky.

Song of the Pilgrim. Felix Mendelssohn, op. 67, no. 3, in B-flat Major, one of the *Songs without Words.*

Song of the Traveler. Felix Mendelssohn, op. 85, no. 6, in B-flat Major, one of the *Songs without Words.*

Songs without Words. Felix Mendelssohn. This collection consists of 48 pieces published in eight books of six pieces in each book composed over a period of two decades. Most of these pieces reflect the sunniest qualities of Mendelssohn's melodiousness, spontaneity, and invention. Mendelssohn gave titles to only five of these pieces: the three *Venetian Boat Songs,* nos. 6, 12, and 29; *Duet,* no. 18; and *Folk Song,* no. 23. Heller supplied some of the other titles, and others came from publishers. Mendelssohn got the idea of the title "Songs without Words" from his older sister Fanny. A definite program is not suggested by each piece but rather an impression, an atmosphere suggested by the composer's imagination.

sonner (Fr.). To sound.

Sonneries de la rose + croix (Trumpet Calls of the Rose + Cross). Erik Satie, 1892. A suite for solo piano: *Air de l'ordre* (Air of the Order), *Air du Grand Maître* (Air of the Grand Master), *Air du Grand Prieur* (Air of the Head Prior).

sonore, sonora (It.). Sonorous, resonant, clear, emphatic.

sonority. The tonal quality (sound) of a pianist produced on a piano; resonance.

Sons et les parfums tournent dans l'air du soir, Les (Sounds and Scents Mingle in the Evening Air). Claude Debussy, *Préludes,* book 1, no. 4, 1910. This seductive waltz ($^3_4$ + $^2_4$) was inspired by a line from Charles Baudelaire's *Les fleurs du mal.*

sopre (It.). Above. A direction for a keyboard performer to play with one hand over the other (crossed hands).

sordina, sordino, sord. (It.). Mute or damper.

sortant de la brume (Fr.). Coming out of the mist.

sospirando, sospirante (It.). Sighing, very subdued, plaintive, sobbing, mournful.

sostenuto (It.). Sustained. 1. In a smooth manner, *legato:* this meaning is valid for the early Romantic composers like Chopin, Liszt, and Mendelssohn. 2. For Brahms it means stretching, broadening, getting slower. 3. For Bartók it means to slow down immediately and keep that slower tempo until the composer gives other tempo instructions, for example, *poco accelerando,* etc.

sostenuto pedal. Sustaining pedal. See pedal.

sotto voce (It.). In an undertone; softly, subdued, without emphasis.

soudain (Fr.). Sudden.

Soul States. See États d'âme.

soundboard. Term used for the thin piece of fir or other resonant wood used in the construction of the piano, placed under or behind the strings to amplify the sounded tones by sympathetic vibration.

soupirant (Fr.). Sighing.

souple (Fr.). Flexible, supple.

sourd (Fr.). Veiled, soft, muffled.

sourdement (Fr.). Subdued, with a dull sound.

sourdine (Fr.). 1. A mute; muted. 2. *una corda* pedal.

sourdine durant toute la pièce (Fr.). Use *una corda* (soft) pedal throughout the entire piece.

sourdine mais f (Fr.). Muted, but loud.

sourdine toujours (Fr.). Use *una corda* pedal throughout.

sous (Fr.). Under, below.

soutenir (Fr.). To sustain.

soutenu (Fr.). Sustained.

Souvenir d'Andalousie (Souvenir of Andalusia). Frédéric Chopin, Bolero, op. 19, 1833. The English edition used this title.

Souvenir de Paganini. Frédéric Chopin, Variations in A Major, BI 37, 1829. The theme of these variations is the Venetian air "Le carnaval de Venise" (Carnival of Venice) used by Paganini as the basis of variations in his op. 10. Ludwik Bronarski suggested that Paganini may have played this opus during his visit to Warsaw on 23 May 1829 and that Chopin heard him play it and was inspired to write these variations (Brown, p. 41).

Souvenirs. Samuel Barber, 1952. Originally for piano duet, solo piano version by the composer. Light and an exploration of dance forms, it evokes ballroom music around the time of the First World War: *Waltz, Schottische, Pas de deux, Two-step, Hesitation-Tango, Galop.*

Spanish Rhapsody. Franz Liszt, S. 254, 1863. Free variations on two contrasting Spanish themes, which are transformed to extraordinary effect. It opens with one of Liszt's finest cadenzas, using blind octaves.

spasshaft (Ger.). Play in a lively, playful manner; jocose, merry, *scherzando.*

sperdendosi (It.). Fading away.

spianato (It.). Tranquil, smooth, even.

Spiel, spielen (Ger.). Play, to play.

spinet (Fr.). Originally a small harpsichord. Today it is used to designate a lower (in height) version of the upright piano with 88 keys. The smallest of modern pianos.

Spinning Song. Felix Mendelssohn, op. 67, no. 4, in C Major, one of the *Songs without Words*. Also known as *The Bee's Wedding*.

spiritoso (It.). Spirited, lively, fire, energy.

spiritual. A type of syncopated religious song especially developed by African Americans in the southern United States. Simple melodies plus rhythmic syncopations make for an interesting body of material. The *Twenty-Four Negro Melodies* by Samuel Coleridge-Taylor are a most interesting collection of pieces based on spirituals.

spiritual (Fr.). 1. Religious. 2. Witty, sprightly.

split keyboard. An electronic keyboard that can be divided into two parts that produce different sounds.

Spring Song. Felix Mendelssohn, op. 62, no. 6, in A Major, one of the *Songs without Words*.

spun string. A string overspun with fine (thin) wire.

square piano. A piano with a horizontal rectangle case that was popular from the late 18th through the 19th century; it varied in size.

staccato (It.). Detached, separated. Indicated with a dot or wedge above or below the note: The opposite of legato.

staccatissimo: as detached as possible. The wedge indication came into use during Beethoven's lifetime. Haydn used the dot, wedge, and slash (') to indicate the same thing (*staccato*).

"Stalingrad" Sonata. Sergei Prokofiev, Sonata, no. 7 in B-flat Major, op. 83, 1939–42. Part of this sonata was composed during the heroic stand and final victory of the Red Army at Stalingrad. Its power and grandeur reflect the heroism that turned the tide at Stalingrad. With this sonata, Prokofiev won the Stalin Prize (Berkowitz, p. 150).

stark (Ger.). Strong, vigorous.

Stark, Lucien (b. 1929). American pianist and teacher, he studied at Drake University, the Paris Conservatoire, The Juilliard School, and the University of Michigan. He toured the United States and Mexico, gaining solid reviews. He taught at the University of Kentucky for many years.

steigern (Ger.). To intensify, increase.

Stein. German firm of piano makers founded by Johann Andreas Stein

(1728–92) in Augsburg. Mozart praised the escapement and damper mechanisms of his instruments. Soon after Stein's daughter Nanette married the Viennese musician Johann Andreas Streicher, the workshop moved to Vienna. Beethoven used a Stein piano when he lived in Vienna.

Steinway and Sons. American firm of piano manufacturers established in New York in 1853 by Heinrich Engelhard Steinway (Steinweg) (1797–1871). A Hamburg branch opened in 1880. It is considered one of the finest pianos in the world.

stendendo (It.). Stretching out, slowing.

stentando (It.). Delaying, retarding, labored, halting.

sterbend (Ger.). Dying away, gradually growing softer.

Sternberg, Constantin (1852–1924). Russian-American pianist, he studied with Moscheles at the Leipzig Conservatory and later with Theodor Kullak (1818–82) as well as Liszt. He toured Russia, and in 1880 he went to the United States. He established the Sternberg School of Music in Philadelphia in 1890 and directed it until his death. Sternberg was highly admired as a piano teacher and taught composer George Antheil and Samaroff.

steso (It.). Stretched, slow.

Steuermann, Edward (1892–1964). Polish pianist and teacher, he studied with Busoni. He toured Europe and came to the United States in 1936, where he taught at The Juilliard School until his death. He was a highly intellectual pianist who played the standard repertoire but who also had a strong interest in music of the 20th century. Steuermann gave the first performance of Schoenberg's Piano Concerto in 1944. He was greatly admired as a teacher. His students include Kenneth Amada, Brendel, Jakob Gimpel, Joseph Kalichstein, Kraus, and Sherman.

Stil (Ger.), *stilo* (It.). Style, manner.

still (Ger.). Peaceful.

Stimmung (Ger.). 1. Mood. 2. Pitch, tuning.

Stimmungsbild (Ger.). Mood picture: a piece intended to express some particular mood. Richard Strauss composed five *Stimmungsbilder.*

stinguendo (It.). Fading away.

Stockhausen, Karlheinz (b. 1928). German composer, he studied with Olivier Messiaen. He is a pioneer in electronic music. In 1952 Stockhausen began a cycle of 21 piano pieces; so far only 11 of the pieces have been completed. In many ways the writing is pianistic, usually taking advantage of the entire keyboard. It is conceivable that these pieces might eventually be considered 20th-century piano classics.

straccinato (It.). Stretched out; same as *ritardando.*

straff (Ger.). Tense, rigid, strict.

strascicando, strascinando (It.). Dragging.

Stravinsky, Igor (1882–1971). Russian composer, he studied with Nikolai Rimsky-Korsakov. He took up French citizenship in 1934 and United States citizenship in 1945. He was one of the giants of the 20th century, but his piano works, while varied and interesting, are not as important as his works in other media. His piano works include *Four Etudes, Les cinq doigts* (The Five Fingers, eight easy pieces), *Piano Rag-Music, Serenade en la,* two sonatas, a transcription of three movements from his ballet *Petrouchka,* and short pieces. For piano and orchestra: Concerto for Piano and Wind Instruments, *Capriccio,* and *Movements.* He also arranged his ballet *Le sacre du printemps* for piano duet.

Streicher. Austrian firm of piano makers founded in 1802 when the daughter (Nanette) of Johann Andreas Stein married Johann Andreas Streicher (1761–1833), a pianist, composer, and teacher. Streicher became the most famous firm in Vienna, and Beethoven gave advice regarding the manufacturing process.

strepitoso (It.). Noisy, loud, boisterous, impetuous.

stretto (It.). 1. Pressing on, faster tempo. 2. In a fugue *stretto* occurs when the subject and the answer follow each other so closely that they overlap.

strictement au même mouvement durant tout le morceau (Fr.). Adhere strictly to the same tempo for the entire piece.

strictement en mesure (Fr.). Strictly in tempo.

strident (Fr.). Jarring, shrill, strident.

stringendo (It.). Hurrying, accelerating the tempo; perform with more intensity.

Structure. Willard Straight (b. 1930). The commissioned piece for the 1966 Van Cliburn Piano Competition.

Stück (Ger.). Piece, composition.

studio piano. A very low upright piano.

study. See *étude.*

Sturm und Drang (Ger.). Storm and stress. An 18th-century movement in German letters which portrayed emotions in a highly dramatic manner (to frighten, to stress, to overcome with emotion), a subjective approach to the arts. It influenced Haydn, Mozart, and Beethoven, among others. Good examples of its influence in their keyboard works would include Haydn's Sonata in C Minor, Hob. 20; Mozart's Sonata in A Minor, K. 310; and Beethoven's Sonata in C Minor, op. 13 (*Pathétique*).

style. 1. The characteristics of a composer's work relating to technical and aesthetic concepts. 2. The choices of the manner of mode of a performance. 3. The comparative analysis of the works of composers of various musical eras.

suave (Sp.). Smooth; quiet, delicate, tranquil, gentle.

subito (It.). Now, quickly, immediately.

subito piano (It.). Suddenly quiet (soft).

subject. 1. The basic theme, motif, tune, or melody of a composition. 2. In a fugue, the theme or subject appearing in the exposition. 3. In a sonata, the first and second themes appearing in the exposition.

Sufferings of the Queen of France, The. Jan Ladislav Dussek, 1793. An unusual piece of program music in 10 movements that expresses the feelings of Marie Antoinette during her imprisonment.

suite. A form of Baroque composition involving a series or set of movements mostly in dance forms; some movements were not dance forms: *allemande, courante, sarabande, gigue* were dance movements. *Bourrée, gavotte, menuet,* and *passepied* were some of the optional dances that were inserted before the *gigue.* The *air, sinfonia, praeambulum, toccata,* and *fantasia* were nondance movements used. J. S. Bach's French and English suites and Partitas are important works in this genre. Later composers also wrote sets of pieces that they called suites, though not always characterized by dance forms.

Suite Bergamasque. Claude Debussy, 1905. A suite of four pieces: *Prélude, Menuet, Clair de lune, Passepied,* reflecting older styles.

suivez (Fr.). Follow, continue, go on. See *attacca.*

suppliant (Fr.). Beseeching, entreating.

sur (Fr.). On, upon, over.

sur la m.d. (Fr.). With the right hand.

surtout (Fr.). Above all, especially, chiefly.

surtout sans ralentir (Fr.). Absolutely without *ritard.*

sussurrando, sussurrante (It.). Whispering.

sustaining pedal. See pedal.

svelto (It.). Quick, nimble.

Sweet Remembrance. Felix Mendelssohn, op. 19, no. 1, in E Major, one of the *Songs without Words.*

syncopation. A shifting or displacement of the usual accent or beat, caused by tying a weak beat to a strong beat. Ragtime and jazz and other popular music make much use of this technique.

synthesizer. An electronic keyboard instrument. Synthesizers can produce a piano sound or an orchestral one and all varieties in between.

Szymanowski, Karol (1882–1937). Polish composer, he studied in Warsaw. He spent time in Russia and was director of the Warsaw Conservatory from 1927 to 1932. Chopin, Scriabin, Richard Strauss, Debussy, and Stravinsky all influenced Szymanowski, and yet he was an original composer. He began to employ Polish folk elements in his music during the 1920s. The later works, which became very personal and unique in style, stamped Szymanowski as one of the most creative artists in the early 20th century. Piano works: *12 Études masques, 20 Mazurkas, Métopes,* nine preludes, three sonatas, *Variations on a Polish Folk Song.* For piano and orchestra: *Symphonie concertante.*

T

T. Abbreviation for trill, *tutti, tempo, tasto.*

tacet (Lat.). "He (or she) is silent," a performer is silent for a time; usually found in orchestral scores.

tack piano. See prepared piano.

Tafelklavier (Ger.). See square piano.

Tagliaferro, Magda (1893–1986). Brazilian pianist and teacher, she studied at the São Paulo Conservatory and the Paris Conservatoire. She had a very successful career as concert pianist and teacher before being appointed to the faculty of the São Paulo Conservatory in 1937. Tagliaferro toured the Americas, where she resided during World War II. She resumed her career in Paris in 1949. She is the dedicatee of Villa-Lobos's *Momoprecoce* for piano and orchestra. Her students include Christian Ortiz, Lennart Rabes, and Tocco.

Takt (Ger.). Beat, measure, time. *im Takt:* rhythmically correct, in strict tempo.

tangents. The brass blades that are activated from the keyboard of a clavichord. Key action causes a tangent to strike a string, and sound will continue as long as the key is depressed.

tango. A moderately slow popular Argentinean dance in duple meter, with a syncopated rhythmic pattern similar to the *habanera*. Piano tangos have been composed by J. J. Castro, Alois Hába, Anthony Hopkins, Martinû, Francisco Mignone, Paul Pisk, Erwin Schulhoff, Nikos Skalkottas, Stravinsky, and Jean Wiéner, among others.

Tansman, Alexandre (1897–1986). Polish composer and pianist, his Warsaw debut was in 1912. He settled in Paris after World War I, and he continued to tour and compose. He settled in the United States during World War II. He was a distinguished pianist and composer whose piano works include *Arabesques, Three Ballades, Eight Cantilenas, Four Impressions,* intermezzi, mazurkas, *Four Nocturnes, Three Preludes in the Form of Blues,* five sonatas, *Sonatine transatlantique* (showing jazz influence), *Suite variée,* and two piano concertos, two *Partitas* for piano and orchestra, and a suite for two pianos and orchestra.

tant (Fr.). As much, much.

tanto (It.). So much, as much, too much.

Tanz (Ger.). Dance.

tape music. Music that uses the phonograph and tape recorder to combine, modify, and store "natural sounds." Numerous composers have written compositions for tape recorder and piano, among them Milton Babbitt, Mario Davidovsky, William Doppmann, Luis Escobar, Jean Ivey, Barbara Kolb, Alcides Lanza, Barton McLean, Luigi Nono, Claudio Santoro, Morton Subotnick, and Anatol Vieru.

taper (Fr.). To strike the key.

tarantella (It.). A lively Italian dance in $\frac{6}{8}$ meter that originated in southern Italy. Composers writing *tarantellas* for piano include Chopin, Mikhail Glinka, Alexandre Guilmant, Liszt, MacDowell, Giuseppe Martucci, Gabriel Pierné, Poulenc, Joachim Raff, Gioacchino Rossini, Anton Rubinstein, and Xaver Scharwenka.

Tarantella. Felix Mendelssohn, op. 102, no. 3, in C Major, one of the *Songs without Words.*

tardamente (It.). Slow. *tardando:* lingering.

tardando (It.). Delaying, slowing, retarding.

tardif (Fr.). Lingering.

tardo (It.). Play in a slow tempo.

Taste (Ger.). A key of a keyboard.

tasto (It.). The keys of a piano or organ; touch. *tasto solo:* play bass notes only with no added harmonies (chords).

tattoo (It.). Touch, feeling, tactile.

Tausig, Karl (1841–71). Polish pianist, he studied with Liszt. Some contemporaries believed Tausig surpassed Liszt and Thalberg in sheer pianistic technique. He had a brilliant concert career and founded an academy for master students in Berlin. Tausig left more transcriptions than original works for the piano, but he did write for solo piano *Two Concert Etudes, Ballade, 10 Preludes, Réminiscences de Halke—Moniuszko* (Reminiscences of Halke), *Ungarische Ziguenerweisen* (Hungarian Gypsy Tunes), and *3 Valses-Caprices d'après J. Strauss* (3 Valse-Caprices after J. Strauss).

Tchaikovsky, Peter Ilyich (1840–93). Russian composer, he studied at the St. Petersburg Conservatory with Anton and Nikolai Rubinstein. In 1865 N. Rubinstein opened the Moscow Conservatory and invited Tchaikovsky to join it as professor of harmony. He composed around 100 pieces for piano including *Album for the Young, Dumka, 12 Etudes, The Seasons,* two sonatas, *Theme and Variations,* plus three piano concertos and a *Concert Fantasy* for piano and orchestra.

Tcherepnin, Alexander (1899–1977). Russian composer, he studied at the St. Petersburg Conservatory and in Paris with Philipp. He made his London debut in 1922 with his own works and his U.S. debut in 1927 and toured extensively. He lived in Paris during World War II. Between the wars he studied music in China and Japan and as a result wrote a *Method for Piano on the Pentatonic Scale.* He taught at DePaul University in Chicago, where his students included Robert Muczynski. Tcherepnin's piano works included bagatelles, *12 Episodes, 10 Expressions,* etudes, *Nine Inventions,* nocturnes, *Petite suite,* preludes, *Four Romances,* two sonatas, *Five Songs without Words, Toccata,* and numerous other character pieces; also six piano concertos and three other works for piano and orchestra.

technique (Fr.), ***Technic, Technik*** (Ger). The purely mechanical part of playing or singing, refers to the individual style and ability of a performer or composer.

tecia (Sp.). Key, keyboard, keyboard instrument.

tedesco (It.). Term for German dances; it was sometimes used for the *allemande,* and by Beethoven for music in the style of a *deutscher Tanz.* See his Sonata in G Major, op. 79, first movement: *Presto alla tedesco.*

tema (It.). Theme, subject, melody.

"Tempest" Sonata. Ludwig van Beethoven, Sonata in D Minor, op. 31, no. 2, 1802. So called because Beethoven said, regarding its meaning: "Read Shakespeare's *Tempest.*"

tempestoso (It.). Tempestuous, stormy.

tempo (It.). Time as regards speed; the pace at which a composition is to be performed.

tempo ballo (It.). Dance time.

tempo commodo (It.). Comfortable, easy movement.

tempo di ronda giocosa quasi presto (It.). In the tempo of a cheerful round, almost presto.

tempo giusto (It.). Strict, exact time.

tempo marcia (It.). March time.

tempo marks. Indications of the speed of a composition or section. Some of these are (from slow to fast) *largo* to *presto*. Gradual changes in tempo are designated by terms like *accelerando* and *ritardando.*

tempo ordinario (It.). 1. Common time, $\frac{4}{4}$. 2. A tempo neither especially fast or slow.

tempo primo (It.). Return to the original tempo.

tempo rubato. See *rubato.*

temps (Fr.). Beat time, beat.

temps de même valeur (Fr.). Keep the beat the same.

temps ont exactement la même valeur, les (Fr.). The beats have exactly the same value.

ten. Abbreviation for *tenuto.*

tender, tendrement (Fr.). Tender, tenderly.

tenebroso (It.). Gloomy.

tenendo (It.). Sustaining.

teneramente (It.). Tenderly.

tenez bien (Fr.). Pay attention to.

tenir (Fr.). 1. To hold, to keep. 2. To perform, to do.

tenir l'accord sans pédale (Fr.). Hold the chord without pedal.

tenir par la pédale (Fr.). Hold with the pedal.

tension. 1. The imbalance created within an artistic work by dissonance, the opposite of consonance. 2. Mental or nervous strain, often accompanied by muscular tautness.

tenu (Fr.). Sustained tone; pedal tone.

tenuto, ten. (It.). Held, sustained. In the 18th century, notes so marked were to be held for their full value, rather than detached somewhat, as was the norm. In the 19th century and following, the term may call for a slight delay of the beat following. A *tenuto* mark is indicated by a short horizontal stroke over or under the note: .

tenuto **touch.** Holding keys longer than the score indicates. This procedure provides textural and tonal contrast and provides a kind of finger pedaling. It is especially helpful in Baroque keyboard music and in Alberti basses in the Classical period.

tercet (Fr.), *terzina* (It.). A triplet.

ternary form. A three-part form or structure (ABA) in which the third part is an exact or varied repetition of the first part. Also called *song form* or *da capo form*. The *minuet* (or *scherzo*, in its early manifestation) of a sonata is in ternary form, the middle section called a *trio*.

ternura (Sp.). Tenderness, sensitiveness.

***Terrasse des audiences du clair de lune, La* (The Terrace for Moonlight Audiences).** Claude Debussy, *Préludes*, book 2, no. 7, 1913. A phrase from the folksong *Au clair de lune* forms the main motive of this imaginative work. It is a masterpiece of symbolic expressiveness.

tertian harmony. Harmony based on thirds, the traditional (before 1900) basis for Western music.

Thalberg, Sigismund (1812–71). Austrian pianist and composer, born in Switzerland, he was called a "god at the keyboard" by Schumann. He was famous for bringing out the melody with his thumbs while surrounding it with elaborate figuration, making it sound as though he had three hands. Most of his piano works were fantasies on popular operas of the day. He contributed to the *Hexameron* variations.

thematic catalog. A list of compositions of an individual composer, using the opening notes as a means of identification. The catalogers of major piano composers are: *J. S. Bach*, (Wolfgang) Schmieder. BWV number stands for *Bach Werke Verzeichnis* (Bach Works Catalog). The Schmieder number and the BWV number are the same. *C. P. E. Bach*, (Eugene) Helm. *Beethoven*, (Georg) Kinsky and (Hans) Halm. *Chopin*, (Maurice J. E.) Brown (the Brown Index abbreviated BI) and Krystyna Kobylanska (abbreviated KK). *Haydn,* (Anthony von) Hoboken (abbreviated Hob.). *Liszt,* Humphrey Searle (abbreviated S.). *Mozart,* (Ludwig von) Köchel (abbreviated K.). *Scarlatti,* (Ralph) Kirkpatrick (abbreviated as K. or Kp.); this replaces the older catalog of Alessandro Longo. *Schubert,* (Otto E.) Deutsch (abbreviated D.).

theme. 1. A subject. 2. A musical motto which serves as the basis of a composition or movement.

theme and variations. A musical form in which the theme (subject) is initially heard, and each succeeding section (variation) offers some variety on or modification of the theme. Sometimes the harmony is the subject of the variation. Many composers have written sets of theme and variations.

theremin. A space-controlled electronic instrument developed by the Russian composer Lev Theremin (1896–1993). "Space controlled" means that it is played by movements of the hands, which do not touch the instrument. The instrument was further developed by Robert Moog and was used by the Beach Boys in their hit *Good Vibrations.* It is purely a melodic instrument.

Third Stream. This term originated with Gunther Schuller to describe a style that attempts to fuse elements of jazz and Western art music. The piano music of Claude Bolling (b. 1930) is an excellent example of Third Stream style.

"Thirds" Etude or Study. Frédéric Chopin, Etude in G-sharp Minor, op. 25, no. 6, 1832–34. So called because of the extensive use of thirds.

Thomson, Virgil (1896–1989). American composer and critic, he was educated at Harvard University and in Paris, where he studied with Boulanger. He was influenced by the writer Jean Cocteau, Satie, *Les Six,* Stravinsky, and his operatic collaborator Gertrude Stein. Brilliant and objective, Thomson was a musical commentator on America. His piano works include *10 Easy Pieces and a Coda,* 19 *Etudes,* 58 *Portraits,* and four sonatas.

Thorn(e), Edgar. Pseudonyms for Edward MacDowell, under which he published the following pieces: *Amourette; In Lilting Rhythm; Forgotten Fairy Tales: Sung Outside the Prince's Door, Of a Tailor and a Bear, Beauty in the Rose-Garden, From Dwarfland; Six Fancies: A Tin Soldier's Love, To a Humming Bird, Summer Song, Across Fields, Bluette, An Elfin Round.*

thorough bass. See *basso continuo.*

through-composed. A composition with no internal repetitions but that goes straight through without repeating any sections.

tie. A curved line placed between a note and its repetition (two notes of the same pitch) that shows the two should be performed as one unbroken note: it should be held for the combined values of the two (or more) tied notes.

tief (Ger.). Deep, low.

tierce de Picardie (Fr.). Picardy third. The practice of ending a composition in the minor mode on a major chord by chromatically raising the third to major of the final chord in the perfect cadence.

Tierces alternées, Les **(Alternating Thirds).** Claude Debussy, *Préludes*, book 2, no. 11, 1913. This brilliant study uses rapid alternation of hands, one more static than the other. It is the only prelude without an extra-musical title and anticipates Debussy's *Études* of 1915.

timbre (Fr.). Tone color, quality of sound. A piano and a clarinet sounding the same pitch produce different timbres.

Timbrell, Charles (b. 1942). American pianist and writer, he studied at the Oberlin Conservatory of Music with Emil Danenberg, the University of Michigan with Dexter, and the University of Maryland with Gordon. He has also worked with Guido Agosti, Monique Haas, and Gaby Casadesus. He has performed extensively throughout the United States and Europe. His articles have appeared in numerous national and international journals. Timbrell has written *French Pianism: An Historical Perspective* and currently teaches at Howard University. His playing is colorful, strong, and focuses on a masterly sense of content and form.

timbrez légèrement la petite note (Fr.). Sound the grace note lightly.

time signature. Normally used for meter, that is, the number of beats in a measure: $\frac{3}{4}$, $\frac{4}{4}$, etc. It is better to use the term "meter" instead of "time," to avoid confusion with *tempo*.

timide (Fr.). Fearful, shy.

Tippett, Michael (1905–98). English composer, he studied at the Royal College of Music in London. His dissonant style stems from Bartók and Hindemith and displays wide skips and other gesticulative thematic elements as well as occasional use of texture and sonority for their own sake. His four piano sonatas are a fine contribution to the repertoire.

tirando (It.). Dragging.

toccata (It.). A "touch" piece. In the nineteenth and twentieth centuries a brilliant composition resembling somewhat the modern etude, generally designed to display a performer's technique and dexterity. Many composers have written toccatas for the piano, including J. S. Bach, Balakirev, Clementi, Czerny, Dohnányi, Debussy, Roy Harris, Gustav Holst, Arthur Honegger, Jacques Ibert, Aram Khachaturian, Benjamin Lees, Liszt, Martinů, Peter Mennin, Robert Muczynski, Paderewski, Poulenc, Prokofiev, Ravel, and Schumann.

toccatina (It.). A short (little) toccata. The *Toccatina* by Kabalevsky is one of the best-known.

Tocco, James (b. 1943). American pianist and teacher, he has had a very successful career. He plays numerous concerts each season all over the world including performances with some of the major orchestras. Tocco has won many awards and gave the first performance of John Corigliano's *Etude Fantasy*. He has made many recordings and taught at Indiana University; he presently teaches at the University of Cincinnati. Tocco is a brilliant and highly sensitive pianist.

tombeau (Fr.). A composition written in honor of someone deceased; a lament. Two well-known 20th-century examples are Debussy's *Hommage à Rameau* and Ravel's *Le tombeau de Couperin*.

Tombeau de Couperin, Le (The Tomb of Couperin). Maurice Ravel, 1917. Piano suite in six movements in honor of Couperin: *Prelude, Fugue, Forlane, Rigaudon, Menuet, Toccata*. Looking back to the French keyboard suite of the 18th century, it is in memory of friends of Ravel who died in World War I.

ton (Fr.). 1. Specific pitch, tone, sound. 2. Key or tonal center. 3. A musical style.

tonal. Exhibiting the characteristic of a system of keys (tonality) as distinct from modality and other systems of organizing pitch; a key center is present. Atonal music is the opposite of tonal music.

tonality. Organizing harmonic system of a piece based around a tonal (or key) center.

tone. 1. Sound. 2. Quality of sound, the good or bad qualities of a sound (gentle, percussive, dry, etc.). 3. American usage for note: 12-tone music and tone row instead of 12-note and note row.

tone cluster. Any group of highly dissonant notes closely spaced together simultaneously, usually produced by striking a large number of keys with the hand or arm. Cowell used the technique in his music from 1912.

tone color. See *timbre.*

tone row. Name used to denote any combination of the notes of the 12-note chromatic scale that may be chosen by a composer as the basis for a planned twelve-tone/serial work. Also called "note row."

Tonreihe (Ger.). See tone row.

Tonsatz, Tonstück (Ger.). Composition, piece.

Totentanz (Dance of Death). Franz Liszt, S. 126, 1849. Work for piano and orchestra, variations on the *Dies irae* (Day of Wrath) plainchant. Liszt creates an unearthly atmosphere of mingled horror and fantasy.

touch. 1. The art of depressing the piano keys so as to produce a musical tone. 2. The resistance of the piano keyboard.

touché baissée sans faire résonner (Fr.). Press down the keys silently.

toucher (Fr.). To touch or play; to finger.

toujours (Fr.). Always, still, nevertheless.

toujours animé (Fr.). Always lively.

toujours retenu (Fr.). Still holding back.

tour (Fr.). Turn, winding; manner, style.

tour de force (Fr.). 1. Brilliant, showy passage. 2. Masterful piece or performance.

tous, tout (Fr.). All.

tout à coup (Fr.). Suddenly.

tout de suite (Fr.). At once.

traduction (Fr.). Arrangement.

traduit (Fr.). Arranged.

"Tragica" Sonata. Edward MacDowell, Sonata no. 1 in G Major, op. 45, 1891–92. It has been suggested that the memory of MacDowell's grief over the death of his teacher Joachim Raff might have given him the idea for this work with its popular title "Tragica." The composer did say that in the first three movements he attempted to express tragic details, and in the finale he wanted to heighten the darkness of tragedy by making it follow closely on the heels of triumph (Berkowitz, p. 164).

traîné (Fr.). Dragged, slurred.

traîner (Fr.). To slur, spin out, drag (out), linger.

trait (Fr.). A brilliant or melodic passage or run.

***Traite d'harmonie du pianiste* (Treatise on Pianistic Harmony).** Friedrich Kalkbrenner, op. 185, 1891–92. Contains etudes, fugues, and preludes with an introduction by the composer.

tranquille et flottant (Fr.). Tranquil and floating.

tranquillo (It.). Tranquil, calm.

Transcendental Etudes. See *Études d'execution transcendente.*

transcription. An arrangement of a piece for some voice or instrument, or combination thereof, other than that for which it was originally intended. The art of transcription is very old. Outstanding transcriptions for piano (keyboard) include pieces by J.S. Bach, Bartók, Brahms, Busoni, Debussy, Godowsky, Grainger, Liszt, Poulenc, Prokofiev, Rachmaninoff, Ravel, Siloti, and Stravinsky.

transition. A bridge passage which leads from one well-defined section to another. A modulation is usually involved.

transporté (Fr.). Moved (with emotion), touched.

transpose, transposition. To write or perform a piece in a different key.

trascinare, trascinando (It.). To drag, dragging.

trattenuto (It.). Held back, *ritardando.*

tratto (It.). Drawn out.

Trauermarsch (Ger.). Funeral march.

Trauermusik (Ger.). Funeral music.

trauernd (Ger.). Mourning, lamenting.

***Trauerwalzer* (Funeral Waltz).** Franz Schubert, Waltz, op. 9, no. 2, in A-flat Major, D. 365/2. Publisher Cappi and Diabelli gave this title to this piece when it was published in 1829. It is no more "funereal" than the rest of op. 9.

***Traümerei* (Dreaming).** Robert Schumann, op. 15, no. 5, 1838. Probably the best-known piece from his *Kinderszenen.* It requires flexible phrasing and sensitive legato.

traümerisch (Ger.). Dreamy.

traurig (Ger.). Sad, mournful.

tre corde (It.). All three strings. In piano music a direction to release the left (*una corda,* soft) pedal.

treibend (Ger.). Driving, hurrying.

tremolo (It.). In piano music the fast repetition of a single pitch in a virtuosic work such as Liszt's *La Campanella*. It also occurs with quickly repeated octaves. String tremolo is sometimes imitated on the piano by fast alternation of several pitches of a chord.

trémolo très fondu, le (Fr.). The tremolo very much in the background.

trepak (Rus.). A Cossack dance in fast duple meter.

trépidant (Fr.). Vibrating, trembling, agitated.

très (Fr.). Very, most.

très allant, gracieux et souple (Fr.). Very spirited, graceful and supple.

très animé (Fr.). Very lively.

très apaisé (Fr.). Very subdued.

très atténué (Fr.). Very soft (quiet).

très calme et doucement expressif (Fr.). Very calm and gently expressive.

très chaud (Fr.). Very warm, passionate.

très décidée (Fr.). Very decisive, *marcato.*

très détaché (Fr.). Very detached, *staccato.*

très doux (Fr.). Very gentle, sweet, soft, delicate.

très doux et sans accentuation (Fr.). Very calm and without accentuation.

très doux et très espressif (Fr.). Very gentle and very expressive.

très éclatant (Fr.). Very brilliant.

très effacé (Fr.). Very much in the background, very subdued.

très également (Fr.). Very evenly.

très ému (Fr.). Deeply moved, moving; greatly excited.

très en dehors (Fr.). Very much brought out, *marcato.*

très enveloppé de pédales (Fr.). Covered with pedaling.

très enveloppé de pédales sans les changer (Fr.). Covered with pedal, without changing.

très estompé par les pédales (Fr.). Very blurred by the pedaling.

très fantaisiste (Fr.). Very imaginative.

très fort (Fr.). Very loud (strong).

très intérieur (Fr.). Very introspective.

très léger et fondu par la pédale (Fr.). Very light and indistinct, due to pedaling.

très léger, pas d'attaques profondes: à peu près sans pédale (Fr.). Very light, no heavy attacks, almost without pedal.

très lent (Fr.). Very slow.

très lié (Fr.). Very legato.

très luisant (Fr.). Very bright.

très mesure (Fr.). In strict time.

très modéré (Fr.). Very moderate.

très peu (Fr.). Very little.

très retenu (Fr.). Very held back: much *ritard.*

très souple (Fr.). Very flexible.

très soutenu de pédale (Fr.). Very sustained by the pedal.

très vif (Fr.). Very brisk.

Trésor des pianistes, Le (The Pianist's Treasures). The most complete collection of keyboard music ever assembled. About 250 of the works are available separately. Twenty-three volumes, compiled by Jacques and Louise Farrenc, published by Leduc (1861–72), reprinted by Da Capo (1977).

"Triangle" Concerto. Franz Liszt, Piano Concerto no. 1 in E-flat Major, S. 124, 1849. The use of a triangle in the finale of the score of this work caused some discussion in Vienna, and the famous critic Hanslick nicknamed it a "Triangle Concerto," intending his remark to be a derogatory one (Berkowitz, p. 165).

trill. An ornament consisting of the quick alternation of a written note with its upper neighbor, frequently ending in a turn. During the Baroque and Classical periods trills normally began on the upper neighbor note and were played on the beat. In later music trills began on the written note.

trill pedaling. See *vibrato.*

"Trill" Sonata. Alexander Scriabin, Sonata no. 10, op. 70, 1913. Bowers, in his biography *Scriabin* (vol. 2, p. 244), nicknamed this sonata. He writes: "Its harmonic symmetry based on major thirds shrinking swiftly into minor thirds sets up a vortex of interior diminution constantly raised by trills and tremolos." The trill plays such an important role that the composer referred to this work as his "Sonata of Insects."

trio. The middle section of the *minuet,* march, or *scherzo* in a sonata or other compositions in ternary form.

trio sonata. A type of Baroque chamber music, written for four performers: two violins, cello, and keyboard.

triple concerto. A concerto for three solo performers and orchestra. Beethoven's is for piano, violin, and cello, but there are also other combinations, such as J. S. Bach's Concerto in D Minor for Three

Keyboards and Orchestra and Bartók's Concerto for Two Pianos, Percussion, and Orchestra.

triplet. A group of three notes to be performed in the place of two of the same kind, indicated by a three and usually a bracket.

triste (Fr.). Sorrowful, sad.

tritone. The interval of three whole tones: augmented fourth or diminished fifth. It sounded so dissonant to early musicians that it was called the "devil in music" (*diabolus in musica*).

***Trois morceaux en forme de poire* (Three Pieces in Pear Form).** Erik Satie, 1903. This set of pieces for piano duet was written in response to criticism that Satie paid no formal attention to his works: *Manière de commencement* (By Way of a Beginning); *Prolongation du même* (Extension of the Same); *I. Lentement* (Slowly); *II. Enlevé* (To Take Away); *III. Brutal* (Brutally); *En plus* (In Addition); *Redite* (Repetition).

Trois mouvements de Petrouchka. See *Petrouchka.*

trois pédale (Fr.). Damper pedal, third pedal.

***Trois valses distinguées du précieux dégoûté, Les* (The Three Distinguished Waltzes of a Disgusted Dandy).** Erik Satie, 1914. *Sa taille* (His Waist), *Son binocle* (His Spectacles), *Ses jambes* (His Legs).

tronca (It.). Cut off, accented.

trop (Fr.), *troppo* (It.). Too, too much.

"Trout" Quintet. Franz Schubert, D. 667, 1819, for violin, viola, cello, double bass, and piano, so called because the fourth of five movements is a set of variations on his song *Die Forelle* (The Trout).

True, Nelita. American pianist and teacher, she was trained at the University of Michigan, The Juilliard School, and the Peabody Conservatory of Music. She is recognized as one of America's most outstanding teachers and has been chairperson of the Piano Department of the Eastman School of Music for many years. She has a discography of over 70 works ranging from Scarlatti to contemporary works written expressively for her. This distinguished pianist has concertized worldwide with highly successful reviews. She has the superb ability to express the shifting emotions within the music. The True "dynasty" includes her brother Dr. Wesley True, his wife Marilyn, and their daughter Carolyn True, all outstanding pianists.

tumultueux (Fr.). Restless, agitated.

tune. 1. Air, melody. 2. To tune a piano means to correct the pitch of each string.

tuning fork. A two-pronged steel fork, tuned to a certain pitch.

tuning hammer. The key used by a piano turner to twist the tuning pins.

Tureck, Rosalyn (1914–2003). American pianist, she studied with Jan Chiapusso and appeared with the Chicago Symphony Orchestra when she was 12 years old. She began giving all-Bach recitals in 1930, and in 1937 she performed a series of six in New York. She also studied with Samaroff during this time at The Juilliard School. She developed an international career. Even though Tureck specialized in Bach, she played a broad repertoire and a large variety of keyboard instruments as well as the theremin.

Turina, Joaquin (1882–1949). Spanish composer and pianist, he studied at the Madrid Conservatory. He also studied piano with Moritz Moszkowski in Paris from 1905 to 1914. Turina taught at the Madrid Conservatory and wrote criticism. During his time spent in France he was influenced by Impressionism. He wrote a large repertoire for the piano, most of his works in a semipopular style, always colorful, exhibiting a fine mastery of form. His piano works include *Album de viaje* (Travel Impressions), *El barrio de Santa Cruz* (The Remains of Santa Cruz), *Coins de Séville* (Remote Places in Seville), *Cuentos de España* (Spanish Stories), *Danzas fantasticas* (Imaginary Dances), *Danzas gitanas* (Gypsy Dances), *Miniatures, Mujeres españolas* (Spanish Ladies), *Niñerías* (Children's Pieces), *Sanlúcar de Barrameda* (*sonata pintoresca:* Turina evokes the atmosphere of the fortified seaport near Cádiz where he spent his summers; one of his most ambitious works), *Sonata romántica* (on a Spanish theme), *Suite pittoresque—Sévilla* (Picturesque Suite—Seville), *Très danzas andaluzas* (Three Andalusian Dances), and numerous other pieces; for piano and orchestra: *Concerto* and *Rapsodia sinfónica*.

Türk, Daniel Gottlob (1756–1813). See *Klavierschule*.

turn. An ornament consisting of a group of four or five notes which wind around the principal note. In the 18th century the turn (the Italian *gruppetto*) normally began on the upper note (thus, four notes in the turn). During the 19th century the turn usually began on the principal note (five notes).

tutte le corde (It.). Release the *una corda* pedal so that all strings sound.

tutti, tutto (It.). All, the opposite of *soli* or solo. It means the passage is to be played by the full orchestra.

Twelve O'clock (*Midi*). John Field, Rondo in E Major, Hopkinson 13K, 1832. This was a revised version for piano of his *Divertissement avec Quartet* no. 1 (Divertimento with Quartet no. 1) (Berkowitz, p. 167). The name "Twelve O'clock" made reference to the clock (indicated in the score, p. 7) striking 12 times to mark the end of the ball.

twelve-tone music. A system of composition in which the 12 chromatic tones are considered equally important and are related one to another and not to a common key (tonal) center. Often referred to as serialism or serial music. This system was developed by Schoenberg around 1924. It is used in his *5 Klavierstücke* (5 Piano Pieces), but for the first time in its integral form in his *Suite* for piano. It is based on the tone row, which contains all 12 tones with no one tone repeated, with no tonic or tonal center. The order in which the 12 tones appear is determined by the composer. The order of tones remains the same as initially written out throughout the piece, but the row can be restated by retrograde, inversion, or retrograde-inversion. Later composers made many modifications in this system. Schoenberg's student Alban Berg managed to combine it with Romantic extended tonality and expression.

twentieth-century music. A catch-all phrase for various types of music that has developed since around 1900. Generally this includes new music under such names as *aleatory, atonal, electronic, Expressionist, dynamicism, musique concrète, Neoclassical, serial* or *twelve-tone,* and *microtonal minimalism.*

Tyson, Alan Walker (b. 1926). American musicologist, he has compiled a thematic catalog of the works of Muzio Clementi.

tzigane (Fr.). Gypsy. Term for a piece influenced by gypsy music. Ravel used the title for a rhapsody for violin and piano.

U

über (Ger.). Over, above.

Übergang (Ger.). Passage; transition.

übergreifen (Ger.). To cross the hands.

übersetzen (Ger.). 1. To pass one finger over another. 2. To translate.

übertragen (Ger.). To transcribe. *Übertragung:* transcription.

Übung (Ger.). Etude, exercise, study. See *Klavierübung.*

Übungen (Exercises). Johannes Brahms, 1893. These 51 finger exercises cover every type of fingering and touch Brahms used in his piano works and are valuable to all pianists, whether they play Brahms or not. Some combine two types of touch in one hand, others use two to four different metrical patterns with both hands, while others focus on developing finger independence. These exercises, plus the "Paganini" Variations, op. 35, and the *Five Studies* present the pianist with a "Brahms Piano Method."

U.C. See *una corda.*

Uchida, Mitsuko (b. 1948). Japanese pianist, she studied in Tokyo and Vienna, where she made her debut. Her teachers included Stefan Askenase, Kempff, and Nikita Magaloff. She has won many prizes and has toured throughout the world specializing in the repertoire of Debussy, Beethoven, Chopin, Mozart, and Schumann with great success.

uguale (It.). Equal, like, uniform.

umore (It.). Humor, playfulness.

un, une (Fr.). A, an, one.

un, uno, una (It.). One, a, an.

un peu (Fr.). A little, slightly.

un peu animé (Fr.). Rather lively.

un peu au-dessous du mouvement (Fr.). Slightly under tempo.

un peu détendu (Fr.). A little relaxed.

un peu en dehors (Fr.). A little in the foreground; a little emphasized, brought out a little.

un peu irrité (Fr.). A little angry.

un peu maniéré (Fr.). A little affected or artificial.

un peu marqué (Fr.). A little marked, *marcato*.

un peu moins hésitant (Fr.). A little less hesitation.

un peu moins lent (Fr.). A little less slowly; slightly faster.

un peu moins rapide cependant (Fr.). A little less fast however.

un peu moins vite (Fr.). A little less rapid, slightly slower.

un peu moqueur (Fr.). Somewhat mocking.

un peu mouvemente (Fr.). Slightly animated.

un peu plus à l'aise (Fr.). A little more leisurely.

un peu plus allant (Fr.). A little more moving.

un peu plus allant et plus gravement expressif (Fr.). A little more moving and more deeply expressive.

un peu plus animé (Fr.). A little more lively.

un peu plus lent (Fr.). A little slower.

un peu plus lent qu'àu début (Fr.). A little slower than the beginning.

un peu plus vite (Fr.). A little faster.

un peu pressé (Fr.). A little pushing forward.

un peu retardé (Fr.). Slightly relaxed.

un peu retenu (Fr.). A little holding back; slightly slowing.

un peu vite de mauvaise humeur (Fr.). Rather fast, in a bad mood.

un poco (It.). A little.

un second piano gravé en accolade (Fr.). A second piano (part) printed in brackets (as in a concerto).

un son nourri (Fr.). A full sustained sound.

una corda (It.). One less string, use the left (soft) pedal; abbreviated *U.C.*

unbetont (Ger.). Unaccented.

und (Ger.). And.

une expression allante grandissante (Fr.). An idea becoming more grandiose.

une fois (Fr.). Once.

"Unfinished" (*Reliquie*) Sonata. Franz Schubert, Sonata no. 15 in C Major, D. 840, 1825. This sonata, which is known by its nickname "Unfinished," is complete except for the conclusion of the main section in the Minuet and the end of the Rondo Finale. The first two movements of the sonata are as perfect in themselves and as nearly related to each other as those of the so-called "Unfinished" Symphony (Berkowitz, p. 168). A number of musicians have attempted to complete the sonata including Ernst Křenek, Walter Rehberg, and Armin Knob. This is probably Schubert's most important unfinished piano sonata.

ungebunden (Ger.). Free, unrestrained.

ungeduldig (Ger.). Impatient.

ungestüm (Ger.). Turbulent, violent.

ungezwungen (Ger.). Free, unbridled.

ungherese (It.). Hungarian.

unheimlich (Ger.). Sinister, uneasy.

uni, unie (Fr.). Even, smooth, unaffected.

uniforme (Fr.). Keep the touch even and unvarying.

unis (Fr.). All (divided parts) together again. This follows orchestral instructions such as *divisi, unison.*

Universal Edition. Founded in 1901 in Vienna, this company published the works of many important 20th-century composers, especially those associated with the Second Viennese School.

Unrest. Felix Mendelssohn, op. 30, no. 2 in B-flat Minor, one of the *Songs without Words.*

unruhig (Ger.). Restless.

unter (Ger.). Under, lower.

untersetzen (Ger.). To pass the thumb under in playing the piano.

Untertasten (Ger.). Lower keys, white keys.

up beat. One or several notes of a melody which occur before the first full measure of music.

upright piano. See piano.

Urtext (Ger.). A text in its presumed original state, with no additions by an editor. Some publishers of *Urtext* piano editions include Alfred, Henle, Peters, Universal Edition, and Vienna *Urtext.*

Uszler, Marienne (b. 1930). American pianist and teacher, she received degrees from Alverno College and DePaul University. She studied with Katja Andy and coached with Fisher, Maier, and Tcherepnin. She was editor of the recent *Piano and Keyboard* magazine and is coauthor of *The Well-Tempered Keyboard Teacher.* She was Professor of Keyboard Studies and Director of Undergraduate Studies at the University of Southern California, where she established the piano pedagogy program. She is currently producing a series of piano pedagogy books.

ut (Fr., Ger.). First tone of a scale, or C.

ut bémol (Fr.). The note C♭.

ut dièse (Fr.). The note C♯.

ut supra (Lat.) As above; as before.

V

va (It.). Go on, continue.

va crescendo (It.). Go on getting louder.

vacillante (It.). To be performed in a wavering, hesitating style.

vaghezza (It.). Gracefully, with longing, with charm.

vago (It.). Vague, dreamy.

vaillant (Fr.). Spirited, brave.

Vallée des cloches, La (The Valley of Bells). Maurice Ravel, no. 5 of *Miroirs*, 1905. Characterized by syncopated bell sonorities, careful pedaling is required for this atmospheric study.

Valley of Rocks. Miriam Hyde (b. 1913), 1975. A strong, brooding, and compelling work. It was inspired by an unforgettable evening when Hyde and her husband came upon the Valley of Rocks while touring in Lynton, North Devon, in 1974. This effective piece achieved great prominence at the 1988 Sydney International Piano Competition.

valse (Fr.). Waltz.

valsetto (It.): little waltz.

Valse, La. Maurice Ravel, 1919–20. This dance poem was originally written for orchestra and arranged for solo piano by the composer as well as for two pianos. It evokes the Viennese waltz and requires virtuoso technique.

Valse triste (Sad Waltz) Jean Sibelius, op. 44, no. 1, 1903. Piano piece from the incidental music to the play *Kuolema*. One of the composer's best-known pieces.

Valses nobles et sentimentales (Noble and Sentimental Waltzes). Maurice Ravel, 1911. This set of eight waltzes derives its name from Schubert's *Valses nobles*, D. 969, 1826, and *Valses sentimentales*, D. 779, ca. 1823, both for piano. They are glittering connected pieces ranging from a forceful opening to a delicate closing that recapitulates the previous waltzes.

vamp. An accompanimental phrase of one or two measures that can be repeated indefinitely until the soloist is ready to begin. If notated, it usually has double bars with repeat sign and marked "till ready."

variations. See theme and variation.

Variations sérieuses (Serious Variations). Felix Mendelssohn, op. 54, 1841. Seventeen continuous variations except for a short pause before and after the fourteenth. The title alludes to the fact that these are "serious variations" when compared to the many "frivolous" variations being written at this same time. Mendelssohn's finest solo piano work.

Variations symphoníques (Symphonic Variations). César Franck, 1885. Work for piano and orchestra in which theme and variation structure is combined with developmental technique.

vaut (Fr.). Having the value of, is worth.

veemente (It.). Vehement, forceful. *veemenza*: with vehemence.

veiller (Fr.). Pay attention to.

velato (It.). Veiled.

velluato (It.). Play in a smooth, legato style.

vellutáto (It.). Velvety, velvet; soft.

veloce, velocemente (It.). Swiftly, very swift (fast), rapid.

velocissimo (It.). With the utmost velocity.

velouté (Fr.). Velvety.

Venetian Boat Song. Felix Mendelssohn, three of the *Songs without Words*, all named by the composer: op. 19, no. 6, in G Minor; op. 30, no. 6, in F-sharp Major; op. 62, no. 5, in A Minor.

Vengerova, Isabella (1879–1956). Lithuanian pianist and teacher, she studied at the Vienna Conservatory and with Leschetizky from

1896 to 1900. She began teaching at the St. Petersburg Conservatory in 1905. She settled in New York in 1921 and was appointed professor of piano at the Curtis Institute in 1924 when it was established and taught there the rest of her life. Her students include Barber, Bernstein, Lukas Foss, Sydney Foster, Graffman, Lillian Kallir, Pennario, Rezits, and Zadel Sokolovsky.

vent (Fr.). The wind.

Vent dans la plaine, Le (The Wind in the Plains). Claude Debussy, *Préludes,* book 1, no. 3, 1910. A six-note pianissimo figure dominates; the alto melody is interrupted by trills and leaping chords.

verhallend (Ger.). Fading away.

Véritables préludes flasques (*pour un chien*) (Genuine Flabby Preludes [for a dog]). Erik Satie, 1912. *Sévère réprimande* (Severe Reprimand), *Seul à la maison* (Alone at Home), *On joue* (Someone Is Playing). Written in barless notation.

verlöschend (Ger.). Dying away.

vermindert (Ger.). Diminished.

Vers la flamme (Toward the Flame). Alexander Scriabin, op. 72, 1914. One chord generates this work: it begins in darkness and moves inexorably toward dazzling light.

Verschiebung (Ger.). Soft pedal (*una corda*), left pedal.

verschwindend (Ger.). Vanishing; play softer and softer as though becoming more distant.

Versetzung (Ger.). Transposition.

version revisée (Fr.). Revised version.

vertical piano. Upright piano. See *piano.*

Verzierung (Ger.). Ornament, ornamentation.

vezzoso (It.). Tender, sweet; play smoothly and gracefully.

vibrante (Sp.). Vibrating. Used in strong, *forte* passages.

vibrato (It.). When used in piano music it means vibrate the pedal (quick up and down movements) to keep some sound continuing. The term "butterfly pedaling" and "trill pedaling" are sometimes used to describe this technique. Also, a strong, full quality of tone, resonant.

vibrer, faire vibrer (Fr.). Allow to vibrate (keep the damper pedal depressed).

vide (Fr.). 1. Indicates an optional "cut," i.e., a passage may be omitted from a composition if desired. 2. Empty.

viel (Ger.). Very, much.

viel langsam (Ger.). Very slow.

Viennese action. The name used to distinguish a piano action perfected in Vienna. In the 18th century the Viennese piano action was lighter in touch as compared with the London piano action.

Viennese School. A name often applied to the Classical period, or to that portion of it when composers like Haydn, Mozart, Beethoven, and Schubert lived in Vienna. A Second Viennese School took place during the early decades of the 20th century centered around the composers Schoenberg, Webern, and Berg, who all lived in Vienna.

vierhändig (Ger.). For four hands, for two performers at one piano.

Vieux sequins et vielles cuirasses **(Old Sequins and Armor).** Erik Satie, 1913. *Chez le marchand d'or* (*Venise 18ème siécle*) (At the Gold Merchant's [Venice 18th Century]), *Dans cuirassée* (*période grecque*) (Dance in Armor [Grecian Period]), *Le défaite des Cimbres* (*cauchemar*) (The Defeat of the Cimbri [Nightmare]). Written in barless notation.

vif (Fr.). Quick, brisk, lively.

vif avec entrain (Fr.). Quick with vigor.

vif et enjoué (Fr.). Quick and playful.

vif et joyeux (Fr.). Quick and joyful.

vif et marqué (Fr.). Quick and marked (*marcato*).

vif et rigoureusement rythmé (Fr.). Quick and very carefully measured.

vif, haletant (Fr.). Quick, breathless.

vigoroso (It.). Vigorous, bold.

vigoureuse, vigoureux (Fr.). Energetic, vigorous.

villageois (Fr.). Unaffected, rustic. Frances Poulenc wrote *Villageoises* (Country Scenes), a set of five pieces.

Villa-Lobos, Heitor (1887–1959). Brazilian composer and pianist, he was largely self-taught although he spent some years in Paris on a governmental grant. His compositional style uses Brazilian folk music, and he developed two types of composition: the *Chôros* (a popular Brazilian dance form, marked by incisive rhythms and a ballad-like melody) and the *Bachianas Brasileiras* (Brazilian rhythms treated in Bachian counterpoint). He has written a great deal for the piano including *Amazonas, Bachianas Brasileiras no. 4, Brinquedo de Roda, Carnaval das Crianças Brasileiras, Ciclo Brasileiro, Cirandas, Cirandinhas, Francette et Piá* (10 pieces based on the story of a little Brazilian Indian who went to France where he met a French girl; combines French and Brazilian tunes), *Guia Prática* (settings of popular Brazilian children's songs), *Prole do Bébé* (2 vols.), *Rudepoema* (Rough Poem; this refers to the rough, unpolished nature of the sentiments he wished to express), *Suite Floral, Ten Pieces on Popular Children's Folk Tunes of Brazil, The Three Maries,* and many more works. For piano and orchestra: five concertos, *Bachianas Brasileiras* no. 3, two *Chôros, Mômo Precoce.* For piano duet: *A folia de um blóco infantile.*

Víñes, Riccardo (1875–1943). Spanish pianist, he studied at the Paris Conservatoire. He was the first virtuoso to feature the works of Debussy and Ravel with his spectacular technique, phenomenal memory, and prodigious repertoire. Dedicatee of *Le fandango* (*Goyescas* no. 3) by Granados, *Noches en los jardines de España* (Nights in the Gardens of Spain) by de Falla, and the *Trois Pièces* (Three Pieces) by Poulenc, who was among his students.

Vingt regards sur l'enfant Jesus (Twenty Contemplations of Looking at the Christ Child). Olivier Messiaen, 1944. A pianistic marathon requiring about one and three-quarter hours to perform. Messiaen lavishes his religious expression on the contemplations of the child Jesus by 20 different personages: the Father, the Virgin, the Star, etc., in a tender and mystic style. "Probably the largest sacred piano work ever written" (Shadinger, p. 125).

violent peu de pédale (Fr.). Excitedly (but with) little pedal.

violento (It.). Violent, vehement, boisterous.

Virgil Clavier. A soundless keyboard for practice, invented by the American A. K. Virgil.

virtuosity. The distinguishing qualities and skills that go into making a virtuoso.

virtuoso. A technically brilliant performer.

Visions de l'Amen (Visions of the Amen). Olivier Messiaen, 1943. A seven-movement suite for two pianos. The composer had in mind to demand from these instruments maximum force and multifarious sonorities. A virtuoso technique is demanded.

Visions et prophéties (Visions and Prophecies). Ernest Bloch (1880–1959), 1940. Five short rhapsodic (Eastern wailing melismas) pieces that are intense and achieve a telling effect.

Visions fugitives (Fugitive Visions). Sergei Prokofiev, op. 22, 1915–17. Twenty short aphoristic pieces, Prokofiev's *Préludes.*

vite (Fr.). Quick, fast.

vite et bien (Fr.). Fast and clear.

vitement (Fr.). Quickly.

vivace (It.). Fast, lively, brisk, animated. *vivacissimo*: very fast and lively.

vivement (Fr.). Quickly, lively.

vivo (It.). Lively, animated.

voce (It.). Voice.

vocifération implacable (Fr.). Relentless, clamoring.

Vogel als Prophet (The Prophet Bird). Robert Schumann, no. 7 of *Waldszenen,* op. 82. The strangeness of this Impressionist-sounding piece is due to the sudden rises and falls of the figuration and the constant use of unessential notes that clash with the bass on strong beats. A masterpiece.

voilé (Fr.). Veiled, subdued.

Voiles (Sails). Claude Debussy, *Préludes,* book 1, no. 2, 1910. The piece oscillates between whole-tone and pentatonic harmonies and requires sensitive tonal balance.

vol joyeux (Fr.). Cheerful, joyful flight.

volée (Fr.). Flight; a rapid passage.

voll (Ger.). Complete, full.

volteggiando (It.). Cross the hands in keyboard playing.

volti subito (It.). Turn the page over quickly; abbreviated *V.S.*

volubile (Fr.). Fluent, free; flowing.

Vortrag (Ger.). Style of performance or interpretation.

Votapek, Ralph (b. 1939). American pianist, he studied at Northwestern University with Guy Mombaerts, at The Juilliard School with Rosina Lhévinne, and at the Manhattan School of Music with Goldsand. He won the Naumberg Award in 1959 and was the first winner of the Van Cliburn Competition. Since then he has toured worldwide earning great success. He continues to be a vital force in pianistic circles in the United States and other countries. He has taught at Michigan State University for a number of years.

V.S. See *volti subito.*

W

W. or Wq. Abbreviation for Wotquenne, used to identify works by C. P. E. Bach in Alfred Wotquenne's thematic catalog. A later and more accurate thematic catalog of the works of Bach is by Eugene Helm.

Wait, Mark (b. 1947). American pianist, he studied at Wichita State University with Paul Reed, at Kansas State University with Robert Steinbauer, and at the Peabody Conservatory with Laires and Wolff. He has concertized throughout the United States, Canada, and Europe with much success. He plays with much authority and presents engrossing and poetic recitals. He has recorded Elliott Carter's Piano Concerto. He is presently dean of the Blair School of Music at Vanderbilt University.

Waldesrauschen **(Forest Murmurs).** Franz Liszt, 1862–63. From *Deux études de concert*. The second etude is *Gnomenreigen* (Dance of the Gnomes). The piece displays the technique of the performer and is not limited to only one technical difficulty.

"Waldstein" Sonata. Ludwig van Beethoven, Sonata in C Major, op. 53, 1803–4. This monumental work was dedicated to his friend and patron Count Ferdinand von Waldstein.

***Waldszenen* (Forest Scenes).** Robert Schumann, op. 82, 1848–49. Eight pieces in this set picture different scenes from the forest.

Walker, Alan (b. 1930). English musicologist and writer, he studied at the Guildhall School of Music and Drama, London, and Durham University. He teaches at McMaster University and is the author of a three-volume biography of Liszt. Walker has also written extensively on Schumann and musical criticism.

Walter. Austrian piano maker of German birth, Anton Walter (1752–1826) was in Vienna by 1780. Mozart liked the Walter pianos in his later years. Beethoven used a Walter during part of his life while he lived in Vienna.

waltz. See *valse.*

Walze (Ger.). A roll for a player piano.

Wanderer, The. Felix Mendelssohn, piece, op. 30, no. 4, in B Minor, one of the *Songs without Words.*

"Wanderer" Fantasy. Franz Schubert, D. 760, 1822. This nickname was given to this piece because most of the themes are derived from his song *Der Wanderer.* Liszt arranged this piece for piano and orchestra in 1850–51 and made an arrangement for two pianos.

wankend (Ger.). Hesitating.

"War" Sonatas. Sergei Prokofiev, three sonatas for piano: no. 6 in A Major, op. 82; no. 7 in B-flat Major, op. 83; no. 8 in B-flat Major, op. 84. Prokofiev himself called these three compositions "War" Sonatas because they were composed during the Second World War (Berkowitz, pp. 173–74).

Wärme (Ger.). Ardor, warmth.

Water Music. John Cage, 1960. Chance composition, for a pianist also using a radio, whistles, water containers, and deck of cards. The score (10 leaves) is to be mounted as a large poster.

Watts, André (b. 1946). American pianist, he studied with Fleischer. He began touring the United States and later abroad; his superb technique shows a preference for the "big" repertoire. His highly charged temperament makes him take risks during his performances. Watts is one of the most successful of his generation of pianists.

Weber, Carl Maria von (1786–1826). German composer, pianist, and conductor, he studied with Michael Haydn. He became a concert pianist and gave first performances of most of his own works. He had a wide stretch (a twelfth), which led to striking effects in his piano music. He is the founder of the German Romantic school, and his piano works are among the first genuine compositions ideally suited to the piano's expressive and technical capabilities. His piano works include four sonatas, six sets of variations, *Invitation to the Dance, Rondo* in E-flat Major, two piano concertos, and a *Konzertstück.*

Webern, Anton (1883–1945). Austrian composer, he was a protégé of Schoenberg. His music was banned by the Nazis, but his influence on 20th-century composition cannot be overemphasized. He is a seminal figure of the century. He first used 12-tone technique as advocated by Schoenberg in 1924. His contribution to the piano repertoire is small and includes the *Klavierstück, Satz, Sonatensatz,* and *Variations.* He was accidentally shot and killed by an American soldier.

Webster, Beveridge (1908–99). American pianist, he studied with Philipp at the Paris Conservatoire. He toured Europe for some years before returning home in 1934, where he developed a successful concert career. He taught at the New England Conservatory and The Juilliard School and edited works for the International Music Co. His students included Michel Block, Jackson, and Thomas Mastroianni.

Wedding Cake. Camille Saint-Saëns, *Valse Caprice* for Piano and Orchestra, op. 76, 1885. This scintillating work is a chain of glittering waltzes which might have reminded Saint-Saëns of a multilayer cake attractively iced and decorated and most appropriate for a wedding (Berkowitz, p 174).

Wedding Day at Troldhaugen. Edvard Grieg, op. 65, no. 6, 1897. Solo piano piece depicting a wedding celebration at Troldhaugen, Norway. One of his Lyric Pieces.

wedge staccato. The small wedge is used over or below a note to indicate *staccatissimo,* the most extreme form of staccato:

. This type of *staccatissimo* came into use during the early part of Beethoven's career (1780–1800).

wehmütig, wehmüthig (Ger.). Sad, sorrowful.

weich (Ger.). Soft, delicate, weak, minor, smooth.

weinend (Ger.). Weeping, lamenting.

Weirich, Robert (b. 1950). American pianist and teacher, he holds degrees from the Oberlin Conservatory of Music and Yale University; he studied with Daniel Winter, Emil Danenberg, Donald Currier, and Claude Frank. He has performed with great success in the United States, Canada, Europe, and the Far East. Active in chamber music, he was the artistic director of the Skaneateles Festival in New York's Finger Lakes District from 1991 to 1999. He has taught at the Peabody Conservatory, Northwestern University, and presently at the University of Missouri at Kansas City. His playing reveals a colorful imagination and superb craftsmanship.

Weissenberg, Alexis (b. 1929). Bulgarian pianist, he settled in the United States in 1946 and made his debut in New York in 1947 with the New York Philharmonic Orchestra. He studied with Samaroff at The Juilliard School and made worldwide tours beginning in 1950. He is a distinguished pianist and chamber music performer.

Well-Tempered Clavier. J. S. Bach, BWV 846–93, 1722, 1744. This two-volume work, often referred to as the "Old Testament" of keyboard repertoire (the Beethoven sonatas are referred to as the "New Testament"), is a collection of 48 preludes and fugues written in the 24 major and minor keys, intended to demonstrate equal temperament.

wenig (Ger.). A little.

White Mass, The. Alexander Scriabin, Sonata no. 7, op. 64, 1911. The curiously color-conscious composer subtitled this work the "White Mass." Terms such as *mysteriousement sonore, menaçant, impérieux,* and *comme des éclairs* point out the mystical element. It is the most elusive, intuitive, and technically complex of all his sonatas. Scriabin considered this sonata "holy," marked some passages *très pur* (very pure), and thought its sonorities to be saintly. The subtitle dramatizes its sacerdotal character, and to him its performance was ritualistic (Bowers, vol. 2, p. 231).

Whitesides, Abby (1881–1956). American piano teacher, she was trained in the United States and Germany with Ganz. Her most important book was *Indispensibles of Piano Playing.* Her concept of rhythm as the driving force of music is basic to her philosophy of teaching. Another book, *Mastering the Chopin Etudes and Other Essays,* was prepared by her students and published after her death.

whole-tone scale. A scale of six different tones, all of them a whole step (whole tone) apart, for example, C, D, E, F♯, G♯, A♯. Debussy was the first to use it extensively although Franz Liszt and other late-19th-century composers experimented with it.

wie ein Hauch (Ger.). Like a breath.

Wieck, Friedrich (1785–1873). German piano teacher and theologian, he started a piano factory in Leipzig and taught singing. Schumann studied piano with him and married his daughter Clara, against his wishes, in 1840. He was a busy teacher who composed studies and wrote textbooks. His students included von Bülow and Clara Wieck Schumann.

wieder im Zeitmass (Ger.). Once again in tempo.

wiegend (Ger.). Swaying motion, like rocking a cradle.

Wiegenlied (Ger.). A lullaby, cradle song.

Wild, Earl (b. 1915). American pianist, he studied at Carnegie Technical College and with Petri. Virtuoso of legendary talent in the late Romantic repertoire, he revived concertos by Xaver Scharwenka and Paderewski. He has also specialized in the piano music of Liszt and Gershwin and has transcribed sets of Rachmaninoff and Gershwin songs, as well as making many delightful transcriptions and paraphrases of other composers' works in the tradition of Liszt and Godowsky. He taught at Ohio State University and The Juilliard School for a number of years.

Winerock, Jack (b. 1945). American pianist, he studied at The Juilliard School with Gorodnitzki and the University of Michigan with Fisher. He has also studied with Fleischer and Shure. He has concertized in Europe, the United States, Canada, and the Far East. He performs early American piano music (especially that of Reinagle) with a special understanding, but he performs a broad range of repertoire. He has also made recordings that demonstrate his ability to perform with profound respect for the composer's intentions.

"Winter Wind" Etude. Frédéric Chopin, Etude in A Minor, op. 25, no. 11, 1834. The constant figuration in the right hand is supposed to suggest the winter wind. The first four measures were an afterthought of Chopin's.

Winterreigen **(Winter Round Dances).** Ernst von Dohnányi, op. 13, 1905. These 10 *bagatelles* are dedicated to a specific friend, make references to personal experiences, and are full of keyboard improvisation.

Wittgenstein, Paul (1887–1961). Austrian pianist, he studied with

Theodore Leschetitzky and lost his right arm in World War I. Member of a wealthy Viennese family (the philosopher Ludwig Wittgenstein was a cousin), he commissioned a number of composers to write works for him: Prokofiev's Piano Concerto no. 4, Richard Strauss's *Parergon zur Symphonia domestica* and *Panathenäenzug*, Ravel's Piano Concerto in D, and Benjamin Britten's *Diversions.*

Wolff, Konrad (1907–89). German pianist and teacher, he studied with Bruno Eisner and Schnabel. He performed in Europe and the United States, giving his New York debut on his eightieth birthday. He taught at Columbia University and the Peabody Conservatory for many years. He edited *On Music and Musicians* by Schumann, and wrote *Masters of the Keyboard* and *The Teachings of Artur Schnabel.*

WoO. Abbreviation for *Werk ohne Opuszahl* (work without opus number), used in the thematic catalog of Beethoven's works compiled by Georg Kinsky and Hans Hahn.

Wotquenne, Alfred (1867–1939). Belgian bibliographer, he compiled a thematic catalog of the works of C.P.E. Bach, usually abbreviated to "Wq." number.

wrest pin. The peg capable of rotary motion by which the pitch of a string may be raised or lowered.

W. T. C. Abbreviation for *Well-Tempered Clavier* by J. S. Bach.

wuchtig (Ger.). Weighty; play with emphasis, vigorous.

wündig (Ger.). Worthy; play in a proper and dignified manner.

würdig (Ger.). Dignified.

"Württemberg" Sonatas. C. P. E. Bach, 1744, W. 49. Six keyboard sonatas so called because they are dedicated to the Duke of Württemberg.

wütend (Ger.). Raging, furious.

Wut, Wuth (Ger.). Madness, rage.

X

Xenakis, Iannis (1922–2001). A Greek composer who worked in many countries, he was one of the truly innovative intelligences in the musical world of the late twentieth century. He incorporated computer-determined probabilities and transferred certain architectural structures into his music. Piano works: *Evryali, Herma*— "Musique symbolique," and *Mists*.

Y

Yablonskaya, Oxana (b. 1941). Russian pianist, she studied at the Moscow Conservatory from 1957 to 1962 and was a student of Alexander Goldenweiser. She won various competitions and was professor of piano at the Moscow Conservatory from 1965 to 1975. She came to the United States and quickly reestablished her reputation as a pianist. She presently teaches at The Juilliard School.

Yamaha. This Japanese manufacturer of pianos was founded in 1887 by Torakusu Yamaha (1851–1916). It makes fine upright and grand pianos plus electronic instruments.

Yankee Doodle. Many variations have been written on this popular late-18th-century tune or incorporated into other pieces. One such piece was the *Federal Overture* by Benjamin Carr (1768–1831), who also composed *Yankee Doodle Arranged as a Rondo* from op. 4, the final section of his battle sonata *The Siege of Tripoli, An Historical Naval Sonata,* in which this famous theme is prominently featured.

Yeomans, David (b. 1938). American pianist who studied with Emil Danenberg, Freundlich, and Sandor and has degrees from the Oberlin Conservatory of Music, The Juilliard School, and the University of Michigan. He has performed across the United States, Canada, and Europe and has elicited critical praise. He is the author of *Bartók for Piano*. Most recently he has investigated Czech piano music. Presently he is Professor Emeritus of Music at Texas Woman's University.

Youth. Dmitri Kabalevsky, concerto trilogy for different instruments: Piano Concerto no. 3, op. 50 (1952); Concerto for Violin, op. 48; Concerto for Cello, op. 40. This trilogy of "Youth" concertos are all in the classical three movements, pose no major problems, and make for delightful listening. Excellent for high-school students.

Z

zapateado (Sp.). Various patterns of stamping the feet characteristic of specific Spanish and Latin American dances. *Zapato* means shoe.

Zaremba, Sylvia (b. 1931). American pianist, she studied with Vengerova at the Curtis Institute. She has concertized extensively in the United States and served as editor for various piano editions.

zart (Ger.). Tender, soft, delicate, sensitive, subdued, suave.

zart aber voll (Ger.). Gentle but full.

Zeitmass (Ger.). Time, tempo.

Zeitmesser (Ger.). Metronome.

zèle (Fr.). Ardor, enthusiasm, energy.

zeloso, con zelo (It.). Fervently, with fervor.

ziemlich (Ger.). Rather, somewhat; moderately.

zierlich (Ger.). Neat, graceful.

Zigeuner (Ger.). Gypsy. *Zigeunermusik*: Gypsy music.

Zimerman, Krystian (b. 1956). Polish pianist, he won first prize at the Chopin International Competition in 1975. His London debut was in 1977 followed by world tours. He is an internationally admired artist, especially as an interpreter of the works of Chopin.

zingarese (It.). Gypsy.

zögern (Ger.). Hesitate, retard, linger.

zortzico (Sp.). Spanish dance from the Basque province in which the rhythm is marked on a percussion instrument.

zu (Ger.). To, too, toward, for. *zu 2:* divide into two parts.

Zumbro, Nicholas (b. 1935). American pianist, he studied with Johana Harris privately and with Rosina Lhévinne at The Juilliard School. He began his major career in London in 1968 and since then has toured the world, receiving critical acclaim as a pianist of the first rank. He has made many recordings and has taught at The Juilliard School, Indiana University, the University of Hawaii, and the University of Arizona for many years. He is also a fine composer.

Zumpe, Johannes (1735–83). English harpsichord and piano maker of German birth, he founded his business in London in 1761. Johann Christian Bach purchased a Zumpe square piano and in 1768 presented on it the first solo performance ever given on a piano in England.

zunehmend (Ger.). Crescendo.

zurückhalten (Ger.). To hold back, *rallentando.*

Zverev, Nikolai (1832–93). Russian pianist and teacher, he was an outstanding teacher in Moscow. He studied with Alexander Dubuc (1812–98) and Adolph von Henselt (1814–89) and was professor of piano at the University of Moscow from 1870 until his death. He had a remarkable talent for working with young students. His reputation for being a tough disciplinarian was well known, but his students respected his inspiration. Some of his students included Rachmaninoff, Scriabin, and Siloti.

zwei (Ger.). Two.

zweihändig (Ger.). For two hands.

Zwölftonmusik (Ger.). See twelve-tone music.

Bibliography

Berkowitz, Freda Pastor. *Popular Titles and Subtitles of Musical Compositions.* Metuchen, N.J.: Scarecrow Press, 1975.

Bowers, Fabian. *Scriabin.* 2 vols. Tokyo: Kodansha, 1969.

Brown, Maurice J. E. *Chopin: An Index of His Works in Chronological Order.* 2nd ed. New York: Da Capo Press, 1972.

Burge, David. *Twentieth-Century Piano Music.* New York: Schirmer Books, 1990.

Clementi, Muzio. *Gradus ad Parnassum.* With a new introduction by Leon Plantinga. New York: Da Capo Press, 1980.

Deutsch, Otto Erich. *Franz Schubert thematisches Verzeichnis seiner Werke.* Kassel: Bärenreiter, 1978.

Dorian, Frederick. *The History of Music in Performance.* New York: W. W. Norton, 1942.

Dubal, David. *The Art of the Piano.* New York: Summit Books, 1989.

Ferguson, Howard. *Keyboard Interpretation.* New York: Oxford University Press, 1975.

Friskin, James, and Irwin Freundlich. *Music for the Piano.* New York: Rinehart, 1954.

Gillespie, John, and Anna Gillespie. *Notable Twentieth-Century Pianists.* 2 vols. Westport, Conn.: Greenwood Press, 1995.

Gilpin, Wayne, comp. and ed. *Student's Dictionary of Music.* Oakville, Ontario: Frederick Harris Music, 1985.

Gordon, Stewart. *A History of Keyboard Literature.* New York: Schirmer Books, 1996.

Bibliography

Hinson, Maurice. *Guide to the Pianist's Repertoire.* 3rd ed. Bloomington: Indiana University Press, 2000.

———. *Music for More than One Piano.* Bloomington: Indiana University Press, 1983.

———. *Music for Piano and Orchestra.* Bloomington: Indiana University Press, 1993.

———. *The Pianist's Guide to Transcriptions, Arrangements, and Paraphrases.* Bloomington: Indiana University Press, 1990.

———. *The Piano in Chamber Ensemble.* Bloomington: Indiana University Press, 1978.

Hitchcock, H. Wiley, and Stanley Sadie, eds. *The New Grove Dictionary of American Music.* 4 vols. London: Macmillan, 1986.

Ho, Allan, and Dmitry Feofanov. *Biographical Dictionary of Russian/Soviet Composers.* Westport, Conn.: Greenwood Press, 1989.

Kaiserman, David. *The Solo Piano Music of S. M. Liapunov (1859–1924).* Ph.D. dissertation, University of Iowa, 1977.

Karp, Theodore. *Dictionary of Music.* Boston: Northeastern University Press, 1983.

Kehler, George. *The Piano in Concert.* 2 vols. Metuchen, N.J.: Scarecrow Press, 1982.

Kennedy, Michael. *The Oxford Dictionary of Music.* Oxford: Oxford University Press, 1994.

Kirby, F. E. *Music for Piano: A Short History.* Portland: Amadeus Press, 1995.

Kirkpatrick, Ralph. *Domenico Scarlatti.* Princeton: Princeton University Press, 1953.

Kobylanska, Krystyna. *Frédéric Chopin: Thematisch-bibilographisches Werkverzeichnis.* Munich: Henle, 1979.

Köchel, Ludwig Ritter von. *Chronologisch-systematisches Verzeichnis sämtlicher Tonwerke von Wolfgang Amade Mozart.* 3rd ed. Revised by Alfred Einstein. Leipzig: Breitkopf & Härtel, 1937. Reprint, Ann Arbor: J. W. Edwards, 1947.

Lyle, Wilson. *A Dictionary of Pianists.* New York: Schirmer Books, 1985.

McGraw, Cameron. *Piano Duet Repertoire.* Bloomington: Indiana University Press, 1981.

Moore, Shirley. *A French–English Music Dictionary.* Atlanta: Leihall, 1985.

Quantz, Johann Joachim. *On Playing the Flute.* Trans. Edward R. Reilly. New York: Schirmer Books, 1966.

Randel, Donald, ed. *The New Harvard Dictionary of Music.* Cambridge, Mass.: Belknap Press, 1986.

Rosenblum, Sandra. *Performance Practices in Classic Piano Music.* Bloomington: Indiana University Press, 1988.

Sadie, Stanley, ed. *The New Grove Dictionary of Music and Musicians.* London: Macmillan, 2000.

———. *The Norton/Grove Concise Encyclopedia of Music.* New York: W. W. Norton, 1994.

Schumann, Robert. *On Music and Musicians.* New York: W. W. Norton, 1946.

Searle, Humphrey. *The Music of Liszt.* London: Williams & Norgate, 1954.

Shadinger, Richard C. *The Sacred Element in Piano Literature: A Historical Background and an Annotated Listing.* D.M.A. dissertation, Southern Baptist Theological Seminary, 1974.

Slonimsky, Nicolas, ed. *Baker's Biographical Dictionary of Musicians.* 7th ed. New York: Schirmer Books, 1984.

Türk, Daniel Gottlob. *School of Clavier Playing.* Translated by Raymond H. Haggh. Lincoln: University of Nebraska Press, 1982.

Waterman, Fanny. *Every Pianist's Dictionary.* London: Faber Music, 1993.

Watson, Jack M., and Corinne Watson. *A Concise Dictionary of Music.* New York: Dodd, Mead, 1965.

Maurice Hinson, Senior Professor Emeritus of Piano at the Southern Baptist Theological Seminary, was founding editor of the *Journal of the American Liszt Society* and is a contributor to the *New Grove Dictionary of American Music.* He is known for his many books on piano repertoire, including the *Guide to the Pianist's Repertoire* (3rd edition, Indiana University Press, 2000), *Music for Piano and Orchestra* (enlarged edition, Indiana University Press, 1993), *The Pianist's Bookshelf* (Indiana University Press, 1998), and *The Pianist's Guide to Transcriptions, Arrangements, and Paraphrases* (Indiana University Press, 2001).